Silences & Images

History of Schools and Schooling

Alan R. Sadovnik and Susan F. Semel
General Editors

Vol. 7

PETER LANG
New York • Washington, D.C./Baltimore • Boston • Bern
Frankfurt am Main • Berlin • Brussels • Vienna • Canterbury

Silences & Images

The Social History
of the Classroom

EDITED BY

Ian Grosvenor, Martin Lawn,
& Kate Rousmaniere

PETER LANG
New York • Washington, D.C./Baltimore • Boston • Bern
Frankfurt am Main • Berlin • Brussels • Vienna • Canterbury

LIBRARY OF CONGRESS CATALOGING-IN-PUBLICATION DATA

Silences and images: the social history of the classroom /
edited by Ian Grosvenor, Martin Lawn, Kate Rousmaniere.
p. cm. — (History of schools and schooling; vol. 7)
Includes bibliographical references.
1. Classrooms—History—Congresses. 2. School environment—History—Congresses.
3. Education—Social aspects—History—Congresses. 4. Classrooms—United
States—History—Congresses. 5. School environment—United States—
History—Congresses. 6. Education—Social aspects—United States—
History—Congresses. I. Grosvenor, Ian. II. Lawn, Martin.
III. Rousmaniere, Kate. IV. Series: History of schools and schooling; v. 7.
LA128.S55   370'.009—dc21   98-53608
ISBN 0-8204-3926-6
ISSN 1089-0678

DIE DEUTSCHE BIBLIOTHEK-CIP-EINHEITSAUFNAHME

Grosvenor, Ian:
Silences and images: the social history of the classroom /
ed. by: Ian Grosvenor, Martin Lawn, Kate Rousmaniere.
–New York; Washington, D.C./Baltimore; Boston; Bern;
Frankfurt am Main; Berlin; Brussels; Vienna; Canterbury: Lang.
(History of schools and schooling; Vol. 7)
ISBN 0-8204-3926-6

Cover design by Nona Reuter

The paper in this book meets the guidelines for permanence and durability
of the Committee on Production Guidelines for Book Longevity
of the Council of Library Resources.

∞

© 1999 Peter Lang Publishing, Inc., New York

Printed in the United States of America

Contents

Acknowledgements

The participants in the *Silences and Images Seminar* were: Richard Altenbaugh, Hilda Amsing, Kevin Brehony, Ron Butchart, Ann Short Chirhart, Geraldine Clifford, Ning de Coninck-Smith, Peter Cunningham, Kristof Dams, Kari Dehli, Marc Depaepe, Noelle Engels, Barbara Finkelstein, Lesley Fox-Lee, Sara Freedman, Lesley Furlong, Philip Gardner, Ian Grosvenor, Thérèse Hamel, Lars-Göran Högman, Ulla Johansson, Martin Lawn, Jaap ter Linden, Dan Littlefield, Valinda Littlefield, Kevin Myers, Don Nethery, Jo Anne Preston, Amy Rolleri, Kate Rousmaniere, Brian Simon, Frank Simon, Harry Smaller, David Vincent, Wayne Urban, Bobbie Wells.

We wish to thank Save Britain's Heritage, the Local Studies Department, Birmingham Central Library, the Nationaal Schoolmuseum, Rotterdam, the Public Archives of Ontario, Toronto, for permission to reproduce images included in this book and Luke Chapman for pre-press.

Introduction

... it is difficult to believe that historians have made almost no attempt to reconstruct the classroom, the culture of the classroom, the social relations of the classroom.[1]

[1] H. Silver, 'Knowing and not knowing in the history of education', *History of Education*, 21, 1, (1992) p.105.

This book focuses on the silence in the history of education about the practice, meaning and culture of classrooms in the past. Classrooms are taken as a major building block in most descriptions of education systems, in historical inquiries in education and in curriculum studies. They are instantly recognisable in their signs and symbols, across cultures and in recent time; and an understanding of their operation, layout and function underlies many historical accounts of schooling. Yet although they are extremely important and central to many historical accounts, they have not been systematically explored. We felt that there have been great 'silences' in the history of education across many cultures, silences about the practice, meaning and culture of classrooms. Across Northern Europe and North America in the past, rows of uniform seating, slates, a blackboard, a high teacher's desk, a globe, and a collection of books and papers constituted the elementary and secondary school classroom. Yet there is a silence in that classroom. What were its routines, what kinds of activities did it contain and what sorts of expressions and lives inhabited its space? What was its pedagogical order, and how was the curriculum mediated in its spaces? What was the lived reality of the teacher's work and the students' lives in and around that classroom? The goal of the book, building on conference papers and discussion on this topic, is to begin to reconstruct the culture of such common social spaces in schools and to ask questions about how historians can begin to piece together the silent social history of the classroom.

This book is based on a series of innovative conferences on the history of classrooms that met in Birmingham

England in 1995 and Toronto in 1996. The conference series, 'Silences and Images: the Social History of Classrooms,' began with a desire to uncover the place of the classroom in a new direction in the history of education. The focus of the seminars was a set of questions about the routines and activities of the classroom, its pedagogical order and the realities of teachers' and students' work in classrooms. The discussion was directed at either particular case studies or the use and interpretation of sources. In this discussion, our silent partner was an unspoken set of questions about the social construction of classrooms as places of learning and places of work.

As well as discussing and deconstructing the idea of the classroom in its variety of spatial, social and work locations, the conference papers and discussions emphasized the processes involved in reconstructing the classroom of the past, including the use of new methodologies and sources, and the questions raised by their use. Several chapters in this book developed methodological issues about the use and interpretation of sources such as teacher and student diaries and notebooks, photographs, school architecture plans and memory. The problems of historical method raised by the use of image and representation are also explored.

The conference was experimental in format: sessions were organised around the study of images and documents, and the group itself encouraged collective exploration and the re-conceptualisation of assumptions and practices. Proposed papers were produced well in advance of the session to allow for group discussion and analysis. As an international conference, the problems and possibilities of classroom history raised crossed cultures and offered the opportunity for cross-germination and collective work between disciplines and nations.

The Meetings

The first conference lasted for three days in mid July, 1995. The conference was held at the University of Birmingham's Hornton Grange, a beautiful Edwardian house. The conference was limited to twenty people. Each attendee had been invited because of his or her interest in aspects of the sociology or history of schooling, be it teaching, children, curriculum or social relations in schools. Some had an interest in a particular period, place or problem; some were involved in a funded research project or private research; and some were interested in an idea. Each was known to be working in school research and to be interested in the subject. The meeting was not intended to be exclusionary but it was felt that the kind of interaction demanded could not be managed with a wider group. The members were a mix of people, seven males and twelve females, drawn from seven countries (Belgium, Canada, Denmark, Holland, Sweden, the United States and the United Kingdom), most of whom had prepared a presentation.

For the second conference in Toronto, over a year later, we tried to maintain its size and intimacy, limiting attendance to thirty people, with first invitations going to the earlier participants. We scheduled the meeting to adjoin the joint Canadian-American History of Education Conference in Toronto in late October, 1996. Our idea was to follow a presentation style similar to the original conference, to keep the group working and living together socially and intellectually, which included a trip to a local archive and changes in the meeting place.

The physical environment of the meetings exemplified our work. At Birmingham, we met in an open room with windows on three sides, looking out into a summer garden. When we first gathered in the room, we arranged chairs in a circle. At first some people felt comfortable pulling desks in front of them, as if to present a table of information, data and resources between themselves and the group. But as the conference unfolded, some of those tables, and those reliances on data too, were pushed aside. Also, in Toronto, we spent one day in the peaceful wood-panelled sitting room of a Quaker meeting house, gathered around a large round table as we collectively discussed a teacher's 1927 written memoir of a Belgian school. This contrasted with the machined environment of the windowless, heavy furnitured, conference room where thoughts were forced out against air conditioned humming and the neon glare of modern hotel architecture, but where we were able to take advantage of the VCR and slide projector to further explore the history of classrooms.

At each meeting, we took a trip. In Toronto, we toured the City Board of Education archives and examined both the artifacts in the archives museum and the museum itself as a presentation of history: what artifacts were chosen to be presented and why? Whose stories were told, and not told, and why? In England, we took one afternoon to visit a reconstructed school outside of Birmingham, in a county museum. We were reluctant to leave the bright countryside sun, but once inside, we all rushed to sit at the desks, feeling ourselves return to our childhood and the patterned behavior of school children: looking inside desks, nudging each other, and calling out to one another across the room. We noticed that we sat in much the same parts of the room where we had sat as children, and that while some of us felt a giggly joy at being back in a classroom, others felt a cloud of malaise, remembering the difficult times of their life in school. Together, as a group of historians, we considered the 'facts' of that reconstructed classroom: the authenticity of the maps and the jumbling together of artifacts from different time periods. But positioned then as students in a classroom, we questioned the importance of those facts and their veracity to our own visceral experiences as former students. We questioned our own memories, and the memories of teachers and students whom we had interviewed as historians, and we wondered what it is that people remember and why.

We began the first meeting at Birmingham with a videotape collage of photographs, drawn from pre- and postwar publications in the United Kingdom, illustrating the shifts in schools. Although it was not formally returned to, this film enabled a number of subsequent discussions to develop, for example, about the images of schooling, the ideas of illustration and source to historians, the creation of narratives and most of all, about interpretations which could be free and yet informed. Visual images and the lenses used to capture and create those images became an important part of the meetings. We examined a posed photograph of what appeared to be a classroom and we wondered how we could ever know if it really was a classroom, or if that question was less important than the question of how and why the photograph was posed in this manner, in this room, with this person appearing as a teacher. What was the intended meaning and message of that photograph, and what might that say about what people thought of classrooms at that time? In Toronto, we continued these questions by exploring a film perspective of a classroom — the opening minutes of François Truffaut's 1959 film *Les Quatre Cents Coups* (The Four Hundred Blows) and examined the depth of the images, the mobile gaze of the filmmaker, the three dimensional view of the classroom, and the characteristics of darkness, dust and mess. As a seminar, we came to life, in effect learning a new pedagogy as academics, when we began to add questions, from quite different perspectives, about what constituted a classroom.

As we questioned the nature of sources, so too did we question the very definition of a classroom, since students and teachers took their experiences and relations outside of the four walls of a room into the rest of the building, the yard, and the community. What we had thought of as classrooms took on life spans of their own: we remembered that in poor and crowded schools, classrooms spilled into the hallway, and in declining enrollments, classrooms became meeting rooms or storage places. To some extent, the building itself seemed to shape the life inside of it. The classroom expanded into peoples' temporal as well as geographical space, shaping their very sense of time and order. The classroom also expanded for us not just geographically, but conceptually, as we heard about teachers who made their classroom their own domestic, personal space, and as we heard about the dynamics of buildings, the way that teachers and students wrestled (sometimes literally) for space, comfort and authority within a physical structure.

Schools and classrooms, we began to realize, are not static points, but whole series of events and social relations over time, rich with personal dynamics. Teachers come in and out of classrooms, hanging posters, contributing an extra bookcase or table. Students run in and out of classrooms, make marks on desk tops, leave shredded paper in their books. Administrators, parents, and other adults associated with the school visit classrooms, leaving their mark in an official book or in the dynamics of the social relations in the room. The classroom seeps in and out of the everyday lives of children and adults. It remains lodged in memories for years afterward so that a ninety-year-old retired primary teacher can describe with acid assuredness, the color and feel of the burlap covering on the bulletin board in her first fifth-grade classroom.

As historians, we questioned the nature of the sources we used: some of those sources were chosen by our own theoretical perspective; some were chosen merely by their survival in the archives. As historians, we come to our work from our own cultural context and perspective, but so too did those people who took the photographs, who remembered their past in oral histories, who wrote their diaries or letters. We realized that we are in a dialogue with those people and their context. We realized also that as historians we are in a position of power, and a position of reflexivity. How can we catch ourselves as we choose our sources and our perspective on those sources? How can we understand, and then describe, the mystery of the classroom of the past?

What is a valid story of the past, if teachers and students remember their classrooms through the veil of their own histories? Some oral histories that we had conducted seemed tinged with sentimentality. Original letters or descriptions tell only the view of one subjective author. Photographic documents had only one lens, and froze in time what was otherwise a rapidly moving picture. Photographs don't tell us what happened before and after the shutter was snapped. The very silences of classroom history can in fact speak very loudly.

Explaining Classrooms
The intentions of the conference's original organisers came out of the problems they had had in studying the work of teachers, itself a surprisingly undernourished area of study. Pedagogic shifts and vernacular meanings are not easy to deduce and we had found an absence of theoretical and methodological discussions about how to proceed.

The commonplaces of schooling are not as valued as the grand narrative or as a subject of study within an empirical case study. Administrative sources and official discourse, legitimized in historical explanation, serve to manage the view of the classroom as it appears in curriculum history and the general history of education narratives. Popular schoolroom reconstructions collect artefacts in a way that suggests relationships and usage but that might be ahistorical, something to be read sentimentally or even to act within a reminiscence therapy. The classroom might be confused with school fabric and construction, it is of course solid, but it is also a work of imagination, regulation and mythology. It is a designed solution to mass schooling and it is a social space that generations have in common.

In addition, it is difficult to discern changes in classroom practice and locating routine meaning is almost impossible in surviving sources. Fragments of data emerge from footnotes, reminiscences, pamphlets, oral histories, photographs and reports. It is easier for the historian to date the arrival of a new textbook in a school or imply value on the basis of the copies sold. As a consequence, classrooms of the past are not easily reconstructed and relived: the technology of the classroom appears discernible, yet this is an illusion. The meaning and practice of work to the teacher lie out of reach, along with the culture and politics of their social and educational existence. Past social and classroom relationships with pupils and parents have gone. Old crafts and routines are barely knowable. Even oral histories, rare enough in teaching, are narratives based on unexplained but ubiquitous terms (like *classroom* or *desk* or *lesson*) as if the meaning could be universally understood across time and context.

So this book contributes to the substantive study of classrooms. It works as a source of new studies of aspects of classrooms, raising questions about the people who occupied them; the constraints and freedoms of this workplace; the place of the classroom in teachers' working lives. It introduces a further set of studies whose implications for the classroom disrupts its common use: what was the classroom designed to do as a technology? What is claimed as its work (and what evidence is excluded about other possible modes)? How did its meanings change during early and late modern periods of educational development?

These chapters add to the methodological debates in historiography, raising questions about discursive analysis of fiction, texts, images and personal writings in studying the idea of classrooms. The history of education struggles to generate new theoretical insights into educational events and practices but appears to be stalled in its methodological evolution. The invention of the footnote was a leap forward in narrative authority in history writing. This book is an attempt to produce new forms of practice in history education and to generate acceptable new ways of working.

Evidence about classrooms doesn't just accumulate within this book. Proof and evidence might co-exist with ambiguity, contrast and layering. We are not looking for absolute 'proof' about classrooms of the past, but justified possibilities. The idea of the classroom investigated through these sources has allowed a useful contrast to develop between descriptions of a fixed space and a struggle over its meaning. Together and within this tension, other possibilities are produced. It isn't a case of either/or but both.

Central to these meetings, and to the spirit of these chapters, was the loose exchange of ideas, the participant's imagination and the way that we encouraged one another to think anew about our professional skills as historians. The conferences were deliberately constructed to mix presentations and experiences in such a way as to create a fluidity of interpretation, opening the subject so as to enable new conceptualizations to be created.

Like the conferences, this book is organised in an experimental way, one that reflects this exploratory nature of the sessions. Its production reflects its experimental and innovative nature. The chapters should be read as open narratives, as works in progress, and as parts of a larger conversation. They should be read relationally, and not as discrete entities. In addition, the relational aspects of the essays are not solely about comparing the broader context of time, space or nationality but about comparing different

conceptualisation of classrooms and different approaches to investigating classrooms.

It is possible to read the accounts and ideas in this book
as a montage, juxtaposing verbal and visual fragments,
a process described (by Alan Pred) as an articulation as
well as a resonation at several levels at once. The study
of classrooms, following Pred and capturing the spirit
of the conferences that created this book, should enable
multiple ways of knowing and multiple sets of
meaning:

by confronting the ordinary and the extraordinary
the commonplace with the out of place
the (would be) hegemonic with the counter
hegemonic,
the ruly with the unruly,
the power wielders with the subjects of power,
the margin definers with the marginalized,
the boundary drawers with the out-of-bounds,
the norm makers with the 'abnormal',
the dominating with the dominated.[2]

2 A. Pred, *Recognising
European Modernities -
A Montage of the
Present* (London:
Routledge, 1995)
p. 25.

Ian Grosvenor
Martin Lawn
Kate Rousmaniere

Part 1
Raising Questions
about
Classroom History

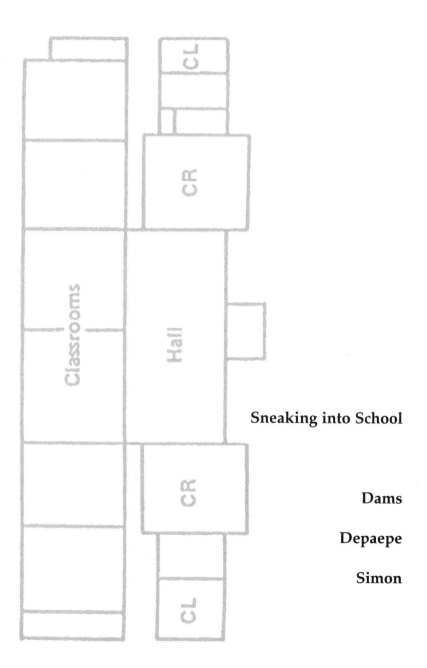

Sneaking into School

Dams

Depaepe

Simon

Sneaking into School: classroom history at work

Kristof Dams, Marc Depaepe, and Frank Simon

The trouble with classroom history

The work of the classroom historian, some say, is seriously hampered by a problem with its sources. Journals, government reports and textbooks - the traditional sources of the history of education - are said to contain merely guidelines and wishful thinking and so have blinded us to 'how it really was'.[1] In order 'to break down the classroom door', the historian must look for other sources, more precisely for reports of eye-witnesses who recorded their observations or of participants who share their experiences with the researcher. We do not wish to cast doubt on the value of ego documents for classroom history, but we do want to question the assumption that casts aside 'normative' sources as of no use whatsoever and that emphasises 'personal testimonies' as the main, or even the only, source. We argue that a well thought-out analysis of normative discourse (and more precisely of educational journals) can contribute substantially to classroom history. To this end, we discuss an element of classroom history that at first sight has most need of personal testimonies, namely the 'climate' in the classroom. This discussion is a practical example of the method for which the theory is presented in another article.[2]

The study of classroom climate has, since the 1960s, established itself as a particular field of specialisation in educational sciences. In historical perspective, however, nothing of any particular significance has been said about it. Larry Cuban in *How Teachers Taught* specifically avoided the subject,[3] and Arthur Zilversmit in *Changing Schools*[4] and Barbara Finkelstein (in *Governing the Young*) also left it aside. Kate Rousmaniere, in *City Teachers*, is the only one who has discussed classroom climate under a separate heading, where she mused that New York class life in the 1920s,

1 B. Finkelstein, *Governing the Young : Teacher Behavior in Popular Primary Schools in Nineteenth-Century United States*, (New York: Falmer Press, 1989) 2nd ed. with a new introduction, p. 35.

2 K. Dams, M. Depaepe, and F. Simon. *Classroom History: Sources and Objectives* (in preparation). The approach presented there is used in a research project supervised by M. Depaepe, M. De Vroede, F. Simon, R. Vandenberghe, and J. Verhoeven and executed by K. Dams, B. Eggermont, and H. Lauwers. We reconstruct the everyday life inside the classroom in Belgium from 1880 to 1970.

3 He intentionally concentrated on visible interaction: L. Cuban, *How Teachers Taught: Constancy and Change in American Classrooms,1880-1990*, (New York: Teachers College Press, 1993) 2nd rev ed., p.9.

4 A. Zilversmit, *Changing Schools: Progressive Education, Theory and Practice*, (Chicago: University of Chicago Press, 1993)

5 K. Rousmaniere, *City Teachers. Teaching and School Reform in Historical Perspective* (New York: Teachers College Press, 1997) pp. 111-32.

6 B. Finkelstein, 'Re-imagining educational reform: Public schools and the nurture of consciousness' *Educational Studies: A Journal in the Foundations of Education*, 14 (1983) p. 103.

7 H. Tenorth. 'Grenzen der Indoctrination' in P. Drewek, K. Horn, C. Kersting, and H. Tenorth, eds., *Ambivalenzen der Pädagogik: Zur Bildungsgeschichte der Aufklärung und des 20. Jahrhunderts* (Weinheim: Deutscher Studien Verlag, 1995).

no matter how hard it was, had its fine moments: there were some good times and some bad times.[5] Finkelstein had already informed us that it was not because the early nineteenth century American public school was the home of ageism, sexism, and racism, where children were kept under control by a 'ministerial force-feeder' that it could not have been a 'haven of liberating possibility'.[6] In the same line, Heinz Elmar Tenorth reported, on the basis of pupils' school memories, that even in the schools of the Third Reich, positive learning experiences were not impossible.[7] He cited Hitler's biographer, J. Fest, who declared somewhat apologetically that he did not dislike reminiscing about his schooldays in the Third Reich. Of course, less pleasant memories about Nazi-controlled schools also emerge, but this ambivalence, according to Tenorth, characterises school recollections of every period.

Thus the verdict on school climate in historical perspective is still out. It is pointed out that things were probably not as bad as they looked, that the 'zero-tolerance policy' that characterised the better part of the history of the classroom probably did not amount to a climate of downright terror and fear. But can one say anything more about it? We think so but we must immediately add that the image will always remain blurred. One thing is clear from the start: the historian is simply not able to penetrate to the core of the child's perception of his or her 'educational environment', and must learn to live with that. In the period of our research into the history of the classroom in Belgium between 1880 and 1970, millions of children passed through school. Every last one of them could, in principle, scrutinise his school experiences (and how they fit into the rest of his life) in a work of the size of Proust's *A la Recherche du Temps Perdu*. When judging the classroom climate in past times, it will have to be with Tacitus' reservation when he described the reactions of the senate, the *ordo equester*, and the people to the death of Nero: 'And such was the mood, at least in Rome, as far as this can be established for a population so large'.[8]

8 Cornelii Taciti, *Historiarum Libri, I, 8*

We must restrict ourselves to what we can know beyond reasonable doubt. We might set out to devise methods to discover the 'truth' about the perceptions of pupils, but we never will succeed. The only thing such an effort can lead to is a torturing of the historical sources to the point that they confess crimes they never committed. The question, therefore, is 'What can we know?' It will be treated alongside another question of some weight: 'What do we want to know?' Or, better 'What are our reasons for conducting research into classroom history?'

Classroom history at the junction of intention and effect

The purpose of classroom history is to investigate what goes on in the black box [9] of educational history, the classroom. Historians have so far studied mainly pedagogical intentions and then linked these to social evolution. But congruency between pedagogical intentions and social change or stability alone does not prove that the school efficiently executed these intentions. To answer the question whether it did or not, classroom practice must be closely studied: What were the intentions? Were they realised and, if so, how and to what extent? And what were the consequences of that realisation?

9 P. Caspard, 'Introduction,' in 'Travaux d'élèves. Pour une histoire des performances scolaires et de leur évaluation', *Histoire de l'Education*, XLVI (1990) p. 1.

This applies to all aspects of classroom history and hence also to classroom climate. It is in fact especially important to keep the broader circumstances firmly in mind when describing the classroom climate because there is a danger of stressing the climate or the experiences of teachers and pupils, the emotions, for no particular reason other than paradigmatic fashion. It is not enough to take a great interest in 'what it meant to people' and 'how they really experienced it' without explaining why this should be worthy of our or anybody's attention. We must point out a danger here

10 E. Terhart,
'Schulkultur.
Hintergründe,
Formen und
Implikationen eines
schulpädagogischen
Trends.' *Zeitschrift fur
Pädagogik,* XL (1994)
pp. 685-99.

that has already affected the educational sciences, at least according to Ewald Terhart,[10] who analysed the emphasis on the 'quality of pedagogical experiences' as an effect of the changeover from a production society to a leisure society in which the affluent fight for less work whilst cultivating distinctions. Previously, the primary school was supposed to prepare its pupils for further education, so that its success or failure could be read in higher-education enrolment rates. Today, the feel-good factor seems to have become crucial.

We feel that the current wave of classroom history should not lead the history of education to limit its scope to a feel-good factor. We plead that the history of education be analysed on the axis of intention, realisation, and effect. In such a framework, the classroom climate becomes important to the historian of education in two ways. First, it is examined how the 'climate' becomes an object of pedagogical reflection and inspires initiatives. Second, the effects, social and otherwise, of these initiatives must be explored. The atmosphere of the Belgian classroom, apart from the realisation or failure of pedagogical intentions, in the few million hours that were devoted to education between 1880 and 1970, in the perception of the roughly 2 to 100 pupils in a class, is irrelevant to our purposes. Only when the creation of a certain atmosphere becomes a strategy, an instrument for realising pedagogical intentions, is the interest of the historian of education aroused.

Consider, by way of an example, fear. The intentions and actions of educators aside, there will always be faint-hearted children. A classic example is that some children break out in a cold sweat when there is no night light burning. These things happen. We do not care. We only begin to notice when someone deliberately turns out the light. This might be meant as a lesson if the educator thinks the child is too old for such foolishness, for such an opinion is part of a pedagogical mentality, just as it is part of a pedagogical mentality to leave the light on. Pedagogical par excellence is when the educator takes measures to make the child gradually unlearn the habit. But when the educator is quite simply unaware of the child's fear, we have no need to know either, even when we later learn from the child about her sufferings. We might sympathise, but the juvenile anguish does not teach us anything about the history of education.

After discovering the intention and analysing the realisation, we are able to start tracing the effects. How do we go about this? Do we measure the effect by the action itself or by the account of the participants? In other words, how do we assess the meaning of a blow struck by the teacher? Do we measure it by the force of its impact? Or do we trust the testimony of the pupil? This is an epistemological but also a heuristic question.

One can say that the pupil's perception is the most important element. This presents two broad problems, however, the first being that the perceptions we speak of are usually reconstructions by an adult. In the war of adults against children, as described by G. B. Shaw,[11] the witness has defected to the other camp. This can already explain the persistent ambiguity of school memories: 'It was hard, but it was for our own good.' The schooled subject who looks back is a different person. He might give vent to anger (and he often does), but is almost predestined to conclude on a positive note. The second problem with the use of personal perceptions in historical perspective is the representativity of the testimony. Certainly for the earlier years of our investigation (the 1880s), only isolated testimonies are available. Through this circumstance, these testimonies gain immensely in weight: one witness becomes the spokesperson for hundreds of thousands of pupils. The problem, then, is: how do we know that this witness is not, for instance, quite simply insane. He might have been paranoid and felt persecuted, pursued, forlorn. He could have been convinced he was the victim of a great and evil

11 As cited by A. Clausse, *Evolution des doctrines et des méthodes pédagogiques. Du conditionnement à la liberté* (Fribourg: Editions Universitaires, 1983) p. 11.

conspiracy. Must we conclude, then, that fear and terror were everyday ingredients of pedagogical practice? The example of a deranged eyewitness may seem far-fetched, but there are other reasons why witnesses can be untrustworthy, as we shall see.

The other method, calculating the force of the blow, is, we feel, the better of the two. This comes down to a study of the environment by which we mean not only the material infrastructure (the pedagogical comfort) but also the mental environment. Part of a mentality, for instance, is the belief that in class there should be silence. We can more or less easily trace historical fluctuations in the desired amount of silence, but what can we decide on these grounds? We can use the following reasoning: many pupils have problems with obligatory silence, preferring to speak, interfere, contribute. Which leads us to the logical conclusion: the climate in schools was restraining. But in pronouncing this verdict, we do not take account of the experience of children who are quite happy as long as they are left in peace, who do not wish to speak out for themselves and contribute. Some people are introverts, others extroverts. We cannot solve this problem by arguing that speaking, expressing oneself, is always good and silence always bad, an inhibition that must be removed even to the discomfort of the taciturn. In this way, one is always correct. Thus, the liveliness of the classroom in a given time, which can be fairly easily established, does not tell us anything about the experience. Again, we cannot get inside the pupils' minds.

But then what can we do? We can investigate socialisation. We can speculate about what 'socialisation in silence' means not in a psychological way but in a social and cultural way. Instead of fruitlessly trying to probe deep into minds, we can simply investigate familiarisation. It is quite obvious that the ability to be silent is of the gravest importance for society, as is the ability to sit still. If tomorrow people could no longer sit still, be silent, and concentrate on an operation that might possibly not appeal to them at all, the system would collapse. Conquering one's aversions is what is learned at school.

Desirable behaviour can be learned without the accompanying conviction that this behaviour is good and honourable. Such conviction is just an extra. The worker who dislikes his job might be feeling tormented and forlorn. These are his feelings. If he followed them, he would stand up and walk out, never to come back. But he keeps still, shuts up, swears only occasionally, and carries on. He has learned to conquer his aversions. Of course, he has also learned at school that working is good. He might start to think that there must be something horribly wrong with him because he feels so bad; perhaps he is not so impressed with the official work ethic and feels not guilty but spiteful. Whatever feelings pass through him, he sits still and works on. Unless, let us not forget, it all becomes too much. He might then do something wild, such as assaulting his boss, or he might find allies and incite a nationwide revolt. There are many possibilities, but what it comes down to is this: people do not perform socially desirable acts because they are deeply convinced they are the right things to do. Such total brainwashing only happened in George Orwell's *1984* because the only place where it can happen is in a work of fiction.

This means that we have to be careful. We must examine relations, behaviour and customs, not deep convictions. We will look at them from two perspectives. First, where do they come from? From what context of ideas do they derive their meaning? Second, what is their social effect? The social effect might differ considerably from the intentions and still be logically explainable from the actions. For this approach, obviously, more is needed than testimonies of experience. We cannot turn directly to the people concerned in the conviction that we can, with our

assortment of devious tricks, extort the full truth out of
them. To get close to the heart of the classroom, we
must be even more cunning and devious than that. We
will have to sneak into the classroom by re-examining
its strategy, thereby avoiding some old pitfalls, such as
seeing the class simply as the missing link in the causal
chain between intention and effect. Indeed, we must be
very careful, for even if we find congruency not only
between intention and effect but also in classroom
behaviour, we still are not certain about the specific
effects of the class. There are two reasons for this. The
first is that education does not consist of schooling
alone; the second is that our actions, are not only, and
maybe not chiefly, driven by education (or the
conscious rejection of parts of education, which we can
also look on in a dialectic scheme as an 'effect of
education', albeit not desired). But we can trace *possible*
effects of the school. We discuss a case.

The Classroom Climate: a reform pedagogue's view
A clear view on, and analysis of, school climate is
found in the following 1927 text by Jozef Emiel
Verheyen, head of the experimental school of
Zaventem. It is taken from the progressive journal
Moderne School, of which Verheyen was editor-in-chief.

> Becoming a pupil: that means being shut up
> with all your friends of your own age during
> the best, longest, and finest part of the day in a
> room that is completely different from all the
> other houses and rooms you know, with
> benches such as exist nowhere else, with
> furniture that you never encounter anywhere
> else, with high whitewashed walls full of
> crumpled maps, worn-out charts, and other
> scraps of paper, such as you never see
> adorning the walls of the rooms in a house,
> with high windows that prevent you from
> looking out, with pen and pencil, slate, paper,
> and books as your toys, which you are not
> allowed to use freely but only on command

and according to particular instructions; becoming a pupil, i.e. learning to sit still and keep quiet, i.e. learning to think and work on all kinds of things for which you have no feeling at all and which you never need in your childhood life outside the school, i.e. above all learning to listen to someone who is older and stronger than you are, who has at his disposal unlimited power and all kinds of torments (such as writing out and copying, staying behind, bad marks, reports, and exams) to keep you in check if the child-in-the-pupil wants to express itself, someone who talks in a different language and in a different way about different things than all the other people you meet daily, who makes you read in books about sunshine when it is raining outside, makes you answer questions about buying a piece of land when you are saving for a scooter, gives a hygiene lesson on the qualities of good heating at the height of summer and at a time when you have stomach-ache from eating too much unripe fruit, someone who...

We all know it and we feel it so well: neither we the teachers nor we the children are the same creatures in school as we are outside school. We all know it, we feel it so well and every time in the conference papers we write full of enthusiasm and in a roundabout way: school must prepare for life,... 'the school for and through life', but what we write down at home as humans, as teachers we do not put into living reality and fertile deeds in front of the class. I do not want to cast the first stone because I know that we are caught in the nets of tradition, of rules and regulations, of timetables, syllabuses and examinations, I know that our own training and the school itself with its buildings, teaching aids, and books, with its orientation, goals, and methods hinders, hampers, sometimes prevents the advance.

And yet! This advance, this merging of school and life must come; the antithesis of teacher and person, pupil and child must disappear; the gulf separating school and life must be bridged; life must penetrate into school, and school must be a natural continuation and form part of life; there, in my view, lies the answer to the question of education. The child's games, his interests in externally observable events and phenomena, his inner drive, his predisposition, feelings, and inclinations must determine the school activities, and it is here that the educator must draw the material and the method for promoting the child's spiritual growth.

We willingly admit that complete implementation of these principles is not possible in the present circumstances with the conditions that now exist in our school with its strictly defined syllabus, with the straitjacket of the timetable, with the official attitudes that still prevail on discipline, examinations, and so on. We must, therefore, first of all try to bring about a change in public opinion on the purpose and essence of the school and also try to capture the freedom that is essential to the teacher and pupil, without which there can never be serious improvement, a change of course, and progress. Does that mean that in the meantime we must carry on as in grandfather's time and cross our arms while we wait? No, because 1) the change we dream of will not fall into our laps like ripe pears; tradition, public opinion and officialdom are not unknown American uncles from whom we can anticipate an unexpected inheritance; 2) the best way of attaining our goal is by furnishing the truth of our views through

Sneaking into School

deeds; 3) the child in the meantime suffers from these unnatural conditions.[12]

The actual drift of this text is least open to misinterpretation. Alongside compulsion, it is chiefly alienation that the author emphasises: he characterises school as an enclosed space turned in on itself in which both teacher and pupil are playing roles which deny their 'true nature'. To evoke the alienation, he cites the separate furniture, the completely distinct 'wall adornment', and above all the windows, which are too high to look through. In interpreting this text, the problem is not what is being said but who is speaking.

Is this an attempt to empathise with the child's mind, or does Verheyen display his own traumas? If it is empathy, where did he start from? His practical experience? But the school of which he was the head was an experimental school and it used different methods from those being criticised. It is true that Verheyen had been an inspector, which means we can read his criticism as being the result of these visits. This would make the source a report on observation. Or is he instead citing memories from his own schooldays? Is he allowing himself to be guided by his own feelings of alienation at that time? This would make the source a report on experience. Or something else again: Is it a matter neither of traumas nor of empathy and must it simply be regarded as a diatribe, the noise that has to be made for one to be fully appreciated by the *avant-garde* intelligentsia?

In our view, it is the last. We cannot interpret this text as the report of an observer or participant, even though over the course of his lifetime Verheyen had been both. We should not try to establish the reality of whatever feeling is expressed within these lines. Rather, we should focus exclusively on the intentions and purposes of the author. There is no feeling here: this is cold, abstract analysis. It is not so much the form of the text that leads to this conclusion. Of course, the text

12 J. E. Verheyen, 'School en Leven', *Moderne School*, I (1927) p.43, translated from the Dutch. This kind of text, with its characteristic rhetoric opposing 'school' and 'life' can be found in many national and international reform-pedagogical journals.

13 Verheyen was also an experimental pedagogue: he incorporated both tendencies. He battled against Catholic normative pedagogy but was himself well aware that the reform-pedagogic striving for freedom, in the society of his time, could not be taken to its limit. Reform pedagogy implied a completely different social orientation. In any case, experimental pedagogy had the effect of tempering Verheyen's reform-pedagogic ideals. This tempering is constantly observed when the principles of reform pedagogy were implemented. The change of direction to meritocracy is striking. See M. Depaepe, 'Experimentelle Pädagogik, Reformpädagogik und pädagogische Praxis. Überlegungen über ihre wechselseitigen Beziehungen, dargestellt am Beispiel der Versuchsschulen von Jozef Emiel Verheyen in Zaventem und Gent (1923-1940)', in J. Oelkers, F. Osterwalder and H.U. Grunder eds., *Die pädagogik des 'Fin de siècle'* (Bern, in press).

14 See M. Depaepe, M. De Vroede and F. Simon, 'The 1936 Curriculum Reform in Belgian primary education', *Journal of Education Policy*, VI

does not look like an ego document; it does not look like a page torn out of a progressive teacher's diary in which he aired his grudges. Verheyen did not merely complain: he argued, identified causes, proposed solutions. The procedure he adopted appears to be identical to one of the two main strategies a classroom historian can follow: he examined the effect on the pupils of the structural elements of class organisation and culture. He measured the force of the blow or so it seems. But the form of the text is irrelevant. It is not unthinkable that personal reflections and convincing empathy might be found at the heart of cold analysis.

But not here. What we have here is straight-out New Education propaganda.[13] The points on which Verheyen focused are too faithful, word-for-word, to reform pedagogy to be revealing genuine emotion. He actually arranged the classroom situations around principles of reform pedagogy. For example, take the point of the lesson about sunshine when it is raining outside. Just a few years later, in 1936,[14] there was an attempt, with a grand design by school policy, to put some reform-pedagogical principles into practice. With a particularly ruthless simplification, we can state that the school reform above all came down to teaching about rain when it was raining and about sunshine when the sun is shining. The principal commitment of the 1936 curriculum was to throw the school gates open and lay out the red carpet for the joyful entrance of 'real life'. It amounted to 'throwing open the classroom windows'. This is a paradox: first, the school was arranged as a differentiated system, with pedagogical approval. Then the educationalists complained that school was not life itself. In the meantime, they did not want to abolish school to 'let life go its way', they wanted to simulate life in school. Or rather to offer such a palette of 'life' that the school would be more 'life' than life itself. It is in this sense that Verheyen's attack on the wall charts is to be understood. Educationalists were satisfied with these facsimiles of 'life' until Verheyen and those of like mind stood up and objected that the charts were a corruption of the true vision. In this spirit, the 1936 plan wanted to drive the masters and pupils out of the classroom, into wide-open nature, to 'environmental studies'.

Verheyen was an active promoter of all these initiatives, and it was on the basis of these concerns that he described the classroom situation. It was not the pupils who demanded a school reform that was chiefly aimed at eliminating 'non-contemporariness'. If we asked them to say what 'cannot any longer be excepted in our schools', would they have complained that there were wall charts hanging on the classroom wall while they did not have any at home? Would they have made the pressing demand that books in which the sun is shining be read only when it was not raining outside?

We must be careful. It is easy to allow oneself to be swept away by discourse as passionate as Verheyen's. His imagery is powerful. In the introduction leading to the quoted passage, Verheyen talked about the teacher who, on his way to school, read in his paper about Charles Lindbergh's transatlantic flight and about a recent flood of the Mississippi. He becomes entranced by heroic exploits and by wild, destructive forces of nature. At his arrival in school, everything seems in comparison narrow and cramped. There's a musty smell in the air. On his way to school, impressions made themselves the better of the teacher, things went through his mind: he was alive. He was a *human being*. In school he hung his 'being a person' on the hat-rack to become a teacher, as the children hung their 'being-a-child' on the hat-rack to become pupils.

Edward Peeters, the journal's former editor-in-chief (it was then called 'Schoolblad voor Vlaanderen') and, like Verheyen, a reform-pedagogue,[15] also used vivid, somewhat agitated prose to sketch the divorce between school and life, but Peeters' examples are less sensational. To depict the narrowness of the school by way of *clair-obscur*, he had no need for trans-oceanic

(1991) pp. 371-83. In the line of the New Education Movement, the new curriculum stressed the importance of the forming of judgement (as opposed to memorising), of an education based on facts and experiences, of social education, and of an ethic that was not based on authority but that arose out of the child. The crux of the new plan was the so-called 'points of interest', which were to have overthrown the traditional school subjects. The plan integrated new developments in child psychology, such as Claparèdes' *syncretism* and Decroly's *globalisation*.

15 Albeit of a different type, Peeters' aim was to stay close to practice and experience, while Verheyen wanted to develop the same principles on an abstract, academic level. Verheyen hence became professor at the University of Ghent, while Peeters never ceased to distrust academic pedagogy. See M. Depaepe, *Zum Wohl des Kindes? Pädologie, pädagogische Psychologie und experimentelle Pädagogik in Europa und den U.S.A.,* 1890-1940 (Leuven/ Weinheim: Leuven University Press, Deutscher Studien Verlag, 1993).

flights or immense, savage powers. He looked no farther than outside the school window where lush grasslands bathed in the summer sunshine. His theme was simple, but his prose all the more exalted. About manuals, benches, and notebooks, he wrote, 'Throw away those instruments of torture! Stop! Stop! Outside! Where between embalming scents a free concerto resounds from thousands of crickets' throats'. He continued:

> How powerful imagination is! Only just have I cried out with a thousand times the power of my lungs or I see, before my mind's eye, the effect of my anti-social performance - for anti-social it is. In schools of all kinds, boys and girls throw away their manuals, jump cheering out of their torture chairs - I mean: out of their benches - storm through the broad gates, hurry through the streets, and throw themselves head over heels in the fresh-green, fluffy grass, walk barefoot, shoes and socks on their back, through the brooks and through the ditches, tossing about and swarming.[16]

16 E. Peeters, *'Vrije Uitingen van een Schoolmeester'* (Nymegen, 's Hertogenbosch, Antwerp: Malmberg, (1920) p. 17. Translated from the Dutch.

Peeters managed to maintain this prose for quite a while longer.

We know now that there is at least one sort of testimony that needs careful treatment, namely, the testimonies of persons with a pedagogical interest, such as teachers, inspectors, and reformers. The asset of their testimony is that they offer ample information on specific techniques and rituals and how they, as pupils, felt about them. Information of this kind does not appear in other testimonies. But there is a real danger that they neatly seal our description of the classroom climate and how pupils experienced it within the framework of a specific pedagogy, of whatever kind. Another example is the Belgian teacher and inspector Leo Roels, who, alongside Léon Jeunehomme, designed the 1936 curriculum, painting an ugly picture of the primary school he visited (his report, somewhat mysteriously though not unexpectedly, concluded with a positive general evaluation). One of his grievances was that the pupils had to sit still in church and listen and did not receive any information on the religious symbols and representations, such as the pictures depicting the Way of the Cross.[17] Must our verdict of the climate in Roels' class therefore be that the pupils were, without any explanation, exposed to images and, in Verheyen's words, 'suffered under these unnatural conditions'? In his article on Third Reich school memories, Tenorth remarked that the testimony of novelists must be treated, in principle, with distrust because of their authors' linguistic talent and knowledge of editing. Professional writers are not naive: they know how to sequence their facts and figures so as to produce a certain, measured effect.[18] This may be true.[19] But it seems that we have to distrust pedagogues at least as much as we distrust literary authors.

In brief, as an eyewitness report or a participant, Verheyen's text is not convincing. His text is only interesting for the information it offers on the drive, the intention, behind it.

Verheyen's war on formality
In Verheyen's text we find many signs of an evolution that took place in the school over broadly the last century as well as in the whole of society: the emergence of informality or the decline in compulsion of form at every level. What Verheyen described as the antithesis between school and 'life', teacher and 'human', we can also describe with Richard Sennett, in his pithy title, as *The Fall of Public Man*,[20]

> The reigning belief today is that closeness between persons is a moral good. The reigning aspiration today is to develop individual personality through experiences of closeness and warmth with others. The reigning myth

17 L. Roels, *Het Vliegenkotje van de Lei,* (Hasselt: Heideland, 1965) p. 65.

18 Tenorth (1995).

19 Although we feel that this might really be an advantage. Candid and artless utterances might, for all their charm, put the researcher quite simply on the wrong foot as regards the feelings and purposes of the speaker.

20 R. Sennett, *The Fall of Public Man* (New York: Random House, 1978) p. 259

today is that the evils of society can all be understood as evils of impersonality, alienation and coldness. The sum of these three is an ideology of intimacy: social relationships of all kinds are real, believable, and authentic the closer they approach the inner psychological concerns of each person.[21]

21 *Ibid.*, p. 268.

In Sennett's view, an intimate society encourages 'uncivilised' behaviour between individuals and discourages a 'sense of play'. The outcomes are 'tyrannies of intimacy'. It is in this context that we must place Verheyen's incentive for the teacher to suppress the formal aspects of his role. Verheyen no longer allowed the teacher to be a 'master', the place where he worked no longer to be a 'school', and the children no longer to be 'pupils'. Such compartmentalisation of the individual, such reduction to a role, was no longer to be permitted. The teacher would, for us, become a human being and the pupil a child. And the school? Life itself.

Rather than concurring with Verheyen's alienation theory by reporting that school alienated the child from his innermost self, we must regard his text as information about a rising distrust of formality and a predilection for what is vague, all-embracing, and 'true'. Verheyen and his allies wanted to scrap the pomp and circumstance of school rites, the outer display of the pedagogical liturgy, in order to put the pupil and teacher in all sincerity opposite each other. Authority in school was to become a matter of human relations.

But did they succeed? In order to succeed, they needed a good plan. In itself, a discipline that is not based on compulsion but on mutual respect is an old pedagogical idea. The educational journals proclaimed it incessantly, but they never showed how to achieve it. They had noble intentions, but noble intentions were not enough in the light of conditions in which the school had to operate. Overpopulated classes were probably the principal objection in the mass of complaints teachers and others endlessly repeated, but they also objected to stress due to additional work, the lack of materials, and the lack of any meaningful in-service training. Under these circumstances, the classroom was a theatre of war in which the pupils had to be pacified by discipline that could not be misunderstood. The luxury of discipline that could be misunderstood was only possible if the structure permitted it.

What interests us the most is not the purple prose of which we have quoted some samples but the plan, the workable initiatives that were developed to change the face of the classroom. For that we have to consult articles on topics other than Verheyen's, whose concern was 'what is wrong with our schools' not 'what are we going to do about it', which he spoke of only vaguely and in passing. The passage by Edward Peeters was a progressive teacher's daydream and, ultimately, so was Verheyen's. To analyse how this drive affected everyday school life, we need articles that spoke directly to teachers, that gave pointers for everyday practice. These articles are not simply 'normative' in the sense of being distanced from practice: they betray the everyday reality, through the clash, on the very pages, of progressive semantics and the need to get on with the job. In the following sections, we will briefly discuss the reception of the two drives that Verheyen stood for: first, the move to outdoor life or, more broadly, the drive to enlarge the 'inside' of the school; second, the need for 'broadness', for 'becoming a person instead of a teacher or a pupil. In our discussion of these drives, we refer mainly to articles in educational journals, but we will also use testimonies of individual teachers.[22]

The inside and the outside of the school

In Verheyen's article, life itself seemed to consist chiefly of destructive forces of nature and unsurpassed audacity, but he also gave a simpler example: the

22 These testimonies by teachers born between 1899 and 1920 were recorded in the early 1980s in an oral history project at the University of Ghent. These interviews with former teachers and pupils were not conducted for this study but are suitable for various uses. Guided by an interviewer with a very wide range of topics in mind (not just the practice and experience in the classroom but also their social background and so on), the intention above all was to let the interview subjects tell their own story, in a structure determined by themselves.

upcoming fair in the village. On his eventful journey to the school, the teacher paused to watch its construction. This choice once again testifies to Verheyen's penchant for the spectacular: a fair might be an event out of everyday life, but at the same time it is a disruption of it, albeit one that is planned for and repeated in a fixed pattern. A fair means pleasure, speed, spinning around, letting oneself go. Edward Peeters, as seen earlier, would get somewhat carried away on the wings of his own inflated prose, but his theme was much simpler: he spoke about the lush meadows surrounding the school. The 'environment' outlined by the 1936 curriculum leaned closest to Peeters. Although the community's economic activity could also be an object of study, the emphasis was fully on the ecological environment. The events around the globe known as 'the news' were not integrated into the child's official 'environment'.

This thematic reduction was the first way in which the outside world could be reshaped to fit the size of the classroom: outdoor life had to adapt itself to school traditions and proceedings. That the observation of nature was heralded as the main 'interest of the child' is understandable, as the classification of fauna and flora was already an important learning goal. Economic activity was also already a study object in geography. To turn the fairgrounds into subject matter, however, would be a novelty: traditional subjects do not abound there. Physical sensations were not included in a learning goal.

That the world news was not subject matter was to be expected because it was beyond the teachers' powers to foresee world events. They could not fit into a previously drawn-up plan because environment studies was not conceived in this way. Already in the 1930s there was an outcry in progressive magazines against the misinterpretation of the 'points of interest'. It was stated that the teacher had to probe for the real interests of the child at a particular moment (in

Verheyen's article: Lindbergh, Mississippi, the fairgrounds) instead of imposing them out of a book. In *Recherches Pédagogiques*, for instance, a teacher boasted that he had seriously inquired about the pupils' real interests to discover that it was labour in all its forms that captivated them most. Considering that the periodical was of Marxist signature, it is not difficult to figure out who really selected the points of interest. Obviously, the 'points of interest' were set beforehand by pedagogical and ideological norms, which was the case not just for Marxist teachers. A simple example: there was no way that teachers were allowed to make use of children's fascination for the burgeoning phenomena of cinema and movie stars; on the contrary, children had to be diverted from this dangerous charm.

The second way that the world could be reshaped for the classroom was the integration of outdoor life in everyday school life: as a guided tour, carefully planned and prepared in advance. There was no place for impulsiveness: everything had to proceed according to plan. A field trip, in the first place, had to be *efficient*, and efficiency meant here that it had to furnish sufficient data to fill a few regular indoor classes. The following procedure was always advised: the field trip was to be extensively prepared in class, and afterwards the results were to be 'processed'. The longer this processing took, the more successful was the field trip. To stress the serious nature of field trips, they were referred to with the meaningfully precise term of 'field-trip lesson'. There could be no mistake about it: it was not a casual promenade.

For all these restrictions and planning, the field trip as a principal practical mode of 'environmental study' remained a bold venture: in open, free nature there were no symmetrically arranged benches. The *ad-hoc* simulation of a classroom in the open air became an important pedagogical problem. Specifically because of the inherent problems of order and discipline, the class field trip was not popular among teaching staff at first glance. The leveling out of the symbols that expressed the hierarchic relationships posed problems for them.

To deal with such problems, a veritable *mise-en-discours* followed. While going on field trips had long been suggested, the incentive gained new weight in the 1930s. Field trips had to achieve new goals; they had to bring schools back to life. The recommendation itself did not change drastically,[23] but what was new was the ubiquity of the encouragement. The problems raised by field trips were dealt with at teachers' conferences and in journals.[24] Opportunities were created to acquire experience in practice, to exchange findings with colleagues, and to acquire a new skill. A problem treated in this way was the question of knowledge. The teacher's authority in the classroom was based in part on her knowledge of teaching rules. In free nature, however, the children were exposed to impulses that might lead to unexpected questions. In order not to suffer a loss of face, the teacher, therefore, had to make the field trip beforehand and look carefully in order to anticipate possible questions and look up answers. In this way, she familiarised herself with the area and knew more about it than her pupils, and, as in her classroom, she had them under her control. The transposition of the classroom to the open air was, in other words, a major exercise.

The journals went out of their way to ensure that field trips would in no way disrupt the proper conduct of affairs. They therefore cannot be expected to have drastically changed the atmosphere in the classroom, except in the very literal sense, of occasionally getting some fresh air. The main principle, which was something of a school law, was that the outdoors could not change the inside of the classroom, for the outside world was only eligible to enter everyday school life insofar as it was compatible with a preceding school structure.

We do not see this changing in the further evolution. In

23 For the history of the incentives towards school field trips, see F. Simon, 'Les acti-vités et les oeuvres scolaires, post-scolaires et parascolaires' in *Histoire de La Ligue de L'enseignement et de L'éducation Permanente* (Bruxelles: Ligue de L'Enseignement et de l'Education permanente, 1990) pp. 139-60.

24 In conference works, for instance, A. Laen, *De Schoolwandeling-Practisch Voorbeeld*, 25 February 1935 (Leuven, Archief Centrum Historische Pedagogiek). Or in a brochure: E. Sneyers, *Schoolwandelingen op de landelijke volksschool* (Lier: Van In, 1931). Also, most journals, *Moderne School, Recherches Pédagogiques, De Opvoeder, Vers L'Ecole Active.*

the 1960s, there was much less theory on school field trips: they seem to have become a standard ingredient of school life. The journal *Le Moniteur des Instituteurs et des Institutrices Primaires*, for instance, was greatly interested in environment and field trips, but a field trip as proposed by the journal does not look like a very attractive event. It was always a prepared expedition that had as its goal the collection of certain things (observations or material) to bring back for analysis. For instance: collecting apples and pears that are counted, weighed and catalogued in class. In short, it dealt with material that could be converted into figures and calculated.

But there is also an important change: world news now became part of the child's 'environment', so it underwent the same treatment as the ecological environment. Thus the classic bicycle race Paris-Roubaix was promoted as school material. The Monday after the race, the teacher was to make clever use of his boys' natural enthusiasm for bicycle racing by having them calculate the average speed of the 1968 winner.[25] The industry and ecology of the French *Département du Nord* also came under close scrutiny. As a reward for having calculated so well, the children were allowed to calculate their own personal walking speed. This appears to be the reaction to Verheyen's assertion that children were not interested in questions about buying a piece of land when they were saving for a scooter.

25 C. De Vriese, 'Onderwijs en Sportactualiteit'. *Persoon en Gemeenschap. Tijdschrift voor Opvoeding en Onderwijs*, XXI (1968-69), pp. 526-28.

Despite such attempts, however, the media were not heartily embraced: there remained a lot of reserve toward the media in general and television in particular. The modern media were seen as a threat because their information overload could make an unformed head spin out of control. Schools had to counter this menace by training their pupils in the old ideal of *la droite pensée*. Cataloguing became something of an obsession. Thus, like the ecological environment, it was not a question of unreservedly opening the school to the outside world but of defending the school against its disruptive and chaotic power. School could not simply make use of the child's interest in television; rather, it had to offer an education *against* television. This school law is still being applied: the same line of argument used against the written press about the dangers of information madness is now being used against the Internet.

Enlarging the assessment

Verheyen may have wished to see teachers and pupils unmask themselves to face each other frankly and openly, but he could not get around the fact that the teacher had a job to do, which was to instruct and to evaluate. The teacher could never be completely open with his pupils, but he could at least try to enlarge his evaluation of the pupil somewhat by transcending the system of attaching marks to achievement. He could try to view the pupil's personality 'in its totality'.

26 H. Mehan, 'The structure of classroom discourse' in T. Van Dijk, ed., *Handbook of Discourse Analysis. Volume 3: Discourse and Dialogue* (London: Academic Press, 1985) pp. 119-31. This form dominates schools all over the world except, curiously, in Hawaii, where a two-step structure deriving from local storytelling practice appears to prevail.

According to Hugh Mehan, classroom discourse (in the sense of the interaction between pupil and teacher) consists of three steps: initiation, response, and evaluation.[26] This scheme pervades the school. It is found at the smallest segment of classroom interaction: when the teacher asks a question, lets the pupils search for an answer, and assesses proposed answers.[27] It is found in the medium-sized segments, such as in the interim reviews of the subject matter by the pupils, in homework, and in tests. It all comes together at the end of the year, when the important question of who is going to be promoted arises. We will discuss the plans inspired by reform pedagogy to enlarge the evaluation at the smallest and the largest level.

27 How this works is analysed brilliantly by M. Hammersley, 'School Learning: The cultural resources required by pupils to answer a teacher's question' in *Classroom Ethnography. Empirical and Methodological Essays* (Milton Keynes: Open University Press, 1990) pp. 27-52.

Immediate assessment

Before Verheyen and his allies stood up, immediate correction of everything the child did wrong was considered a fundamental law of education. Errors had to be wiped out immediately lest they become fixed and claw into the flesh like an ingrown nail. Verheyen and his colleagues thought differently. They considered immediate correction as no more than simple harassment, as a constant interruption of the pupil's natural development. Still, they could not get past correcting errors, for otherwise education would be meaningless. The question was never to correct or not to correct, but when was the right time to intervene. If a mistake was made, the teacher could (a) immediately interrupt the child in the middle of a sentence, (b) let the child first finish her sentence or story and then correct her, or (c) not correct the child at all, because she could not yet know she did anything wrong, according to the curriculum. This meant that the correction had to come a few months or years later.

If we analyse when and under what circumstances the reform pedagogues advised intervention, it is not impossible to see why their recommendation came down to letting the child finish his speech, even if it was full of mistakes, and then to correct him, preferably in a discreet way, such as by using the right word or expression in an obvious manner. There were many other methods, which all came down to correcting the pupils without discouraging them. This had already been advised, but no one ever said how: it was left to the insight or the tact of the teacher. We can assume that it meant using a soft tone of voice and a gentle look in the eyes, as opposed to calling the erring pupil a hopeless blockhead. But the delay in correction opened up many more possibilities, such as watching out for general mistakes and then taking time to correct them without mentioning names. We will limit our discussion to one effect of overcoming the problem of immediate correction, namely, the creation of breathing space within the tight framework of assessment by means of 'classroom discussions'.

This was certainly an important breakthrough. Reasoning with children has always been an important pedagogical problem, certainly since Rousseau begged the question with his famous reasoning in a circle. As the 'founder of modern pedagogy' saw it, children understand only one language: not that of reason but that of force. His position was that, as the goal of education was to make the child 'reasonable', if you can reason with the child, he is already educated and therefore no longer a child. *'Employez la force avec les enfants et la raison avec les hommes: tel est l'ordre naturel'.*[28] The teacher in Martin Lawn's 'Encouraging license and insolence in the classroom: Imagining a pedagogic shift', who in 1969 denounced the idea of classroom discussions in strong words: 'Do we have to make them feel their callow opinions are important when most of them can't spell?'[29] This teacher is a *bona fide* follower of Rousseau. As were most educators before (and, indeed, after) the 1930s.

We can take the stance of ideology criticism and point to the internal contradictions in the pedagogical discourse. No matter how severe and inflexible classroom interaction might be (even in idealised prescriptions), spreading democratic virtues has always been one of the official purposes of education. At the origins of mass education, we always find a conjunction of democratic and civic ideas. This is clearest in France, where the Third Republic teachers acquired a reputation of being an aggressive lay phalanx, always eager to spread the gospel of civic ideals.[30] In Belgium, too, at the roots of the liberal initiatives of mass education, we find motives of preserving and expanding democracy against, mainly, the dark forces of Ultramontanism.[31] We would argue that, as there is no trace whatsoever of democracy in classroom interaction, all this talk about democracy can be no more than an ideological haze to camouflage the power structure. Indeed, it is difficult to see how children can be brought up to support democracy when they are socialised in a power structure that owes more to despotism, enlightened or not. But the position of early democratically committed pedagogues has its own logic, which has to be understood in the light of Rousseau.

This can best be clarified by a remark in the Tony Scott

28 J. J. Rousseau, *Emile ou de l'Education,* (Paris: Garnier, 1964) p. 79.

29 M. Lawn, 'Encouraging license and insolence in the classroom: Imagining a pedagogical shift', in M. Lawn, *Modern Times? Work, Professionalism and Citizenship in Teaching* (London: Falmer Press, 1996) p. 83.

30 This group has been analysed by J. and M. Ozouf, *La République des Instituteurs* (Paris: Gallimard, 1992). They qualify the view of the sectarian phalanx, but the Third Republic teachers most certainly had their ideals.

31 The liberal-democratic tradition was especially strong in Brussels and was embodied in the *Ligue de L'enseignement,* whose leading figures, Charles Buls and Alexis Sluys, were both active in Brussels city politics. See *Histoire de la Ligue* (1990) and J. Lory, 'Libéralisme et instruction primaire 1842-1879', *Introduction à l'Etude de la Lutte Scolaire en Belgique* (Louvain: Nauwelaerts, 1979).

film *Crimson Tide*, where an American nuclear submarine is on a mission to save the western world against post-Soviet Russian rebels. The senior officer, meanwhile, has a problem with the way the captain runs the operation and confronts him with this. He gets a clear answer: 'We're here to preserve democracy. Not to practice it'. Like the submarine captain, we can admire the austere teacher for his mission to preserve democracy without practising it. The idea was to build a citizen who, once grown, could make up his mind about the things that mattered to him. Before that, he had to learn how to make up his mind. There is nothing particularly undemocratic in this line of reasoning, considering that democracy is a system based on few principles that are democratic in themselves, regardless of what an opinion poll of general views would produce. Respect for these principles, against which there can be no democratic protest, has to be learned. There can, of course, be markedly undemocratic effects of this approach when children are dissuaded from making up their own minds and are taught simply to follow the *magister dixit*.

The French philosopher Pascal Bruckner manifested his belief in the positive effects of preserving democracy without practising it when he argued in *La Tentation de L'Innocence* that children's parliaments and such can never be anything more than a meaningless satire of adult democracy, and that the only way to safeguard democracy is to give children a good, solid education with nothing of this modern rubbish. With Kant, Bruckner stated that children must be made 'ripe for freedom': 'This is the paradox of education: the little human must be prepared for freedom by way of obedience to adults who help him to be no longer indigent and guide him in his progressive emancipation.'[32] Bruckner is convinced that a cult of the child, which takes all the child's witless utterances to be a treasury of poetic wisdom, is spreading and gnaws at the roots of the institutions that should educate the child instead of worshipping him or her. In

32 P. Bruckner, *La Tentation de L'Innocence* (Paris: Bernard Grasset, 1995), pp. 102-3.

the first place, the school appears to be in danger. Bruckner criticised the 'thousands of pedagogical reforms' not meant to educate the child ('Oh, sacrilege!') but to enhance its free expression, its 'genius'[33].

33. *Ibid*, p. 101.

In reality, Bruckner is deluded by a successful progressive rhetoric that blinds one to what really happens in schools. It has been known to happen before, which is understandable because, as Jurgen Oelkers pointed out, reform pedagogy has become the single, broad language in the public discussion about school reform, ruling out any alternative.[34] Arthur Zilversmit has spoken of the 'air of unreality' of the major offensives against progressive education in light of its poor results. The ultimate failure of progressive education, he contended, was that most of its success was purely rhetorical.[35] Therefore, those who worry about the unsettling effects of progressive school reforms need not worry too much.

34 J. Oelkers, 'Break and continuity: Observations on the modernization effects and traditionalization in international reform pedagogy', *Paedagogica Historica* XXXI (1995) p. 710.

35 Zilversmit (1993), p. 167.

In any event, the effect of classroom discussions, to return to our subject, does not appear to have been revolutionary. We have an example of an application of discussion technique by the Belgian rural teacher Alphonse Battiau.[36] Throughout his career, which spanned forty years from the late 1930s to the late 1970s, this teacher relied on a rigid discipline, that he characterised by himself as 'militaristic': during his classes, pupils had to sit perfectly still with their hands behind their backs. Nonetheless, toward the end of his career, Battiau became interested in classroom discussions. From time to time he allowed his pupils to argue freely and openly on some subjects and tried himself to stay as much as possible in the background. During such a discussion hour, discipline was lax: pupils could even walk around freely without permission. When the discussion hour was over, however, they had to return to their benches, put their hands behind their backs, and again keep perfectly quiet.

36 A transcript of interviews taken from Battiau in 1982 is in the *Historische Onderwijscollectie* of the University of Ghent, Transcript 82/009/4.

This was a way of lifting the ban on immediate correction, but while the occasional and heavily checked cessation of immediate correction might have 'freed' and 'empowered' the pupils under certain circumstances, the evaluation grid quietly and surreptitiously was being fortified. We can see this in a non-theorised and therefore almost invisible technique of question asking, which in the 1930s was still marginal but spread quickly. This technology consisted of fill-in sheets or a blackboard diagram that gave precise instructions: 'fill in', 'transpose', 'adapt', 'change the structure', and so on. With dotted lines, diagrams, and grids, they look technical and were easy to correct. It was a polyvalent technique that could be used for maths, language, grammar and reading comprehension. For checking 'comprehension (a broad assessment par excellence), no 'conversation' between pupil and teacher (as adult to child, in all openness) was necessary, just a cluster of brief questions drawn up by the teacher. Of course, this did not rule out 'wider' questions: traditional essays were still given as homework, which gave the pupils some space to work out their own vision. And there was discussion. On the whole however, the 'creative genius' was hardly ever really promoted: the teacher was not urged to find poetry in the 'witless utterances' of the child. The teacher's task remained to knock some sense into the child, whose progression in grammar, maths, and so on became more closely and more formally checked by the new technique of asking questions, with the teacher in control of it all.

The Great Assessment
In a sense, the reform-pedagogical endeavour to go beyond examinations and grades as a means of assessment was old-fashioned or at least nostalgic. It is only around the time of Verheyen's article that a form of non-reflexive and self-evident broad assessment was dying out. In the previous decades, the system of formal evaluation through examinations and grades on homework and daily work had established itself only

slowly and painfully. A teacher who went to school in the second half of the 1920s and the first part of the 1930s reported about an enigma that puzzled him all his life: although there were no examinations or any type of formal evaluation whatsoever, at the end of the year the teacher would produce a list in which the pupils were ranked for the distribution of prizes.[37] There is a difference in this between city and countryside: the city schools were quicker to establish formal evaluation.

Thus we cannot agree with Verheyen's equation of narrow, formal assessment with the 'old' school, with routine and rut. Everything considered, the reform pedagogues in this respect were not, as they liked to see themselves, modernists attacking soul-killing routine but rather nostalgia buffs denouncing modernity. It has been pointed out how reform pedagogues begin to defend the value of the old at the precise moment of its perishing. This was the case with the German popular schools, where the last bastion of collective-individual instruction, handwork schools for girls, finally abandoned their age-old system in favour of class instruction at the same time that the reform pedagogues rediscovered the value of the old ways: an *'Ironie des Schiksals'*.[38]

So it was with examinations. Edward Peeters described in a largely autobiographical novel (published under the pen name Paul Kiroul[39]) the old way of assessment, when it was still largely the custom in the countryside. To decide promotion, there were no examinations. At the beginning of a new year, the previous year's pupils returned to their old class, and the master looked at them one by one and reflected personally each pupil's aptitude for promotion. The criteria were not achievement or even intellectual ability but broader, 'mental' maturity. Thus he would retain a pupil he considered smart enough for promotion on the grounds that he was not emotionally prepared for a change of master.

37 University of Ghent, *Historische Onderwijscollectie,* Teacher Interview Transcript 82/009/4 (Alphonse Battiau), p. 149.

38 C. Jenzer, *Die Schulklasse. Eine historisch-systematische Untersuchung* (Bern: Peter Lang, 1991) p. 73.

39 P. Kiroul, *Rond een kleine klas. Scènes uit het schoolmeestersleven.* (Brussel: Libertas, s.d., early 1920's).

But such a solution was certainly not satisfactory: a plea for letting the teacher alone decide who would be promoted would never be accepted. One possible alternative was psychological testing, as promoted by Verheyen's soul mates of *Recherches Pédagogiques*.[40] This journal discovered an unusual problem, namely, pupils who try their best to be a 'good pupil' according to the norm. This aspiration was considered to betray a lack of character. And character for *Recherches Pédagogiques* did not mean moral and intellectual constancy but rather originality and authenticity. These qualities could not be expressed in grades: those who received high grades only proved that they were good at getting high grades, which was considered a special gift that told nothing about real intellect. Psychological testing was the solution that *Recherches Pédagogiques* proposed.

But they failed utterly. All that happened was an outcry in pedagogical circles for a greater role for psychology in education. In the second decade of this century, psycho-pedagogical guidance bureaus started to be established, but they kept aloof from everyday class life. Psychology did not enter the field of assessment. And, unlike what could have been expected after reading the works on modern power by Michel Foucault, psychology did not even enter the system of punishment in schools. Insofar as psychology was used in punishment, it remained a question of everyday knowledge of human character rather than scientific psychology, of popular wisdom rather than technical expertise, in short, of La Rochefoucauld rather than Foucault. The famed seventeenth century French moralist certainly seems to have loomed largely in an extensive series of articles on character observation published in the 1960s in *Le Moniteur des Instituteurs et des Institutrices Primaires*. The author presents a few ideal types of human character, which he describes in such terms as 'vain', 'brutal', 'timid', 'cruel', 'dominating', and 'backbiting'.[41]

For all the development of the science of psychology,

40 They were soul mates, in the sense that both warmly welcomed the 1936 curriculum, but with the qualification that *Recherches Pédagogiques* remained more critical: as Marxists, they reproached the plan (and its spiritual father, Ovide Decroly) for its bourgeois nature. But they never tired of showing how the plan still was a good foundation for raising the children to that higher level of insight that is historic materialism.

41 M. Mosray, 'Recréation et éducation' in *Le Moniteur des Instituteurs et des Institutrices Primaires*, XV (1962-63) pp. 233-37, 265-74.

42 J. Degent,
'Quelques
constatations dans
l'emploi de la
méthode globale,' *Le
Moniteur des
Instituteurs et des
Institutrices Primaires*
XIII (1960-61) pp. 4-9.

the descriptions do not differ from those used in the 1880s, except in the omission of some Catholic terms that had become unfashionable even among the faithful, such as 'original sin' or 'evil'. We seldom see the human mind described in technical terms, such as *'une psycho-motoricité defectueuse'*,[42] which another author in the same journal saw as a reason for slow progress in reading. Slow progress in reading was still more likely to be attributed to 'laziness', 'slowness', or the all-embracing 'lesser talent'. One of the side effects of the systematisation of psycho-pedagogical knowledge was the segregation of the 'normal' from the 'abnormal', but once psychology had effectuated this exclusion, it retreated from view and left the class to the insight of the teacher as far as punishment was concerned and to the insight of impersonal formality that stressed achievement rather than the innermost self as far as assessment was concerned.

Formal examinations meanwhile spread and became integrated from the highest level to everyday interaction, in which the narrowing technology of precise questions established itself. There was no psychological component. If we want to draw conclusions on this for the climate, we might say, that with the reform pedagogues, the grid of examinations hindered the natural development of the pupil. We might also say that the pupil has obtained at least some degree of 'legal security', which was lacking with the old way and in psychological testing. If the pupil did what had to be done, he or she would succeed rather than being sneered at by *Recherches Pédagogiques* as a mindless careerist.

By way of conclusion

The response to Verheyen's desire for informality was the further formalisation of what schools actually did: instruct and evaluate. Meanwhile informality was more often allowed on the periphery. It was more visible: the teacher abandoned his stately three-piece suit and stiff collar and no longer stood on a raised platform, at least not in newer schools. Everyday intercourse became more easygoing: the pupils were no longer needed to compose their answer in a strict formula, that involved part of the question 'Why were you late for school today? Sir, today I was late for school because...'[43] There was also, as noted, the possibility of free discussion. Also, relations on field days became more relaxed: a class on excursion was no longer a regiment on the march.[44] Despite all this, the evaluation became more tight and formal.

Schools formalised their instruction and evaluation and loosened up at the same time. This was a question of changing mentality but also of infrastructure. In our period of research between 1880 and 1960, 'pedagogical comfort' most certainly increased. The classrooms became better equipped and less crowded. But alongside these tangible factors there was also the effect of the school itself. By 1960, we had through schooling (among other things) been 'civilised'. The nature of the 'clientele' had consequently changed. We can see this as an important part of the infrastructure: the attitude of the pupils, their mentality, or in Foucault's mischievous term, their *'gouvernmentalitié'*.[45] Thus if testimonies and juridical sources point to a marked decrease in violence, we have to consider why. In the 1880s we have sources, admittedly heavily biased, telling of children being beaten with sticks and umbrellas and anything else at hand until the blood flowed.[46] This practice appears to be more or less authorised by a judge ruling in 1885 that the teacher, *in loco parentis*, had the right to inflict corporal punishment, 'within measure'.[47] The reason that these things disappeared resided certainly in the mentality, in the inspection service, and in the infrastructure. But the teachers also said that the need to inflict corporal punishment no longer existed. When they entered the school, the pupils were already convinced that learning was for their own good and that they should co-operate, give or take some mischief and pranks.

[43] L. Roels, *Twintig Jaar Boeman* (Lier: Van In, 1966) p.29.

[44] As seen in the film 'Methodische film. Onze kleintjes leren sommen'. Recorded in the first year of the Gemeentelijke Jongensschool nr. 2, Mortsel, s.d. 1936 (University of Ghent *Historische Onderwijscollectie.*).

[45] J. D. Marshall, 'Foucault and educational research' in S. J. Ball ed., *Foucault and Education: Disciplines and Knowledge* (London: Routledge, 1990) p. 14.

[46] L. Vanderkindere, *Rapport sur l'Etat de l'enseignement primaire public et privé* (Bruxelles, 1884), pp. 27-9.

[47] E. Picard, N. d'Hoffschmidt, J. De Le Court et al., *Pandectes Belges: Inventaire Général du Droit Belge à la Fin du XIXe Siècle* (Bruxelles: Larcier, 1901-1920), p. 1157.

48 A. De Swaan, Kinderen in de verschuiving van bevelshuishouding naar onderhande-lingshuishouding, *Tijdschrift voor Orthopedagogiek* XIX (1980) pp. 153-65.

We see, in the words of Abram De Swaan, more or less a shift from a 'command' relationship to a 'negotiation' relationship.[48] But in the reception of the ideas of Verheyen and his colleagues, we can also see that the social *détente* of the last half-century did not interfere with a better organisation of school. The school went on quietly organising itself as a separate institution, in which specific rules were followed. Real life did not enter the school, it remained where it already was, which was, of course, nowhere at all.

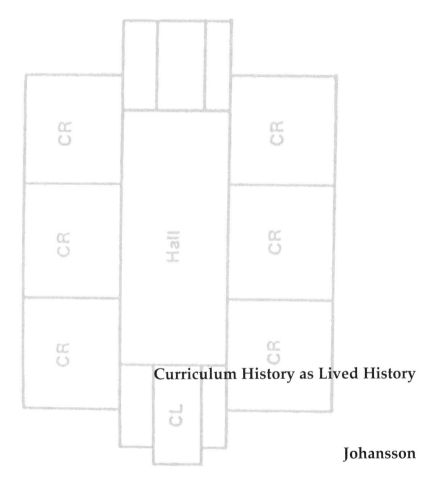

Curriculum History as Lived History

Johansson

Curriculum History as Lived History

Ulla Johansson

The history of 'education' has been of a certain kind of education, one that is divested of complexities, in which children exist only in a set of conceptual stereotypes, are involved in no relationships, belong only to an 'emergent system', and can by and large be ignored by historians.[1]

This volley was launched by Harold Silver in 1977 as a way of describing English research into the history of education. His critique could also perfectly well have included Swedish research. That is, it was top heavy, concerned with the provision and administration of education (and even then with a very narrow focus). Swedish research into the history of education was empty — education was seemingly a void and no attempts were made to take educational processes into account. It was uni-dimensional, in that it failed to consider the impact of schooling, or how pupils and parents responded to, and even resisted, educational reforms. It was isolated, as no serious attempt was made to explore the relation between education, on the one hand, and family, work, or local community on the other.[2] The classrooms in the past were totally silenced with no human beings appearing in research reports, except for influential politicians and great thinkers, mostly men, who were seen to have had a crucial impact on educational reform. Thus, intentions, motives, and school policy were implicitly synonymous with school 'reality'.

In the 1970s, in Sweden as in other countries, a new paradigm of educational research emerged. Previously, psychological approaches had been predominant, but now there was a growing interest in the sociology of education. Marxist inspired

1 H. Silver, 'Aspects of neglect: The strange case of Victorian popular Education' in P. Gordon and R. Szreter ed., *History of Education. The Making of a Discipline* (London: Woburn, 1989), p. 207.

2 *Ibid*, p.198.

theories focused on schooling as a means of reproducing an unjust society, and questioned the liberal notion of education as a democratic enterprise. In the history of education there was a corresponding trend of revisionist historians. For example, the rise of mass schooling was regarded as a response to changing patterns of social control.

Human beings, however, were completely absent in the sociology of education. Structures operated seemingly regardless of human thoughts, feelings, hopes, and fears. Critical voices drew attention to the fact that structures ultimately were supported by people, and that structural theories left much unexplained, such as how education reproduces ideology, culture, social classes, or labour power. What mechanisms are operating, and what role do teachers and pupils play in the process of reproduction? In order to find answers to such questions, the researcher has to collect information on what goes on in the classroom and, as for a historical study, is obliged to try to break the silences of the classrooms of the past. The difficulties one is left with are not only about how to find relevant sources of evidence; there are also theoretical and methodological problems involved. In this chapter I will give a few examples by reviewing my own research in retrospect.

Schooling for the home
I began to work on my doctoral thesis in the early 1980s, and at that time I was markedly influenced by sociological theories about schooling as reproductive of society. These theories dealt with the reproduction of knowledge, skills, norms, and moral standards. They also focused on the way school sorted pupils into different positions in the labour market. But they had neglected still another aspect of labour reproduction, namely, that which concerned the daily restoration of the human beings and their physical and mental health. This process of reproduction

largely takes place in the home, and includes clothes, food, and so on. Cooking and making and mending clothes clearly require certain skills and knowledge, but these activities are also influenced by ideological notions of the good home life.

The overall question of my thesis was: What was the significance of elementary school for this aspect of reproduction? Eventually I decided to study four different school subjects, gardening, handicraft, domestic science and temperance instruction between 1842 and 1919. These subjects had one thing in common: to prepare pupils for home life. The aim was to analyse the content of the teaching and also to discuss the importance of these subjects for the ability of the worker's family to support itself.[3]

3 U. Johansson, *Att skolas för hemmet. Trädg̈årdsskötsel, slöjd huslig ekonomi och nykterhetsundervisning i den svenska folkskolan 1842-1919 med exempel frän Sköns förasmling* (Umeå: Umeå universitet, pedagogiska institutionen, 1987), pp. 8-9.

These questions took me into the classroom, and more exactly to classrooms in the parish of Skön, in northern Sweden. Skön lies in the heart of the Sundsvall region, where the rapidly expanding sawmill industry during the final decades of the nineteenth century symbolizes the breakthrough of industrial capitalism in Sweden. The first major battles between labour and capital in Sweden were also fought here. Another subject of study was the schools financed by the sawmill owners for the children of their employees. Like the sawmill society in general, these schools were established according to the patriarchal principles of earlier periods. But the elementary school code and other state regulations applied to these schools too.

The following sources were used in this study:

• Records and other documents of the local school board. Among other things they contained directions for the teaching of handicraft to girls.
• A diary kept by a woman teacher of domestic science and gardening during the First World War, when Sweden was severely struck by food shortage.

• Journals on lessons in domestic science from one company school, where the teacher had noted what had been taught. A former pupil had also saved a notebook in which she had recorded recipes and the teacher's instructions.

• A questionnaire, issued in 1914 by a state committee and kept at the National Archive. In the questionnaire 265 teachers from different parts of Sweden had answered questions about how they treated temperance issues.

• Records of meetings of the local teacher union in Skön. Sometimes they discussed issues of instruction, e.g. a local curriculum for temperance instruction.

• Interviews with thirteen former pupils born between 1899 and 1910.

• Photographs of sawmill society and of the life of schools.

• Written recollections of sawmill workers in the Sundsvall district, kept in the Nordic Museum in Stockholm. These described in detail daily life at home and work, but revealed little about experiences of schooling.

• Research on this socio-economic environment, which provided information about the conditions of the working class family.

These sources gave a multi-faceted picture of my research questions. Crude contours could be nuanced. For example, in debate many voices claimed that instruction in domestic science and handicraft was absolutely necessary as the working man's wife lacked both time and ability to educate her daughter in domestic matters herself.[4] These opinions were shared by the sawmill owners. One of them was a member of Parliament and an eager proponent of state subsidies for domestic science in elementary school:

4 *Ibid,* p. 119-30.

> I have at close distance watched small families not being able to support themselves in spite of high incomes, while large families

with lower incomes can manage to keep their
homes neat and tidy and the children proper
and clean. How does it come? I would say
that it all depends on the house wife.[5]

5 *Ibid*, p.147.

Accordingly, it was argued that the workers would
benefit more from instruction in domestic science for
girls than from raising salaries. However, there is
reason to question the accuracy of these statements.
At least they seemed not to have been valid for
women in Skön. The interviewees and written
recollections of sawmill workers give a picture of a
very highly competent house wife, who managed to
keep her family clothed and fed on extremely meagre
resources. Moreover, she initiated her daughter into
the difficult art of housekeeping by making her take
responsibility for a share of domestic work at an early
age. Against this background, it can be argued that
lessons in handicraft and domestic science in schools
were of only marginal importance.

The interviewees also made me reconsider my
structuralistic way of thinking. For instance, ideology
reproduction was not only a matter of imputing
bourgeois ideals into working class people. Let me
give but a few examples. In the debate surrounding
elementary school teaching in the four school
subjects, there was a common and recurrent theme:
with the help of these subjects the ideals of thrift,
tidiness, and cleanliness would be impressed on
young people, and the chaos of the worker's home
would be dispelled. Evidently the school spread this
moral gospel. As these virtues are usually regarded
as essential parts of a bourgeois ideology, one could
claim that schooling exerted a form of symbolic
violence. But if this was the case, it was hardly a
question of a simple process of transmission of
ideology. It is most likely that these ideals belonged
just as much to the working class and were rooted in
their material conditions. Cleanliness was not only a
virtue but also a necessity. There was no other

weapon in the struggles, say, against lice. Thrift was certainly promoted by the instruction in domestic science, but this lesson was probably more effectively taught by the harshness of reality. The former pupils spoke of the poor conditions of their childhood, which left their mark on their present behaviour although they could afford to be more extravagant now. Order and discipline were also imperatives for a family in overcrowded conditions. One of my interviewees recounted experiences of her childhood as follows:

6 Quoted in *ibid*, p. 243.

7 The research project is reported in C. Florin and U. Johansson, *'Där de härliga lagrarna gro ...' Kultur, klass och kön i det svenska läroverket 1850-1914* (Stockholm: Tiden, 1993). There are also a few articles in English dealing with different parts of the study. See U. Johansson and C. Florin, 'Young Men: Old Institutions. Culture, Class, and Gender in Swedish Grammar Schools. A Comparative perspective', *Scandinavian Journal of History*, 18 (1993) pp. 183-198; U. Johansson and C. Florin, 'Order in the (Middle) Class! Culture, Class, and Gender in The Swedish State Grammar School 1850-1914', *Historical Studies in Education*, 6, 1 (1994) pp. 21-44; U. Johansson and C. Florin, '"Where the Glorious Laurels Grow . . ." Swedish Grammar Schools as a Means of Social Mobility and Social Reproduction'. *History of Education*, 22, 2 (1993) pp.147-62.

> We were not allowed to throw our clothes all over the place. No, we were told to put the clothes into neat piles so if anything went wrong, if there was a fire for instance, everyone would immediately pick up his clothes and shoes. [6]

Virtues such as order, thrift, and cleanliness were part of a bourgeois ideology and they were certainly promoted by school. But the pupils did not passively internalise the moral message; they transformed it and adjusted it to their material conditions. And when I had finished my thesis writing, the field of social science had also shifted. The agent and the human subject had been restored.

Where the glorious laurels grow [7]

My next research project would take me into the classrooms of grammar schools, accompanied by the historian Christina Florin. The nineteenth century grammar school was a privilege of but a few. First, all girls were by definition excluded. Second, only a small proportion (about three per cent) attended these schools. In the nineteenth century, Sweden rapidly changed from an agrarian to an industrialised capitalist society, with the aristocracy's power broken and a bourgeois hegemony established. The main research question was: What part did the grammar school play in this process? Did it contribute to the cultural formation of the middle classes?

According to our definition, the middle classes consisted of four bourgeois groups: grand entrepreneurs, professionals with an academic degree, white collar workers, and small enterpreneurs (artisans and tradesmen). Thus the middle classes were heterogeneous social groupings. They earned their living in various ways, were more or less wealthy, and more or less powerful. But they had one thing in common: their sons who were seated in the grammar school classrooms. Against this background several questions were raised:

• How did the years spent together in school affect this motley crowd?
• What was the impact of instruction in different school subjects, the daily routines of school work, the formal and informal rules of order, modes of punishment and reward, and the fine old traditions of grammar schools? 8
• What did the girls' absence mean?
• What ideal of manliness was officially promoted in the school, and in the unruly pupil culture?

8 The grammar school dates back to the medieval cathedral school, established by the Catholic church in the thirteenth century.

The answers to these questions could only be found inside the school walls, in the classrooms, in the school yards, and in the extra curricular activities of various school societies. Thus, we wanted to analyse curriculum history as lived history. For this purpose the following sources were used:

• Records of staff meeting at Vasteras grammar school, a middle size town in central Sweden, which provided important information on modes of discipline and order, as the teachers discussed how to punish pupils who had seriously offended the rules.
• Diaries kept by two pupils in Vasteras, and diaries of two pupils from other grammar schools.
• Published recollections from grammar schools.
• Jubilee publications containing information on

teachers and school life.
• Memoirs and autobiographies of men who attended grammar school.
• Photographs.

These sources give a highly complex and contradictory picture of daily life in school. They tell us of teachers' violence, pupils' bullying, and education for war, with military exercises. We also learn about affectionate and broad-minded teachers, brotherhoods and life-long friendships among the pupils. The discipline was hard and brutal, and the principle 'Each thing at its proper place and time' was celebrated. At the same time, an unruly subculture existed, as the boys openly defied the order and prohibitions of the school. They used their imagination to challenge the timetable, and to seize hold of spatial control of the classroom.

The modes of punishments and rewards promoted bourgeois virtues such as a rational and method-ological way of life, logic and reason, diligence, honesty, and perseverance. Meritocratic ideals, the hallmark of the bourgeoisie, was effectively comm-unicated in school. The boys were repeatedly assessed, and the results of the evaluation were made visible; the boys were placed according to scholastic attainment in the class room, where the brightest boy sat in the front and the 'black sheep' sat at the back. At the end of the term, the headmaster officially announced the results of the examinations in the assembly hall and also the fact that everybody was not up to the required standard.

The study concluded that the grammar school was a means of achieving the cultural formation of the middle classes, but we also realised that such a cultural formation was intrinsically linked to gender formation. The bourgeois ideals of rationality, logic, and reason and the pronounced support of the individual performance were basically male ideals.

Grammar school also transmitted a double message of love and violence as constitutive of manliness. The unruly boy culture could also be regarded as a preparation for power; it provided an environment in which the boys questioned and tested the limits of rules and norms. With increasing age they progressed in rank and dignity at the same time as discipline was relaxed. Eventually, at the Abitur party, they were allowed to call their teachers by name, and they drank toasts to this.

Memoirs and autobiographies in curriculum history
Memoirs or autobiographies are usually written late in life when the author is looking back into the past. Therefore many researchers argue that these documents are unreliable historical sources. It is not only a matter of a failing memory, or of the effects of nostalgia or bitterness on memories. The fact is also that the story of a life is a totally different thing from life itself. A story has a narrative structure, a plot with a beginning and an end. The events are arranged into a causal chain according to the inner logic of a coherent narrative. Life, however, is neither coherent nor logical. It consists of many disparate and coincidental events.[9] Jonas Frykman claims that life is lived at random or by instinct, but in retrospect one describes it as a path.[10] Philip Jackson has a similar view of autobiographies. Most memoirs are written by prominent men, and an autobiography is the story of a hero, whose childhood is regarded as a preparation for a career 'which develops like a sky rocket'. Anything that deflects from the rising trajectory is ruthlessly cut back, or ignored.

However, there are also researchers who defend the value of memoirs as historical sources. According to them, the preceding critique is primarily relevant for autobiographies with literary ambitions. Many memoirs are not narratives in the true sense of the word as they do not have a narrative structure. They are rather descriptions of concrete and incoherent

9 See E. Nurminen, 'En jämförelse mellan skriftliga och muntliga livshistorier' in C. Tigerstedt *et al.* eds., *Självbiografi, kultur, liv: Levnadshisotriska studier inom human- och samhällsvetenskap* (Stockholm: Symposion, 1992), pp. 224-25.

10 J. Frykman, 'Biografi och kulturanalys' in *Självbiografi, kultur,* liv, p. 249.

practices. The author certainly chooses to focus on certain events, while others are not mentioned. But a plot is often lacking, and causality is not visible. Memoirs are consequently more like surveys of events than they are narratives.

Most of the memoirs which we read for the grammar school project lacked a narrative structure. This is especially true for those parts dealing with pupils' schooldays. Teachers pass by, whose appearance and clothing are described in detail. To be sure, every teacher is not remembered equally well, and eccentric individuals and originals probably take up a larger part of the accounts than in reality. You can find many substories of disparate but obviously memorable events from classrooms and schoolyards. They usually do not represent the author (that is, the ex-pupil) as a hero, or in a particularly favourable light. All these events taken together do not give a reliable picture of daily school life. The author describes certain events while others are left out. The reader must divine the principles of selection, for the writer wants the events to have an entertainment value, to amuse and disquiet the readers, to touch their hearts, and stir their minds. To fulfil these aims, the ex-pupil probably carries things too far, at the same time as trivial events and ingrained patterns are neglected or toned down. In retrospect, however, even trivia can be worth mentioning, for example, from the outlook of today, several parts of ordinary life in the past seem bizarre. Furthermore, there are those who prefer to shed light on the monotony of school life. Some of them hated school, and in their attempts to transmit their feelings of detestation, they focus on deadly boring cramming, lack of freedom, and the slavery of school routines.

Even if stories of life and school in memoirs must be taken with several grains of salt, they can describe social practices, though not necessarily by means of a narrative structure. Their literary weaknesses accordingly increase their strength as historical sources. All problems, however, are not solved by such a statement. In the grammar school project we wanted to find out what school meant to individual boys, but we also wanted to catch the essence of their experiences of schooling. The main purpose was to analyse the collective concordances and cultural patterns that emerged from these concordances. And we might have most seriously distorted the past in order to fulfil this aim.

Billy Ehn calls attention to the fact that researchers using written or oral life histories pick and choose among the events that comprise the story of a person's life. They sort out events related to a research problem in order to answer their questions. Individual life stories are thereby cut into pieces, and the fragments are transformed into empirical raw data. A sort of data bank is thus produced, on which the analysis of a certain cultural or social phenomenon is based.[11] In our grammar school project, for example, we collected events in order to analyse the social construction of masculinity. This meant that individual personalities are objectified, private experiences are typified and transformed to exemplify main tendencies. The only thing remaining of a single life story was thus at most a few quotations, disconnected from their context.[12]

Ehn raises the question of what kind of knowledge will come out of such a procedure, but he also claims that this remains a legitimate way of doing research. What is demanded is that the researcher gives a detailed description of the research process, of principles for data analysis, quotations, and reporting. Validity is regarded as crucial to and built into the research process, rather than merely a mark of the quality of the research's outcome.[13]

11 B. Ehn, 'Livet som intervjukonstruktion' in *Självbiografi, kultur, liv*, pp. 201- 06.

12 Ibid.

13 See S. Kvale, 'To validate is to question' in ed., S. Kvale, *Issues of Validity in Qualitative Research* (Lund: Studentlitteratur, 1989), pp. 77-8.

The history of silence

Some of the sources which I have used do not communicate anything about life in school and what has been going on in the classroom. For example, two diaries written by boys in Vasteras grammar school give detailed information of what happened in the schoolyard on breaks and in leisure time. My interviewees in Skön had very sharp memories of certain elements of instruction, but they could not remember anything at all, for example, of temperance instruction. How could such silences be interpreted? Also, why did not a pupil write about school work in his diary? Does this mean that school only played a marginal role in his life? I suggest that this is not a reasonable conclusion. The diary writers spent several hours a day in the classroom, and according to laws of psychology, their school experiences certainly left marks on them. The silence of the diaries can therefore be an indication of many things. The school might have been such a self-evident part of their life that they neither reflected on or spoke about it. Perhaps they reserved the diaries for events or elements of existence in which they played an active part and in which they were at least partly their own masters. As far as can be judged from the diary, pupils showed a richness of initiative and ingenuity outside school, while they were not supposed to take any initiatives of their own in school but just listen to the teachers and obey orders.

The local curriculum for temperance instruction in the parish of Skön prescribed in detail how issues of temperance should be treated in such subjects as religion, mathematics, biology, and history. Furthermore, many teachers had attended various courses on how to conduct temperance instruction. Among the junk in a storeroom in which teaching aids were kept, I also found wall charts illustrating the damage done by alcohol on human organs, and books on how to teach temperance. Despite that, however, the ex-pupils I interviewed did not remember any lessons on that matter. This may be evidence of the inevitable discrepancy between written and experienced curricula. Another explanation can be that the quality and quantity of temperance instruction depended on the individual teacher's personal commitment. This opinion was, for instance, widespread among the school inspectors, who regularly paid visits to elementary schools to assess the quality of the teaching.

As I have only interviewed a relatively few ex-pupils, their teachers could coincidentally have belonged to the uncommitted group of teacher. One could also divine another explanation from the answer of one interviewee to the question about whether he had been taught temperance: 'No, not as far as I remember. But we were taught morals. One had to be completely perfect, you see, so I guess temperance was part of it'.[14] Perhaps the pupils internalised the gospel of temperance in such a complete way that it became self-evident. If this was the case, it might be difficult for them to remember afterwards how it happened.

[14 Quoted in Johansson (1987) p. 199.]

The restoration of the subject and paradigms in curriculum history

As mentioned I entered the history of education with a baggage of structural theories. Accordingly I presumed that school history essentially dealt with education as the reproduction of various conditions in society. I had not taken into consideration the role that human beings played in that process. But my case study in Skön taught me that people are not passive puppets to the strings of structures. And I also soon realised that my research questions actually concerned the creation of something new — the establishment of a new life mode in the family sphere of reproduction, a mode adjusted to the conditions prevalent in this particular sawmill district. In the construction of a new reproductive order, many social forces were at work. Elementary education controlled by the state, the sawmill owners' actions to ensure profit as they tied the workers to the work and to themselves by building modern schools for the workers' children, and the working class family's ambitions to make life as pleasant as possible, are only a few factors which were active in the construction of the new order. A structuralist theory cannot possibly take such a complexity into account.

The starting point of the grammar school project was the notion of change. The formation, not the reproduction, of the middle classes was central, and the project principally dealt with the role of the grammar school in the immense transformation of Sweden in the nineteenth century. But today the field of social sciences and humanities has again shifted — postmodernism and poststructuralism are paradigms that cannot be neglected; at least one has to take a position on them. What are the consequences of a postmodern approach to the history of education? Is such an approach fruitful for curriculum history as lived history?

The postmodern rejection of straightforward models of explanation and its emphasis on the complexity of reality are very well in line with my own opinions of how to write curriculum history. To break the silence of the classroom, we are thus urged to listen to many different voices, even the weakest ones.[15] To do that, however, the researcher cannot confine himself or herself to postmodern analyses of discourses, but must continue to look for information on discursive practices in which teachers and pupils took an active part. Otherwise we will run the risk that human beings will once again disappear from curriculum history.

15 However, the heavy emphasis on local contexts may collapse into biographical accounts of educational history which, in my opinion, would bring another deadlock.

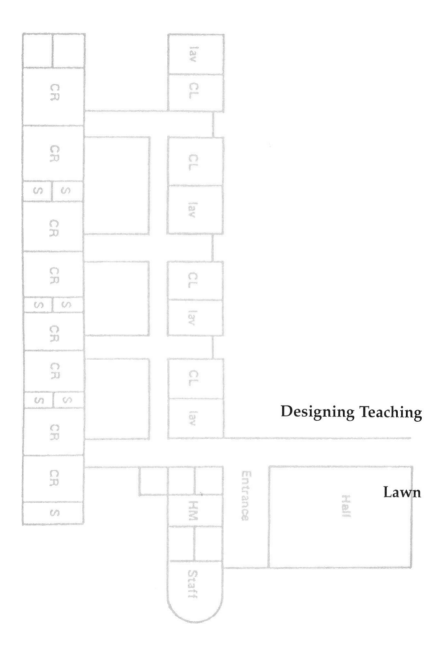

Designing Teaching

Lawn

Designing Teaching: the classroom as a technology

Martin Lawn

During the first seminar discussions of the 'Silences and Images' meetings, especially those built around artefacts and photographs, I became interested in the special tools of classrooms, their presence in rooms and cupboards and the ways in which they were used by teachers and pupils. I remembered from my own teaching experience the epidiascope I had used in my first year in an innovative social studies department my final encounter with a Gestetner printer, the use of coloured pens, the two day closing of a wing of the school to make a film recording of a single teaching lesson, the whistle used in the corridor to change social studies topics. Then I thought of the form of the lessons in social studies, the combination of discussion, worksheets and groupwork, that took place across the age range within late Edwardian classrooms and how it emerged and was kept in place. Past accounts I had collected from teachers followed: were there stores of now unused educational film slides somewhere? What did it mean when it took a 1950s school forty years to finally replace its original class furniture? Why did school inspectors tell teachers that only mature children could use an ink pen, and where did this information come from? Had the design of a board duster ever changed? What happened when the designed purpose of a classroom tool is overtaken by a shift in practice? For example, desks with inkwells and storage space, windows placed high on the wall, a teacher's dais, partition walls, and most readily to hand, textbooks and readers. In the social studies department, we regularly amalgamated classes to watch films together and ordered films that were often unconnected with current class work. Only later did I recognise the circle of meanings of which the film was the centre, and that this was not a random act or a whim. Film, motivation, interest, new technology, 'these kind of children' and social studies were all linked together and produced its practice and reaffirmed meaning. The tools appeared to operate within networks of meaning although these networks could be obscured, deteriorate or be reinvented in new ways over time. For example, I knew no longer the pedagogic function or curriculum innovation that epidiascopes were invented to sustain or that came into being through their invention, yet I used it for my purposes anyway.

This chapter emerged from a recognition that I was treating the classroom as a known but invisible part of teaching, and yet, as a pupil or teacher, I had worked in very different classrooms (a Victorian-period elementary classroom, a 1950s designed primary room and so on) and should have been sensitive to setting and design. Concentrating on recovering the histories of teachers from administrative narratives, I had taken either the individual life or some form of collective life, in which the classroom was the place they occupied briefly or less significantly than other places. These 'places' could be the marriage bar, strikes, social associations, activist campaigns, and so on. So, while the idea of the classroom was ubiquitous, I realised that I had not treated it as significant. I think this was partly because I had no way to develop a conception of it. Nor had I thought through my relation to it. I recognised the classroom as a place of work, I recognised that inhabiting it might mean domesticating it, and I recognised its privacy. My underdeveloped recognition of the way the physical environment (read classroom) affects me might be shared by others; for example, Malcolm Seabourne, the specialist historian of school building in England, who began a book by stating that teachers were much more influenced by the physical environment than they often realised – 'at any rate consciously'.[1]

1 M. Seabourne, *Primary School Design* (London: RKP, 1971) p. 1.

Yet in the early 1980s, I had co-written an essay, 'The

Educational Worker? which had argued a version of the Braverman labour process thesis on teaching. Within this argument there was a strong emphasis on the technologies of teaching and the relationship between them and the teacher. In the Braverman thesis, technology is used to harness and control the worker and cheapen the cost of production. At the time, my questions were about computers and their ability to replace workers, speed up work and remove craft knowledge from the worker. The worker and the machine constitute a powerful coupling in other fields of research but this image did not easily fit the idea of the teacher in the classroom; a teacher who seemed to lack sophisticated tools but was nonetheless in charge of the environment's pace and modality. The failure of technical innovations, such as programmed learning and microteaching, and the teacher's fear of technology seem to give little substance to the idea of such a powerful relationship within education.

I want to use this chapter to raise questions about how to define teaching tools, designed environments and teachers, and the relations between them through a necessary argument about the scope of technology in the classroom. Such questions enable the development of a new perspective on classroom technologies allowing the tool to be placed within a methodological context in which its creation and use, and its relation to ideas and pedagogy, and teachers and networks are available to historians.

Technology/ Classrooms
Technology has become synonymous with hardware and earlier, with physical objects, which have tended to be seen as quite separate from the teacher; they appear to play a subsidiary and minor role in the classroom, although when marketed they might seem capable of replacing the teacher. But technology is more than sets of educational objects. Technology can be defined as a tool and as an approach. It is the

science of the practical, the systematic application of solutions to the practical situation. The systematic solution might not result in new hardware but a redesigned sequence of events or a rearrangement of people and objects. Technology can be defined as a tool, and the thinking the tool represents: actually it is both. In a simple way, the classroom is a technology; it is a design solution, or series of solutions, to a problem. It is, at the same time, a simple machine, a process of systematic solutions and a particular way or thread of thinking about using technology.

Bijker *et al.*, in a collection of essays on the new sociology of technology, argue that it is possible to use the term *technology* in a number of ways. Technology can mean simple objects or artefacts (a reading primer, for example), a process (a production process) and the know-how or tacit knowledge used in creating the tool or managing the process.[2] In education it tends to be used mainly in the first sense and rarely in the second. Street's definition is helpful:

> technology refers to the way in which the parts are organized, through the application of knowledge, to realise their particular purpose.[3]

So technology is the tool and the social processes within which it is created, contained and used.

When Dreeben used the idea of technology to explore the nature of teaching, he did so within the sense of a systematic solution, a means by which a job gets done. While not excluding hardware, teaching technology means organizing the instructional process, motivation and control, and varying classroom design and social relations. The latter included:

> numerous attempts, both architecturally and

2 W. Bijker, T. Hughes and T. Pinch eds., *The Social Construction of Technological Systems: New Directions in the Sociology and History of Technology* (Cambridge, Mass.,: MIT Press, 1987).

3 J. Street, *Politics and Technology* (London: Macmillan, 1992) p. 8.

socially, to vary classroom design; by unscrewing desks and chairs from the floor, by permitting pupils to move more or less freely around the room, by dividing the members into numerically smaller units to provide ability and interest groupings, by introducing more than one teacher into the classroom, by introducing inanimate teaching components (such as teaching machines and computers), and by widening the age span of pupils assigned to one teacher. [4]

4 R. Dreeben,*The Nature of Teaching - Schools and the Work of Teachers* (Glenview, Illinois: Scott Foresman 1970) p. 100.

This is a wider usage than is now common when technology is explained yet it stays within the proper meaning of the term viz the systematic application of solutions in which incipient networks of social arrangements and inanimate components are used to create teaching solutions in the classroom.

Returning to the idea of physical objects used by human agency in the classroom as a means of educating and controlling, however, there is a gap in our knowledge about why these objects were constructed and consumed or how they were used within single or integrated solutions. Kulikowski offers a fascinating list of necessary inventions used in 'study and instruction'.[5] The list is of general teaching tools, for example, '1780 steel nib pen, Samuel Harrison, England'; '1795 graphite pencil, Nicholas Conte, France'; and 'c1940 overhead projectors in bowling alleys, AMC Inc, USA'. Kulikowski is interested in the the acceleration in the technical requirements demanded of teachers. In a short preface to the list, he discusses the necessary invention of chalk for the classroom. Chalk allowed the teacher to manage a larger group, to display text and graphics simply and to allow the pupils to sit and see from a distance. The list is of value as it draws attention to the technologies of the classroom but there are difficulties associated with it. Why is the

5 S. Kulikowski, A timeline of technology used in study and instruction. (1995) [www document] URL http:// www.newsgroups: bit.listserv.edtech

invention of the electric light excluded? It is not a teaching tool, according to the list criteria, yet it is an essential element of other tools, for example, the movie projector. The exclusion of electricity renders a part of classroom history invisible. In what way was the classroom designed or organised differently because light was available in a new, accessible form?

The list raises other questions. What significance does the cost of an invention have? While the invention of the standard rule can be related to new pedagogical flexibilities, did the cheapness of its production affect its spread? Again, is there a presumed relation between the tool and its use in the classroom? So the invention of the tool does not explain its adoption, its use and its relational capacities in the classroom. The exclusions from the list helps to obscure the wider question of how the tools are placed in relation to one another to create a system. The tools can be observed in the classroom but often not the whole technology that relates them together, a point I would like to return to later.

From a strongly technological determinist per-spective, McClintock argues the case for printed texts as education's single greatest invention, enabling the rise of modern schooling from the sixteenth century. Schooling was created by the technological breakthrough of the printed text. In his argument, it wasthe invention of the printed text that enabled the city bourgeois to create the prototype school which then, McClintock says, grew with developments in transport technology:

6 R. McClintock, *Power and Pedagogy : Transforming Education through Information Technology* Institute for Learning Technologies, University of Columbia (1992) Chapter Four para. 165, http://www.ilt.columbia.edu

> Printing gave rise to the technical strategy employed in modern schools: to use inexpensive printed texts as effectively as possible as a foundation for educational efforts, redefining the task of education.[6]

McClintock treats the printed text as much more than

a simple tool for enabling the formation of systematic instruction. Instead, he sees it as a complex technological development that created a raft of material conditions affecting the ordering of schooling. For example, the physical nature of books 'necessarily influence the way that educators organise schools'. The centrality of the book determines the entire system for McClintock; it involved problems of physical distribution and transport, classification and division of texts, ordering sequences and shifts in groupings. The use of the text created problems that the shape and evolution of the modern school resolved. Indeed, as this is part of an argument about the power of new learning technologies, McClintock argues that the school has ossified around the book; the physical load of the book necessitated a limit per subject and the schools are now ordered by this original technical problem (load and distribution) so that self-direction is thwarted by the lockstep of the class.

Although the final reasoning might not convince, the argument about technology and the classroom has advanced again. A tool (in this case the book) is not just invented and used; it may determine the shape of the school. Its use involves a number of problems that must be resolved. The interrelatedness of technologies creates complex problems that affect how schooling is designed or evolves.

In his interesting book on technical learning in the nineteenth century and the way it shaped school practices, pedagogical thinking and tools, Stevens showed how the necessity to teach sciences in school created problems of explanation that new texts had to overcome. In addition, teachers or small manufacturers had to invent new apparatuses to explain visually the abstract natural forces. First a 'cabinet' had to be provided, to display models and other necessary materials:
Everything from stones to skeletons, levers

and electrical apparatus found a place... The essential equipment needed for demonstration was listed by one lecturer in 1830 as a timepiece, maps and globes, a blackboard and an abacus or a numeral frame.[7]

7 E. Stevens, *The Grammar of the Machine* (Boston: Yale University Press, 1995) pp. 73-75.

Stevens shows why certain tools were invented, how a new pedagogy of visual demonstration developed that needed these tools and how teachers and others became involved in their manufacture. A fuller version of technology is present here so that a network of people and objects originate and manage a systematic solution to a problem: tools, processes and know-how enable the science classroom to work.

Form, Space and Function
Widening the scope in these areas, it is possible to see the classroom in a further way. As a unit within schools, it is not just the home of technological processes; it is also a designed technology itself. As part of a building designed for a purpose, it contains particular forms, spaces and functions, all of which express intentional usages by teachers and pupils.

For the purposes of this argument, it can be said that historians of education have privileged the actor over the wider technology so that a focus on the teacher or the curriculum (or, more often, on regulation and site narratives) has treated the classroom as invisible. Sometimes this is a difficulty a historian has because of the complication of classroom reconstruction; more often it might be that remaining sources are not available for this type of research. The problem of classroom reconstruction from the perspective of a sociology of technology is that physical tools may be left but become separated from their located meanings: for example, in their operation, their place, their interrelationship, their necessity and their value to the teacher. In this case, the difficulty is worsened by the invisibility of the classroom as a technology. It is a common occurrence in teaching narratives for the shape, awkwardness, irregularities, exits, convenience, site periphery and heat/light qualities of the classroom to be mentioned. These aspects are significant to the teacher and can be treated as part of a discussion on work, resources or learning. Design is treated as a quality of the architecture and building. Yet there is a level of analysis missing, I think.

If the classroom was designed with built-in values and purposes, which shape the work and behaviour of the teacher, then what were those ideas and how were they turned into machined solutions?

There is a limited but interesting field of study on schooling in the United Kingdom that has created a narrative history of postwar architectural developments in school building and design. Concentrating on the innovations in school design and construction in a period of massive educational reconstruction, this field is a formal record of the use of new technologies of aluminium on site construction, fibre panelling and shaped wood. The contemporary English primary school, usually in the city suburbs, built in the building boom of the 1950s and 1960s, is a creation of these material innovations. This period of school building is now finished and these schools now exist alongside the other distinctive English schools, usually in the inner city or town, which were created in the building boom of the late Victorian period (1880-1900). These schools are brick inside and out, have high ceilings and poor natural light; classrooms have either part glass partition walls (looking into a shared hall) or brick walls. A primary school teacher in a large city is likely to have worked within both of these designed environments.

The postwar schools are represented in the numerous photographs taken to illustrate the rebuilding of society and are symbolised by children playing/working in sunlight in friendly, well-lit classrooms. The Victorian schools are less well represented but exist in contemporary photographs of ordered classrooms and curriculum improvement. Taken together, the contrast is of light and dark. In each case, the photographs are to be read as a sign of the material improvements in schooling, at the start of state schooling and at a significant stage in its development. School architecture study tends to work with biography, technique, regulation and administrative policy and reveals the solutions to problems of construction and design and the social ideas present in the design of schools. And the latter are fertile ground for an inquiry into the classroom as a technology.

According to Thomas Markus, the material evidence an educational historian should look at in studying schools, for example,

> is in the buildings which were adapted or purpose built, the space thus created, and the material contents of this space - furniture and equipment. Above all, it is in the order imposed on the human bodies in this space, down to their tiniest gestures, including the gaze of their eyes.[8]

8 T.A. Markus, 'Early Nineteenth Century School Space and Ideology' in *Paedagogica Historica* vol. xxx, 11 (1996) p. 12

9 Seaborne (1971) p. 1.

Markus is almost echoing here one of Seabourne's teachers who told him 'that in his experience the building made the teaching method'.[9] In this material evidence there is a fixity of form and space; in the Victorian school design there is an emphasis on control of movement and visual surveillance. When Markus 'reads' the Victorian school as a text, he finds evidence of a concern for moral force in its architectural symbols and ordering of space, a cost benefit analysis of necessary institutional cost and an emphasis on hygiene and hierarchy expressed within structure. The separate classroom was a sign that teachers 'suffered less supervision, were trusted to be more independent, and had greater privacy'.[10] In other words, the classroom was designed and built to represent and shape a particular form of teaching behaviour. Markus, drawing on a spatial analysis of nineteenth century schooling reformations (such as the Wilderspin school), argues that the simulation of the predictable order of the machine was one of the ways in which social control and power relations were built into the fabric and design of schools. Such a spatial examination of schools would concentrate on how the building is designed for use (flow, observation and constraint) and the way in which the fixedness of the material technology shapes its function through order, classification, compartmentalization, segregation and so forth. This argument is not just about the late nineteenth century Board schools of England. The way a school is designed to work reflects social ideas about institutions and the education these institutions are created to further.

In David Hamilton's history of forms of schooling and the creation of the classroom, the social ideas expressed within the form of the classroom were mass production and social efficiency.[11] The classroom emerged from the confluence of two forces, the social and the technological. The social philosophies, such as the social efficiency or industrial efficiency movements, emphasised this particular form of school organization , social control and differentiated courses. For Hamilton, the technological refers to school architecture, time and resources, placed together within a particular pedagogic form. He describes a system of schooling as 'batch' production to show how it resulted from the expression of industrial efficiency, social control and technology to produce a managerial and material form and to reproduce a specific practice. The classroom, together with a teacher, furniture, texts and aids, was invented to produce a designed effect. Markus and Hamilton raise questions about the operation of the classroom that focus less on the

10 Markus (1996) p.50.

11 D. Hamilton, *A Theory of Schooling* (Lewes: Falmer Press, 1989).

teacher controlling the space and form, and more on being controlled by it. When Cuban researched questions of constancy and change in classrooms, one of his categories was concerned with organizational structure. In one passage he tries to isolate this category, referring to it as teachers' working conditions:

> about which decisions are generally made by others far removed from the classroom. Design of classroom space, how many students required courses of study, district tests, report cards, supervisory rules - all of which are concrete realities over which teachers are seldom consulted yet their presence penetrates classrooms daily influencing in large and small ways what teachers do.[12]

12 L. Cuban, *How Teachers Taught* (New York: Longman, 1984) p. 48.

In this section, Cuban is trying to explain the lack of innovation in classrooms because of these conditions yet the separation of designed space from the regulations that flow into it might be a false distinction. Whereas space and form remain fixed, function might alter. In later passages, Cuban explains organizational structure through the continuing pressure of productivity; teachers need to produce order and teach a testable content in a confined space and with a large group of people. The classroom and its regulations are one; the organizational structure is material and produces a certain pedagogic form. This is no accident and to call it a choice is mischievous. He is describing teachers worked by their classroom -

> Organizational structures drove teachers into adopting certain instructional strategies that varied little over time. By structure, I refer to the way a school space is physically arranged; how content and students are organized into grade levels; how time is

allocated to tasks; and how rules govern the behaviour and performance of both adults and students.[13]

13 Ibid, p.242.

Here Cuban explains how the organizational structure, this mix of the material and its ordering, shapes teaching. It drives routine, constructs efficient teaching practices and rations energy and space.

Markus, Hamilton and Cuban are describing teachers *worked* by their classroom. What they have in common is an argument, derived from social ideas expressed in material and organizational structures, about the shaping of teaching through a school/classroom technology.

Social Technologies

In 1973, Daniel Bell used a phrase that is helpful in securing the argument about the classroom as a technology. He differentiated between machine and social technologies:

> The organization of a hospital or an international trade system is a social technology as the automobile or a numerically-controlled tool is a machine technology.[14]

14 D. Bell, *The Coming of Postindustrial Society* (New York: Basic Books, 1973) p. 29.

Technology has been defined as a tool, the process that contained tools and the knowledge about the process or use of tools. In this chapter, technology has been more widely defined than is customary in education so that a new perspective on the classroom enables technology to be conceptualized in a new way. The classroom fits within wider material and social (organizational) structures.

Is the classroom a social technology,[15] seen as a set of artefacts and structures, and as a set of socially constructed principles, procedures and processes, devised to function effectively and realise its purpose? It will be necessary to see the classroom as

15 Although I am making the case for a wider definition of technology, the idea of a social technology is a useful way of making a distinction between tools and the social context in which they operate.

a hardware and a software; it is the material structure (spaces, walls, furniture, tools) and the working procedures, series of ideas and knowledge systems, operating within it. The classroom is the integration of artefacts and rules and teachers. Within the sociology of technology the artefact is not seen as inactive: it may be an actor in a network of which it is part. The meanings of schooling are constituted by the network of actors (computers, displays, desks, teachers, ancillaries, rules, and so on) that constitute the classroom. It is a social technology in which the elements cannot be easily separated even though we have tended to think of it as a space in which the teacher operates freely.

Function, choice, actor, discretion and cultural realignments are all concepts used in architecture, sociology or history to denote the effect that people and ideas have in managing, disrupting and reordering their surroundings. Histories of education are full of the means by which teachers have been influenced by social movements, new pedagogies and new practices. This chapter is not about to recreate the idea of a total institution, the classroom, which has been designed to operate in a 'teacher proof' way. Indeed, the way teachers or new tools alter older networks of meaning is at the heart of this approach.

The English Primary School
As a test of the interpretation offered earlier, I want to look at the postwar history of the primary school in England. It is an interesting test because the representations of the classroom and school in the 1950s, in image and words, are among the most powerful in English educational history. The photographs of children in well-lit classrooms or in pleasant playgrounds came to stand for the optimism and resolve of the postwar reconstruction of education and the political establishment of a new partnership with teachers. The images and words

about teachers, particularly primary teachers, came to symbolise the new public and democratic space of education. The professional teacher, empowered by society, is helping to rebuild England, by developing the citizens of tomorrow. They are seen to be growing, inquiring and creating in new, well-lit, friendly classrooms with a caring woman teacher to the fore. This whole view of the teacher and the classroom seems to be in stark contrast to a view of teaching as part of an earlier social technology network, certainly Hamilton's view of 'batch processing'. The image is so pervasive that it has taken a deliberate campaign by English politicians, beginning in the early 1980s, to lever it apart from descriptions of primary education.

In 1957, the Ministry of Education, in a review of its postwar school building, stated that 'we see the school no longer as a mere machine for giving lessons but as a social unit concerned with the all round development of boys and girls'.[16] This was a review of the response by planners, especially the Ministry's Development Group of architects and planners, to incorporate into their school designs the curriculum philosophies of the prewar education reports such as Hadow. Buildings were designed to manage the shift to care functions, groupwork, fields of experience (topic work and the like) and new forms of discipline. The Ministry and its advisors did this by seeking to identify the leaders in educational thought, translate their ideas into architecture and then convince clients to try them out.[17] This translation of current social philosophies (Hamilton's phrase) of education into space and form occurred in several ways.

Maclure saw this as an industrialization of building, using steel fabrication and a design reflection of Modernist concerns with democratic, mass-produced buildings.[18] The flexibility and fast construction of prefabricated buildings for primary schools, combined with new regulations on natural daylight

16 Ministry of Education, *The Story of postwar School Building* Pamphlet series 33 (London, 1957) p. 2.

17 A. Saint, *Towards a School Architecture - the role of school building in post war England* (Boston: Yale University Press, 1987) p. 192.

18 S. Maclure, *Educational Development and School Building: aspects of public policy 1945-73* (London: Longman, 1984) p. 112.

areas in schools, produced new kinds of primary schools. They were often single storey buildings, with glass and wood fibre panelling as key structural features; they were based on a grid system that broke down long corridors and staggered paired classrooms. By reducing the need for corridors (by cutting down pupil circulation through the school), pairing classrooms and decentralising toilet and cloakroom space, they could increase the number of classrooms. They invented the idea of the teaching space (a phrase first used by one of the influential planners); it was a classroom plus a practical activity/wet area plus care facilities. This design was intended to offer

19 Saint (1987) p. 71.

> the options of privacy and intimacy, by decentralising lavatories, or of community and integration, by staggering the corridors and opening them up to classes. [19]

Planners worked with paint manufacturers to create new colour schemes for rooms and with steel and panel manufacturers to make structures and cladding. Manufacturers produced technical innovations in materials. A range of furniture, specially constructed for schools, incorporating new data about child ergonomics was 'designed to encourage the modern teaching methods of group work, activity and movement'.[20] These innovations were created by partnerships of manufacturers, architects and a consortia of local authorities and several Ministries. Led by architects/planners, and used extensively after a while on other forms of public buildings, these integrated schemes were designing schools for new functions and in a quite comprehensive way. They were integrating the material into a social system.

20 Ibid, p.192.

John Newsom, a key figure in this process, saw it as a 'thinking about what good primary education might be and how it could be made possible in building'.[21] They used the 'best' or 'imaginative' teacher as the model for good educational practice and designed the building that this teacher could use effectively. They even saw the increase in natural light as a way to increase teacher performance; they were trying to 'design in' a teaching performance which they calculated against daylight factors.

21 Ibid p.62.

Hamilton, studying a later open-plan school describes the planned flexibilities of space this way:

> Particular attention was focussed on the relative disposition of space within a school, on the distribution of resources which could be shared, and on the utilisation of unused areas inside and around the building. In turn, there was a blurring of the architectural boundaries that had previously separated indoors from outdoors, corridors from cloakrooms, and classrooms from halls and dining rooms.[22]

22 Hamilton (1989) p. 33.

Material resources, such as books, equipment, writing, and painting materials, were very important in this newly designed practice of primary schooling. The new pedagogy depended upon these new resources. Hamilton offers an interesting insight into their new prominence in the classroom:

> [the] increased importance of material resources means that they must be located much closer to the child's working milieu... (though too costly to be in each classroom). [They] become shared rather than guaranteed.[23]

23 Hamilton (1989) p. 105.

In a distinctive way, new primary schools were designed to be operated to produce a new kind of teaching and learning. In fact, it is unclear whether they were to be operated by teachers or were to perform teaching by creating and shaping responses.

Pedagogy might have had to follow or rub against or be contradicted by the designed space it occupied.

Conclusion

In this short chapter, I have set the scene for new possibilities in classroom histories in which the designed tool can be broadly defined, placed in relation to others and to teachers/designers, and its meanings and usage verified at different points. In addition, the classroom might be seen as constituting a social technology. Tools and aids, furniture and walls, space and form, rules and meaning all create teaching and are inseparable from it. This view is not technologically determinist as it recognises the way networks of buildings, artefacts and rules/meaning establish the classroom.

Historically it might be possible to discriminate between a classroom as a site of simple technologies and as a complex technology. Design has got closer to the point of production and is not just concerned with the school as a machine of control and social efficiency. As in other kinds of work, it might soon be possible to recognise that teaching has been redesigned itself and that the emphasis will be less on the Markus' building shaping a particular form of teaching behaviour and more on the technologies that can make teachers improve themselves.

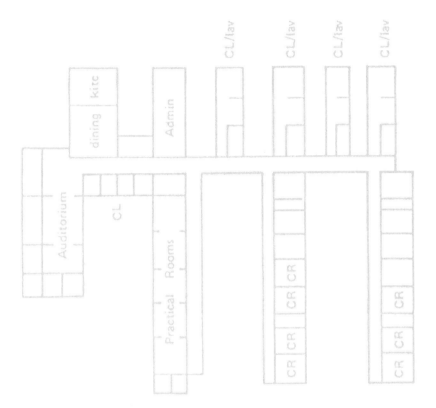

On Visualising Past Classrooms

Grosvenor

On Visualising Past Classrooms

Ian Grosvenor

Taking Photographs

Photography has been called 'light-writing'.[1] Reflected light from an object passes through a small hole in a camera, alters the molecular structure of the surface of the photographic plate or film and produces a pattern of light and dark which is chemically fixed. The image which is produced by 'light-writing' is one of autogenesis, as a nineteenth century photographer remarked: 'the sun was the artist, the camera the vehicle and the silver plate the canvas'.[2] The 'camera eye' was thus considered to be like 'a mirror held up to Nature'. Similarly, the photographer Margaret Bourke-White, commenting on her documentary work in 1930s America, observed: 'with a camera the shutter opens and closes and the only rays that come in to be registered come directly from the object in front'.[3] It was this link between nature as author and chemical technology which gave photography its objectivity: 'light printed pictures produced by the operation of natural laws and not by the hand of man'.[4] The photographic process from the mid-1850s was held to be inherently objective. Photography offered a way of observing the world without bias. The photographic image had truth - value, it was self-evident and evidence of the 'real'; it was a witness, and had documentary status.[5] As the photographer Roger Fenton observed at the first meeting of the Photographic Society of London in 1853:

> The principal objects of the Society [are] the collection and the diffusion of information, the verification and explanation of new discoveries, the comparison of processes and of their results, and the improvement of the mechanical and optical machinery of the Art.... One of [our] simplest, but not least

1 G. Clarke, *The Photograph* (Oxford: OUP, 1997) p. 11.

2 Mr Berry, 'On Photography, Retrospective and Prospective', *Liverpool Photographic Journal*, (March 8, 1856) p. 34.

3 Quoted in W. Stott, *Documentary Expression and Thirties America* (Oxford: OUP, 1973) pp. 31-32.

4 This description of the self-evident truth captured by the photographic image was given in an American court of law in 1906. For details of the case, *Porter v. Buckley*, and a discussion of photographs as evidence in law see J. Green-Lewis, *Framing the Victorians. Photography and the Culture of Realism* (New York: Cornell University Press, 1996) Chapter 6.

5 For a critical discussion of the 'documentary' nature of photography see A. Solomon-Godeau, *Photography at the Dock. Essays on Photographic History, Institutions, and Practices* (Minneapolis: University of Minnesota Press, 1991) Chapter 8.

Silences and Images

6 R. Fenton, 'Upon the Mode in Which It Is Advisable the Society Should Conduct Its Labours', *Journal of the Photographic Society of London* (March 3, 1853) pp. 8-9.

7 Stott, *Documentary* (1973) p. 14.

8 R. Samuel, *Theatres of Memory. Past and Present in Contemporary Culture* (London: Verso, 1994) pp. 328-29.

9 A. Sekula, 'Photography between labour and capital' in B. Buchloch and R. Wilkie eds., *Mining Photographs and Other Pictures* (Halifax: Nova Scotia College of Art and Design, 1983) p. 198.

important offices will be to define what is already known... Next it will be a register of all new facts, and herein will consist much of its value.[6]

Photography, mechanically and objectively, suspended a 'real' event/subject in time and offered the viewer empirical knowledge and visual 'truths' of, and about that event/subject. The image defied comment, it imposed meaning, and confronted its audience with empirical evidence which made 'dispute impossible and interpretation superfluous'.[7]

Historians and Photographs
It follows, therefore, that a photograph of a 'past' event has both a temporal and a physical presence. It records what was real. What was in front of the camera existed and is captured as a moment. It is a moment open to historical scrutiny. It allows us, as historians, to become 'eyewitnesses' to a historical event, to see the past as it was. It is an image which presents a 'transparent reflection of fact'. It shows us, 'in lifelike detail, history "as it was" '.[8] The viewer, as Sekula has said, 'is confronted not by historical-writing, but by the appearance of history itself'.[9] The photograph acts as a bridge between the past and the present. It turns distant historical subjects into intimate 'human' contemporaries.

A photograph may suspend a past moment, but the process of historical scrutiny of photographs is problematic for several reasons. First, as Raphael Samuel tellingly observed in the early 1990s,

> It is a curious fact that historians, who are normally so persnickety about the evidential status of their documents, are content to take photographs on trust, and to treat them as objective correlatives of fact... All that appears is a mere credit -'Mansell Collection', 'Mary Evans Picture Library', 'Museum of

English Rural Life' as though a depository had the same authority as a source... [T]here are not even the rudiments of an agreed scholarly procedure which would allow photographs to be treated with the high seriousness accorded to much less problematical sources. As one curator puts it caustically, most of them are treated as 'eye-wipes'.[10]

Second, and relatedly, the conception of photography as inherently objective has, as Solomon-Godeau writes, 'long since been abandoned. We... now take for granted that the camera produces representations — iconic signs — translating the actual into the pictorial'.[11] The idea of photography as an objective medium and as 'an innocent tool' has been rejected in favour of the belief that it functions 'as an active means by which society is structured' and is implicated in a whole set of power relationships that exist within society.[12] A photograph may capture the 'truth' of a moment in the past, but in stopping time the photograph takes its subject out of history: every photograph 'has no before or after: it represents only the moment of its own making'[13]. Third, and again relatedly, there continues to be among many historians a reluctance to depart from what Peter Burke has described as the 'parochialism' of historical study.[14] Historians are suspicious of theory and wary of borrowing conceptual tools and approaches developed in other academic disciplines. Yet, it is in such works — the theoretical writings of Michel Foucault, the writings of Walter Benjamin, Roland Barthes, Susan Sontag, John Berger, John Tagg, Allan Sekula, Victor Burgin, Abigail Simon-Godeau, Graham Clarke and John Pultz on photography; Jennifer Green-Lewis and Annette Kuhn's work in the field of cultural studies; writing associated with the 'new' anthropology; and the phototherapy work of Rosy Martin and Jo Spence — that historians can find answers to some of the difficulties of using photographs as historical sources.[15] In sum, it is in

10 R. Samuel, 'The "eye of history" ', *New Statesman & Society* (18 December 1992/1 January 1993) p. 41.

11 Solomon-Godeau, *Photography*, p.169.

12 J. Plutz, *Photography and the Body* (London: Weidenfeld and Nicolson, 1995) p.10.

13 Clarke, *Photograph*, p. 24.

14 P. Burke, *History and Social Theory* (London: Polity Press, 1992) p.2.

15 See W. Benjamin, 'The Work of Art in the Age of Mechanical Reproduction' in *Illuminations* (London: Jonathan Cape, 1970) and 'A Short History of Photography' in A. Trachtenberg ed., *Classic Essays on Photography* (New Haven: Leete's Island Books, 1980); R. Barthes, *Camera Lucinda, Reflections on Photography* (London: Jonathan Cape, 1982); J. Berger, *Ways of Seeing* (Harmondsworth: Penguin, 1972); V. Burgin, *The End of Art Theory: Criticism and Postmodernity* (Basingstoke: Macmillan, 1986); J. Crary, *Techniques of the Observer: On Vision and Modernity in the Nineteenth Century* (Cambridge, Mass.,: MIT Press, 1992); A. Kuhn, *Family Secrets. Acts of Memory and Imagination* (London: Verso, 1995); R. Martin and J. Spence, *Double*

Exposure: the Minefield of Memory (London: Photographers Gallery, 1987); S. Sontag, *On Photography* (Harmondsworth: Penguin,1978); J. Spence and P. Holland, *Family Snaps: The Meanings of Domestic Photography* (London: Virago Press, 1991); A. Trachtenberg, *Reading American Photographs: Images as History, Mathew Brady to Walker Evans* (New York: Hill and Wang, 1989).

16 Central to this critical practice must be an acknowledge-ment of the importance of Raphael Samuel's writings of the early 1990s in establishing the need for social historians to review their use of photographs.

17 Burke, *History*, p.19.

18 Ibid.,.p.165.

such works that the elements of a critical historical practice can be found.

In this sense, this study was conceived as a contribution to the development of an agreed critical practice among historians in using photographs as historical evidence.[16] This critical practice recognises that photographs exist both in history and as history, that they are products of cultural discourse, that they do not offer a transparent window into the past, that photography constitutes a site of production and representation, and that a photograph must be read not as an image, but as a text, and as with any text it is open to a diversity of readings. In particular, the study focuses on the visualisation of past classrooms. The study attends to concrete detail, but utilises social theory, socio-linguistics and literary criticism. In short, it accepts Burke's position that 'without the combination of history and theory we are unlikely to understand either the past or the present'.[17] Indeed, to be open to new ideas, to be capable of adapting them to one's own purposes, and of finding ways to test their validity 'might be said to be the mark of a good historian and a good theorist alike'.[18]

On Visualising Past Classrooms (1)

What is the objective reality captured in the photograph reproduced here? It is a photograph that through the process of 'light-writing' faithfully records a school event in the past. It captures a moment in classroom life and its internal clues enable us to locate it both in time (late nineteenth century) and in space (Somerville Road Board School, Birmingham, England). It reflects a natural state of affairs, although it is possible by looking at the writing on the blackboard to recognise an element of 'staging'. Statements can be made about the teaching body, and about their dress, roles can be ascribed (to the headteacher, the teacher, the visitor); observations can be made about the composition of the pupil body (girls only), their number, age and condition, and the

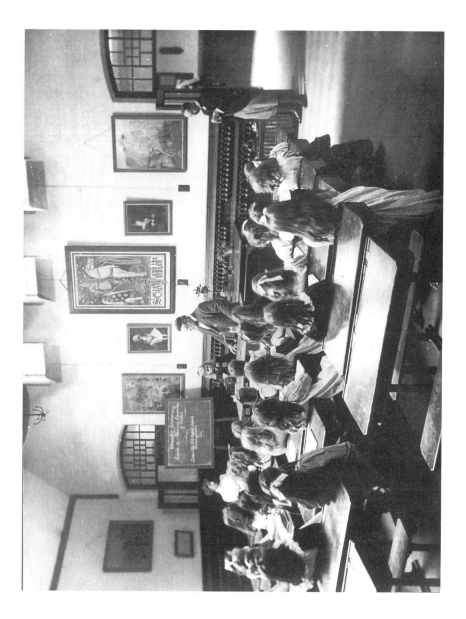

On Visualising Past Classrooms

visible classroom resources (desks, table, teaching equipment, pictures and so on). Internal clues allow the viewer/reader to identify the subject being taught (Domestic Economy), and the lesson content (the Chemical Composition of Water) and this can be related to the rise of practical science in the school curriculum in the 1880s. It is an image which a viewer/reader could readily expect to encounter in a book on nineteenth century pedagogy or in a museum display on the iconography of past classrooms.[19] In both cases, it would commonly be treated as social fact. The image would speak by, and for, itself. In both cases, it would be afforded a non-subjective, non-interpretative testimonial power.

19 See, for example, the photographs reproduced in P. Horn, *The Victorian and Edwardian Schoolchild* (Gloucester: Alan Sutton, 1989).

On Visualising Past Classrooms (2)

The content of a photograph — this photograph of a classroom — is chemically fixed on the negative, but the process of recording is never innocent. A different reading — indeed plural readings — is possible if the beguiling nature of the photographic image is recognised and its documentary status questioned. The potential for alternative readings becomes readily apparent if this photograph is 'looked-at' and the following question posed: What is the relationship between the classroom and the photographer's creative lens?

This question can best be explored by translating it into a series of sub-questions and observations. These can be grouped under six headings: the photographer's gaze, technology, purpose, meaning[s] and audience, title/caption, and presentation. As the purpose is to work towards the development of critical practice, some issues will be raised under these headings, which do not directly relate to the image being analysed here, but are nevertheless relevant to the overall project.

The Photographer's Gaze

Where, when, and by whom was this photograph taken? Photographs are bounded, that is, they are framed. Framing is a mechanical function of the camera's eye, but what is included, what is framed, what is excluded, is determined by the gaze of the photographer. The photographer controls the construction of the image and the relationship between objects positioned within that frame. Thus the decision to set the limits, the edges of the framed image, are neither arbitrary nor an artefact of technique. They define what is *in* the photograph and what is *not*.

What is not shown in this classroom? What exists outside the frame? What do absences signify? What determined the framing of this photograph?

Is what is portrayed actually what went on in school classrooms, or what the photographer wanted to show the audience? In other words, what was the photographer's *intention* in constructing the significance of what the photograph presents?

What are the aesthetics of the image? What factors governed its composition? Does it conform with certain photographic conventions?

Photographs are not made and cannot be understood 'outside of the context from which other kinds of pictures derive their significance'.[20] They are texts inscribed in a 'photographic discourse' and achieve

20 J. Snyder and D. Munson, *The Documentary Photograph as a Work of Art: American Photographs, 1860-1876* (Chicago: University of Chicago Press, 1976) p. 8.

21 See V. Burgin ed.,
Thinking Photography
(Basingstoke:
Macmillan, 1982)
passim.

meaning through a language of codes.[21] Is the photograph representative of a genre? Is it part of a systematic recording of classroom behaviour? Does it coalesce with other photographic texts? Is there mutuality, which reinforces the 'real'? In short, does the photograph constitute an element in a discursive production which delimits and structures classroom normality?

Technology

What photographic technologies were used and how did they affect the image? What was the camera angle? What lighting was used? Can we see where the light is coming from? What was the range of the lens? What was the exposure time? What type of film was used? Was the camera hand-held or attached to a tripod?

How is the photograph printed? Is it matt or glossy? Is it in black and white or in colour? Tinting and colour processes were available early in the history of photography, but black and white was the preferred medium of documentary realism. Does the presence of colour/tinting question the image's 'truthfulness', and authenticity? Does the photograph's shape or size affect our understanding of its meaning?

Purpose

Is it a record for future memory or a document for possible use? If it was produced for use, was it official or private? Who was the intended audience? Who saw it? Was it circulated? Photography was one of the mechanisms of surveillance used by the state in the late nineteenth century and the compilation of photographic records became common practice.[22] Was the photograph inserted into a cumulative archive of documents recording and surveying schooling. Was it catalogued and then filed? Where is the photograph now?

If this photograph was produced for commercial purposes as a memento of a child's progress through school which could be purchased and preserved in the family album/collection to what extent does it present a teacher-authorised version of the school child? Is the setting neutral, or has it been chosen to convey the values the school sought to promote?

Audience and Meaning[s]

Meaning is given to a photograph by our gaze: 'the reading of the photograph is... always historical; it depends on the reader's 'knowledge'... intelligible only if one has learned the signs'.[23] How do we make sense of what is going on? Is it through internal clues or is it the knowledge we bring to the photograph? Does this make it historically significant, 'transforming a more or less chance residue of the past into a precious icon'?[24]

Closely related to this, is the photograph perceived as 'real', as 'true' because that

22 See J. Tagg, *The Burden of Representation* (Basingstoke: Macmillan, 1988); D. Green, 'On Foucault: Disciplinary Power and Photography', *Camerawork* , No 32 (Summer 1985).

23 R. Barthes, *Image-Music-Text*, trans. Stephen Heath (Glasgow: Fontana, 1977) p.28.

24 Samuel, *Theatres*, p. 328.

25 E. Edwards ed.,
*Anthropology and
Photography 1860-1920*
(New Haven: Yale
University Press, 1992)
p. 8.

is what the viewer/reader expects to see? Is it a case of 'This is how it should be' becoming 'this is how it is/was'? [25]

What happens when if we, the viewers/readers, visualise ourselves as a subject in the photograph at the moment it was taken? Whose position do we choose? What happens if we take up the position of another subject in the photograph? Does our understanding change? It is interesting to notice that in this particular photograph no one returns the gaze that addresses him or her.

To what extent is knowledge produced by the creation of this image? Does the photograph define, or seek to define, normal classroom behaviour? Does it codify pedagogical practice? Does it reinforce stereotypes? If it was circulated, would it have contributed to and defined pedagogical practice? Does it represent the exercising of a normalising disciplinary power?

To have visual knowledge of an object is to have power over it. Is the photographic image an element in a 'regime of truth'? Indeed, does the detail created by the photographer become a symbol for the whole and tempt the viewer/reader to allow the specific to stand for generalities? This is a late-nineteenth century classroom?

What was the relationship between the image and its audience in the past? How did the photograph speak to its historical viewer? What meaning did it hold? How did it engage with the wider social and cultural practices which defined and gave meaning to a 'world view'? What constitutes the cultural framework which enabled the image to be taken and understood. According to Sekula 'the meaning of a photograph, like that of any other entity, is inevitably subject to cultural definition'.[26] Was there a shared reading, a shared understanding among the audience of what constituted classroom reality or was there a potential diversity of readings? What does the photograph tell us about the ideas in circulation in the late nineteenth century with regard to education and schooling?

What does it say to us now? How do we discursively position ourselves to respond to the image? What are the implications of gender difference in terms of photographic practice and the 'reading' of photographic texts? When we find a photograph meaningful 'we are lending it a past and a future'.[27] Meaning is discovered in what connects, 'the lens of the camera is, in effect, the eye of the person looking at the print'.[28]

Title/Caption

Does the photograph have a title, if so, when was it given and by whom? Written text can help the viewer, both historical and contemporary, make sense of an image, but titles and captions can equally function to control the possible meanings of a photograph, they can be projected into the image. 'A title', as John Fisher has written, 'is not

26 A. Sekula, *Photography against the Grain: Essays and Photo Works, 1973-1983* (Halifax: Nova Scotia College of Art and Design, 1984) p. 3.

27 J. Berger and J. Mohr, *Another Way of Telling* (London: Writers and Readers Publishing Co-operative Society, 1982) p. 89.

28 The American documentary photographer Arthur Rothstein quoted in Stott, *Documentary*, p. 29.

29 J. Fisher, 'Entitling',
Critical Inquiry 11,
(1984) pp. 289-92.

30 E. Margolis, 'Mining
Photographs:
Unearthing the
Meanings of Historical
Photos', *Radical History
Review* 40 (1988) p. 42.

31 M. Baxendall,
Exhibiting Intention' in
I. Kard and S. D.
Levine eds., *Exhibiting
Cultures; The Poetics and
Politics of Museum
Display* (Washington:
Smithsonion Institute,
1990) pp. 35-36.

only a name, it is a name for a purpose...
[it] tell[s] us how to look at a work, how
to listen'.[29] Captions similarly direct the
viewer's reading: 'we are told what to
see', they force meanings on the picture
that are neither explicitly nor implicitly
part of the image. [30] Does the title tell us
what we are to see and how we are to
see it?

If the photograph has no title, what
would be appropriate? If we give it a
title, to what extent would 'our'
entitlement be an act 'of interpretation
masquerading as [a] verbal aid'?[31]

Presentation

How is our understanding of a
photograph's meaning altered by its
presentation? Does a change of context
alter its status? If it was placed side by
side with other photographs of past
classrooms, as is often the case in
monographs about nineteenth and
twentieth century schooling, is the
narrative which it individually generates
for the viewer/reader significantly
altered?

An 'exhibition' is a particular space into
which objects are collected for viewing,
but it is also 'a discursive practice,
constituted through selections and
omissions, captions, titles, hanging,
spatial lay-out, catalogue introductions
and essays and the decisions underlying
all these things which are determined by
the institutions or groups which have the
power and resources to put on
exhibitions'. If the photographic text is

read / consumed in the institutional context of a museum, how is that reading influenced by the curators who define the discursive frame for viewing the image.[32]

The History of a Photograph: Somerville Road Board School

No reading[s] will be offered here of the photograph of Somerville Road Board School; that creative role will be assigned to the viewers/readers of this essay. However, the following data about this particular photograph are known. On the reverse of the print is the name of the photographer: W. Woollaston. There is no date on the back. It is one of a series of twenty school photographs attributed to Woollaston which are held by the local studies department in Birmingham Central Library. All but two of these photographs are interiors; they were taken in at least four different locations and all but two of them are dated 1896. The twenty photographs are catalogued among the Warwickshire Photographic Survey, but were never part of it. This photographic survey was undertaken in the late Victorian period by a group of amateur photographers living in and around Birmingham, who wished to record the fast disappearing village environment of rural Warwickshire.

There is no correspondence about the photograph's provenance, except a librarian's memory that it was deposited with other education records of Birmingham City Council and was added to the Warwickshire Photographic Survey collection for reasons related to administration and record linkage. Woollaston is not listed among known professional Birmingham photographers and no reference to his studio could be found. There is no reference to Woollaston or the taking of photographs in the

32 G. Pollock, 'Three Perspectives on Photography', *Screen Education* 31 (1979) p. 49. See also T. Bennett, *The Birth of the Museum. History, theory, politics* (London: Routledge, 1995) and R. Krauss, 'Photography's Discursive Spaces' in R. Bolton ed., *The Context of Meaning: Critical Histories of Photography*, (Cambridge, Mass:, MIT Press, 1989).

School Board Minute Book for 1896 (or 1894, 1895, 1897) or in the single extant Somerville Road School Log Book for 1896 or in the school's Visitor's Book for 1896 (or 1894, 1895, 1897). Finally, the space that is shown in the photograph is not strictly a classroom. The lighting is coming from above when according to traditions of board school design, it should be coming from the left side. If the two doorways visible in the photograph are added to this, then it must have been a hall not a classroom. However, this realisation prompts a further question, in terms of teaching and learning: What determines what can be defined as a classroom?

Towards a critical historical practice

Photographs — if they are to be used for 'knowledge' of a subject, if they are to be used to help discover the silences of past classrooms — require historians of education to engage critically with issues relating to their production. Woollaston's photograph of Somerville Road Board School, Birmingham ca1896 has been used here as a representative of the thousands of images of school life which are held in archives and collections. It has been used to promote/provoke a series of questions about the nature of photography, of photography as production, of the photographer as an image producer, of photographs as constructed pictorial representations of reality, of photographs as texts inscribed in a photographic discourse, of photographs as complex and ambivalent artefacts. Photographs, like written documents, are always produced for a purpose, they are always in context and like all other constructions are open to deconstruction. In developing a critical historical practice in using photographs as evidence, it is clear that historians need to follow John Berger's advice and construct a radial system around an image so that the viewer/reader can deconstruct the photographic text in terms which are 'simultaneously personal, political, economic, dramatic, everyday and historic'.[33]

33 J. Berger, 'Uses of photography' in *About Looking* (New York: Pantheon Books, 1980) p.63.

Any critical practice must of necessity be continually re-viewed and re-defined. To this end this chapter will close with both an activity and a further set of questions. First, the activity: four other photographs of past classrooms appear at the end of this text for readers/viewers to further develop and explore the configurations of a critical historical practice. Three of the photographs are from Europe and the other from North America.[34] Second, the need for review is particularly true of a practice directed at the use of a source which is now mass-produced. Photographic realism and objectivity are generally associated with the documentary photographer, the professional recorder of events who visualised history in a series of discrete black and white images. It is with their photographs that historians traditionally engage. By the last decade of the nineteenth century, however, photography as a cultural practice changed dramatically. The development and successful marketing of Eastman's relatively cheap 'You press the button, we do the rest' Kodak camera in 1888 and the production of the inexpensive Brownie box camera in 1900 changed photography from being a privileged pursuit of a professional minority to being open to potentially everyone. The camera — the means of photographic production itself — was put into the hands of the many to tell and record their own life stories, to become active producers of unique personal photographs and family albums. As collections of people's memorabilia grow, so too does the volume of photographs available to researchers. The critical practice outlined here has in the main focused on the professionally produced documentary photograph. Will the same questions serve to guide historical practice using this universalised source? Will family 'snapshots' and personal photographs require extra questions to be posed? Indeed, will the use of photographs from the family album alongside the professionally produced visual record of past schooling have the potential to

34 Those interested in critical discussion can reach the author at I.D.Grosvenor@bham. ac.uk

bring us closer to people's everyday experience of classroom life by unlocking memories, half-forgotten conversations, whispers, and anecdotes?

On Visualising Past Classrooms

On Visualising Past Classrooms

On Visualising Past Classrooms

On Visualising Past Classrooms

Words about Classrooms

Smaller

Words about classrooms: what can one letter tell us?

Harry Smaller

Lansdowne P.O. CW
16th. Dec 1865

Sir

We have a small school, average attendance about 20; an able young man for a teacher (that is able in a physical point of view) who has come to the conclusion that it is not his duty to sweep and dust the school room as laid down in the school manual as pertaining to the duties of masters. Some of the trustees think that it is the masters duty to sweep and dust the school every evening, the teacher and one of the trustees hold that the trustees must hire some one to do it. Now when it is swept at all, the children have been compelled to do it, in many cases very much against the wish of their parents. Up to this time there never has been any dificulty [sic] about the matter. The teacher has always kept it sweep [sic] and considered that it was his duty [. F]rom this out it will be necessary to have the masters duties more clearly defined. I have therefore been instructed by the trustees to write to you and ask for your decission [sic] in this case.

    I am Sir

        Your very Obt Servant
        William Thomson
        Secy Treasurer
        School Sec No 9
        Leeds and Lansdowne Front
the Chief Supt of Education
        Toronto
P.S. Is it the duty of the teacher to make the fires in the school house - after the wood is del'd.

        W.J.[1]

1 RG 2 C6C Thomson to Ryerson, Dec. 16 1865, Public Archives of Ontario, Toronto.

Lansdowne P.O. CW
16th Dec 1865

Sir

We have a small school, average attendance
about 20; an able young man for teacher (that is
able in a physical point of view), who has come to the
conclusion that it is not his duty to sweep and
dust the school room as laid down in the School
manual as pertaining to the duties of Masters.
Some of the Trustees think that it is the masters
duty to sweep and dust the school room every
evening, the Teacher and one of the Trustees hold
that the Trustees must hire some one to do it,
now, when it is swept at all, the children have
been compelled to do it, in many cases very
much against the wish of their parents,
up to this time, there never has been any
dificulty about the matter, the Teacher has always
kept it swept and considered that it was his
duty, from this out it will be necessary to have
the Masters duties more clearly defined. I have
therefore been instructed by the Trustees to write
to you and ask for your decision in this case

I am Sir
Yours very Obt Servt

William Thomson
Secy Treasurer
School Sec No 9
Leeds & Lansdowne Front

The Cheif Supt of Education
Toronto

P.S. Is it the duty of the Teacher to make the firey in
the school house — after the wood is delt
W.J.

What is to be made of this letter? What does it tell us? By comparison, what does it allude to, but not 'tell' us? On the basis of this one letter, what might we conclude, or conjecture, about the trials of one student, or one family, or one teacher, during these times? What might we conclude or conjecture about schooling during these times – in the classroom, or at higher levels of government? What might we conclude or at least conjecture about social groups, social structures and social relations during these times? What other information would we like to have in order to put this letter into some larger perspective and or to 'test' our conjectures?

This letter, while unique in itself, is certainly not unusual in the history of schooling in North America. Bureaucrats and officials at all levels of schooling systems were continually inundated with similar missives for much of the nineteenth century and well into the twentieth. Where they have been conserved (and are accessible to the curious), they form an astounding array of information about the people, issues and events of the past. This letter, for example, is housed in an Ontario Public Archives collection of letters (Record Group Two, C-6-C) that were written specifically to the provincial Superintendent of Education by parents, school trustees, teachers, ratepayers, clerics, local school superintendents – and even a few students – over a 32-year period from 1842 to 1876. While they have never (to my knowledge) been counted, the boxes in which they are stuffed occupy 150 feet of shelf space in the archives. Clearly they number in the tens of thousands, and this is just one collection, in one jurisdiction of North America!

As my preceding questions suggest, these letters can be read and interpreted in many ways. These interpretations can then be tested, using information from other letters, teachers' diaries, minutes from meetings, classroom attendance records, annual reports, and so on. This is 'doing' history – whether as a hobby or an occupation. From these documents (and other evidence) come interpretations, ideas, and theories that in turn spawn further search for evidence and new interpretations that may or may not support the earlier ones. The purpose of this chapter then, is to take a closer look at Mr. Thomson's letter in two ways: to examine the possibilities and limitations of such a document, and to use it, directly and indirectly, to explore a number of issues and themes related to schooling during these times.

Lansdowne was (and remains to this day) a small village half-way between the historic towns of Kingston and Brockville in Canada West ('CW' in the letter heading), as Ontario was known before national confederation in 1867. It was probably typical of many settlements in this area of the province. Being close (five kilometers) to the transportation corridor of the St. Lawrence River, with fairly fertile soil, it would have been an early destination for European immigrants. Well before the end of the eighteenth century, they had successfully pushed out the aboriginal population and 'settled' the land. Some of these 'settlers' would have come directly from Britain and other parts of Europe. Others would have come as refugee 'United Empire Loyalists' from the United States, after it seceded from Britain in the 1780s.

One could also conjecture, based on the letter, that the school over which Mr. Thomson and his trustee colleagues presided did not actually sit in the village of Lansdowne but rather somewhere in the surrounding rural area. It was located in 'School Sec[tion] No.9' which, in those days, were small geographic areas, each containing one, single room schoolhouse. Their outside boundaries were generally determined by the maximum distance a student could be expected to travel daily (by foot or otherwise) to attend school – three to five kilometers (two or three miles) on each side, with the schoolhouse somewhere in the middle.

The language of 'school sections' came into being as part of colonial government regulations introduced in Ontario during the 1840s. From that time on, local parents who wished to receive financial support from government coffers for schooling were required to advertise, hold a public meeting and elect three school trustees, who in turn were to notify the authorities of their request to be considered an official 'section.' As they were established, these school sections were numbered chronologically within each township (an area approximately 18 to 20 kilometers, or 11 to 12 miles, per side). Given that this was school section number nine, one could surmise that, like many areas of the province, it might well have been established after residents in the more populated areas of the township had found it possible to do so. (Given their size, townships in Southern Ontario rarely ended up with more than 10 to 15 school sections each). Thus Mr. Thomson and his school could well have been situated in the outer reaches of the township, with Landsdowne merely containing the nearest post office ('P.O.') from which Mr. Thomson could send (and ideally receive a reply to) his letter, on that undoubtedly cold day in mid-December 1865.

And who was Mr. Thomson? Clearly he was one of thousands of adults across the province who participated in local ratepayer meetings that were held each January to elect school board trustees. Given that more than 82 percent of Ontario's school-age population lived in 'rural' areas during this era (a category that did not even include settlements officially designated as 'villages') and that only 'ratepayers' were eligible to vote, the chances are high that Mr. Thomson owned a farm or was otherwise employed in a manner that would allow him to own property. In any event, we can assume that he was seen, by a sufficient number of other ratepayers, to be worthy of serving on the school board. Whatever other criteria these electors may have considered important in a candidate, being a male was certainly one of them. Although the regulations governing these elections did not specifically mention gender, there is certainly little, if any, record of women being selected during these times. The reasons why he was subsequently selected by his two elected colleagues to serve as Secretary Treasurer – a position often considered as one of special influence within these structures, and in the larger community – are also open to some conjecture. The fact that he could read and write may or may not have been a factor.

Even though Mr. Thomson's school was the ninth in the township to be officially declared as a result of the 1840s regulations, this is not to suggest that his community did not have formal educational settings for its children before that time. In fact, like other provinces and states in North America, educational settings in Ontario developed almost concomitant with European settlement itself. Reports abound of schools and other educational settings which were in operation in various centres in Upper Canada, even before the beginning of the 1800s. By 1813, even more distant counties in the western reaches of the province were reporting that every township therein had anywhere from one to four schools, and four years later (1817) a statistical survey showed that, in the forty-six townships reporting complete information, 34,069 inhabitants supported 165 common schools, giving an average of over three and one-half schools per township, or one school for every two hundred residents. Reports of individual towns are equally impressive. For example, by 1818 more than a dozen schools were in operation in Kingston alone, and in 1834 it was reported that the small town of Hallowell (in the same area as Lansdowne, but no longer listed on Ontario government maps) boasted 'several elementary schools' taught 'by men who seem enthusiastic' in their work. In addition, the town possessed 'an extremely well selected library.'[2]

2 *Hallowell Free Press* July 21st 1834.

As significant as these figures are, it is important to remember that many of them were drawn from official government records. Therefore, they usually did not include many local schools that were not officially reported, and did not appear on official records. In fact, education historians Susan Houston and Alison Prentice point out that 'even by mid-century,' these schools 'may still have been the majority... in Upper Canada.' They cite the example of Kingston which as late as 1849 found 738 students in common schools, at the same time as 826 others were enrolled in non-grant aided programs.[3]

3 S. Houston and A. Prentice, *Schooling and Scholars in Nineteenth Century Ontario* (Toronto:University of Toronto Press, 1988) p. 112.

Whether or not they appeared in official records, these schools were different from their later counterparts in one main way. They were established and operated by parents themselves, with little or no government involvement or control, and very little, if any, financial support. Teachers were hired on the basis of qualifications that parents themselves deemed important. They were directed and supervised by these parents, who also, for the most part, paid their salaries directly from their own pockets.

By 1865, however, if Mr. Thomson's letter is any indication, it is clear that things had changed considerably. Not only were elected school trustees officially responsible for running the school and determining the behaviour of the teacher, but they in turn found it necessary to consult a higher governmental authority to fulfill this function. Why this dramatic change in control over education during these times?

In many respects, the answer is simple. The 1840s marked a turning point in schooling in many parts of Canada. During the previous decade, the political and economic elite had been shaken by a number of social disruptions - severe economic depression, increased migration of the poor from the Britain, and serious armed rebellions by local residents across the colony against colonial rule. Colonial leaders were determined to introduce new social structures to prevent further rebellions and unrest, and schools were increasingly viewed as one way to achieve this task. As historian Susan Houston has pointed out, the 'equation of ignorance and vice, schooling and virtue, would appear in the arguments of spokesmen of various political hues throughout this period.' Reverend Robert Murray, the first Assistant Superintendent of Education for Upper Canada, explained it well:

> ... unless the provision for the support of education is made certain and permanent, this great country must rapidly sink deeper and deeper in ignorance and vice. No man possessed of property in this Province, who attends for a little to the state of ignorance which pervades the great mass of the many thousands in which our native youth are growing up around us could hesitate for a moment to pay any reasonable tax for the support of education, as he would be thereby increasing the value of his estate, and securing himself and his posterity in the possession of it.[4]

4 As quoted in S. Houston 'Politics, Schools and Social Change in Upper Canada' in M. Cross and G. Kealey eds., *Pre-industrial Canada* (Toronto: McClelland and Stewart, 1982) p. 93.

What was not acceptable to the elite, however, were the existing schools, embedded in local communities across the province, and controlled everywhere by local parents. Rather, what was required was a universal, uniform, centrally managed schooling system, one that, as Reverend Murray suggests, emphasized above all else the importance of character development and subservience to the British crown, traditional forms of government, and, a concept often heard being exhorted during these times, 'manly virtues'. Achieving this change would not be an easy task however – given the local community investment in, and control over, their own schools, as well as the mounting opposition to any incursions of the colonial government into local structures.

Few would deny, however, that this task was largely accomplished over time. By the end of the nineteenth century a system was in place that, although still left with the appearance of local involvement, was highly regulated by a centralized Department of Education, with standardized curriculum, textbooks, examinations, teacher training and certification, school rules and regulations, all overseen by a province-wide platoon of school inspectors who were ultimately responsible to the Department. The complex ways, often subtle, but invariably powerful, in which this agenda was achieved is certainly worthy of study. Mr. Thomson's letter, I would suggest, offers many insights into this complex process.

Even on the surface, Mr. Thomson's letter shows poignantly how local officials, supposedly in authority in such seemingly trivial matters, were left deferring to higher state officials. Political scientists and historical sociologists (among others) use these kinds of examples to theorize on the ways in which relations between local and higher state authorities evolve and crystallize, despite continuing (then and now) opposition from others in the community. Mr. Thomson's letter also provides wonderful (albeit singular) evidence for further investigation into a large array of historical (and contemporary) schooling themes, concepts that now carry such labels as school governance, school-community relations, teacher-parent relations, student-teacher relations, teacher evaluation, standards of practice, and so on.

For the purposes of helping to understand Mr. Thomson's missive, however, I have chosen to engage another theme that, while encompassing important aspects of many of the issues just mentioned, occupies a special place in the evolution of the centralized schooling systems now found across the western world. It will provide, I believe, useful ways in which to understand and relate the activities and concerns of a number of different 'actors' in (and beyond) School Section 9 of Leeds, Lansdowne and Frontenac in 1865, trustees, parents, a teacher, higher schooling officials and the students themselves. For lack of a better label, I will categorize this theme as 'the professionalization project'.

Professionalization

What is entailed in sweeping a schoolhouse? What does it mean to those who do it and to others who watch, or know? Was five or ten extra minutes of work at the end of a school day the only thing at stake here, in this particular conflict among and between students, parents, trustees and a teacher? It's possible, but highly unlikely, I would argue. For starters, even Mr. Thomson's postscript ('P.S.') suggests otherwise. Similarly, did asking a teacher to sweep a floor become an issue only for this one small Upper Canadian school community at one point in time? Definitely not, as anyone who has perused the C-6-C collection in the Public Archives of Ontario well knows. It is inundated with similar letters from across the province and across the decades - complaints and inquiries from all 'sides' about the nature of teachers' 'extra-curricular duties'.

Based on letters like Mr. Thomson's, one can safely conclude that it was not the five or ten minutes of extra work that was at stake in these matters. Rather, what was invariably at issue was the nature of the work involved. Before the 1840s, teachers had traditionally been responsible for the entire operation of the local schoolhouse. When the schooling legislation of the 1840s came into being however, it was replete with many references to the 'professionalism' that teachers needed to adopt in order to assist in the development of these new forms of (centralized) schooling. Over the ensuing years, in letters, speeches and publications, the schooling elite were prodigious in their declarations about the nature of this 'professionalism' and the many levels at which it was to operate. Some aspects involved legislation and regulation, but much of it operated at the ideological level - advertising the importance of 'proper' deportment and social relations. These values were explicitly tied to gender and class relations with the community and the importance of the newly-evolving school system in 'schooling' such proper subjectivities among young people. Thus at one important level professionalism was (and remains) deeply intertwined with 'status' within communities, status in relation to others. In this regard, it is certainly not surprising that, by 1865, after at least 25 years of continuous state propagandizing, a 'young' male teacher would balk at being required to engage in such clearly gendered and 'classed' labour, even at the risk of sanction, including summary dismissal, with little or no provision in those times for recourse.

At another important level, Mr. Thomson's letter also exemplifies the ways in which the development of state-supported professionalism in Europe and North America in the eighteenth and nineteenth centuries resulted in a major shift in the way in which clients and their communities were allowed to relate to the providers of public and private services. Clearly, by 1865, parents of this school section were no longer able to determine a simple matter of work responsibility for their employee. Much more intriguing, however, are the actions of the elected trustees in this matter. Despite provincial regulations explicitly allowing them to direct teachers in matters such as these and despite the absence of provincial regulations governing or limiting teachers' extra-curricular duties (something that at least one of the trustees or community members would surely have been aware of), and even though there was clearly written local policy on the matter ('as laid down in the School manual'), these elected officials still felt it necessary to consult with higher state officials before finalizing their strategy with the teacher in question. Such were the ways in which the ideology of professionalization was able to influence, and even on occasion determine the political agendas and decisions within communities across the province.

To be sure, Mr. Thomson did not make it clear (intentionally or otherwise) as to how many of the parents were actually complaining about this matter. Nor was he clear whether those who were complaining wanted the teacher to sweep floors, or simply that they did not want their own children performing those tasks or being compelled rather than asked to do so. This matter does raise other complexities about school governance in those times. Given that trustees were elected by all ratepayers, and not just those with children in school, concern for the public purse often rated at least as high as concern for the 'adequate' (however judged) funding of schooling. Parents as compared with other taxpayers could well have been in favour of hiring someone to perform the extra tasks.

Mr. Thomson's appeal to higher authority also provides insight into larger agendas of state officials in relation to developing their centralized schooling system. While these officials would not necessarily have relished the social disruption that these differences over schooling matters caused, the thought of one teacher insisting upon achieving status above that of most local residents, certainly aligned with their overall project. Their campaign to ensure that schools served the interests of the state rather than the interests of local communities included a vigorous denunciation against teachers remaining socially and culturally embedded within the communities in which they were raised and worked. One official claimed that teachers' 'minds have become dissipated' as a result of not being able 'to choose either their place or their company' in the community. For the same reason, 'boarding around' with families (an economic necessity for most teachers given the salary levels offered during this time) was also seen as an evil by higher authorities. One local school superintendent complained that teachers 'often ingratiate themselves with members of the families', and thus 'go out and blight the growing intellect of the youth of our Country'. Ironically, those teachers who could afford to stay in local inns were equally suspect. In the words of another official of the time, 'they insensibly become assimilated to them [other clients of the inn] in their manners, views and habits, and are thus rendered utterly disqualified for conducting the education of youth'.[5]

5 J.G. Hodgins *Documentary History of Education in Upper Canada* Vol.13 (Toronto: L.K.Cameron 1894-1910) p. 71.

Clearly, professionalization meant, among other things, separation from communities or, at least social separation (and elevation) from the majority of the residents thereof. On this basis, one could correctly conjecture that Mr. Thompson's opinion on the matter would not have been well received by the Chief Superintendent in Toronto. Ironically, since the beginning of the state system in the 1840s, officials had been generally evasive when confronted with demands for rulings on precisely these kinds of issues, partly because they were wary of the backlash caused by their impositions on local traditions. By the mid-1860s however, the centralization process developed to the point that opinions and even regulations were being promulgated at the centre in support of the 'professional authority' of teachers.

Mr. Thomson's letter certainly tells us much about teacher-employer-parent relations in School Section #9 during those times. For one thing, I am left with the opinion that, whatever the final decision on the particular task of sweeping floors (not to mention the making of fires), it would probably have done little toward resolving the underlying, long-term tensions that undoubtedly existed. Indeed, one wonders whether Mr. Thomson's implied solution to the immediate 'problem' (his threat to 'have the master duties more clearly defined') would have had much ameliatory, or even practical, effect given that he started the letter by stating that this duty was already clearly defined.

Finally, and perhaps most important, what can we learn from Mr. Thomson's letter about what was happening in the classroom of School Section #9 in 1865? What did this larger struggle mean to students there? Can we conjecture things about the nature of the social relations between students and with the teacher? Was he really compelling students to sweep the floor or was this just some parents' interpretation based on what their children chose to tell them? Did the students mind doing these tasks? How did they interpret and respond to the manner in which these requests and demands were being made?

More broadly, what were these students supposed to be learning and what were they really learning? How did a struggle over control, being played out at a number of levels in and beyond this community, impinge upon and even constitute their experience in the classroom? Is it really possible that all of this was a 'learning experience' and that the students came to understand the 'hidden curriculum' through which power is exerted and contested within and between groups and structures in our society?

Part 2
Seeking Answers:
Case Studies in a New
Social History of the Classroom

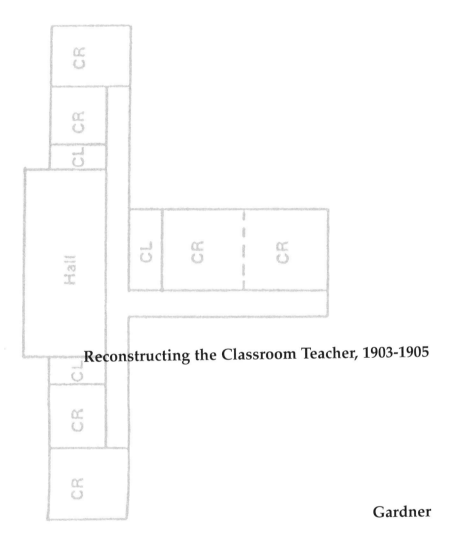

Reconstructing the Classroom Teacher, 1903-1905

Gardner

Reconstructing the Classroom Teacher, 1903-1945

Philip Gardner

The classroom has been an increasingly important site of shared national experience since the early nineteenth century. By the end of that century its impact had become universal. The classroom was established as the locus of an effectively inescapable collective experience shaping the lives of each successive generation of British children from then until now. The dominant figures in the construction of that experience were, as they remain, teachers. Any attempt to understand life in the classrooms of the past must therefore find some way to understand the teachers who both regulated and participated in that life. This is less easy than it sounds.

The central difficulty in approaching the teacher in history is presented by a superabundance of preconception and a dearth of appropriate historical evidence. From the inception of a structure of formal training and certification for elementary school teachers in 1846, there has been no shortage of public and political pronouncements about the nature of teaching and the perceived characteristics of those who have undertaken it. Over the years, teachers have been variously constructed as selfless missionaries, as intellectual upstarts, as ambitious status seekers, as social isolates, as cruel authoritarians, as well-meaning dupes unwittingly serving this interest or that, as emergent professionals, as trade union fighters, or as a disparate occupational constituency divided against itself. In each of these assertions, there is of course some truth.[1] Each could be supported by compelling documentary evidence. By extension, each could also be challenged in similarly persuasive terms by drawing on different sources of evidence. If our goal is to understand the classroom teacher historically, then stereotypes or unwarranted generalisations will not do. They certainly have

1 M. Lawn *Servants of the State* (Lewes, UK: Falmer Press, 1987) p. ix.

importance, but this lies more in their practical contribution to social constructions of teaching over time and less in any putative analytical utility.

The supposition that broad or exclusive categories defining teacher identity are legitimate tools of historical investigation has been sustainable largely because those to whom such categories have been attached - the classroom teachers - have historically had little to say about themselves. This reticence is itself a further significant factor in understanding the constructed character of teacher identity. But, in the present context, the salient point is that, to the extent that the teachers of the past have been relatively silent about themselves and their work, this has made it easy for others to do their talking for them.

A career teacher who began his or her elementary schoolteaching life in 1903 would be coming to the end of it in 1945. The span of these years saw mighty transformations in every sphere of wider social and political life, as well as two catastrophic world wars. But what changes did they bring to the ways in which classroom teachers perceived themselves and their work? What sense did this generation of teachers have of the reconstruction of their professional identities over these four decades?

To address this question, we must focus our enquiry on the classroom teacher, which means concentrating on a surprisingly distant figure in an unexpectedly far-off landscape. And as the historian seeks to resolve this indistinct picture, he or she becomes aware that the historical sources available to the task are challenged in ways which parallel the researcher's central difficulty. Such sources, though contemporary with the subjects of which they speak, remain effectively the products of outsiders attempting to make sense of what they perceive to be going on within.[2] This is particularly the case for official government papers and policy documents on

2 D. M. Copelman
London's Women Teachers: Gender, Class and Feminism 1870-1930
(London:Routledge 1996) p. 36.

the one hand and popular press reports on the other.[3] To a lesser degree, it also applies to the public pronouncements of the organised unions and associations through which teachers were represented and to the assessments of those who formally inspected the work of teachers. In each of these cases, the understanding of the figure of the pre-war teacher is veiled by the distance of culture, experience or place, just as that same figure is obscured from the historian by the distance of time.

Increasingly after the turn of the century, the work of teachers was widely debated in the public arena.[4] Teaching itself, however, remained an intensely private and often solitary craft.[5] It was not difficult for individual teachers, locked in the confined spaces of their classrooms, to conclude that they were more or less widely misunderstood by the world outside and that the rhetoric of the public discussion of education and the reality of their teaching lives were two quite different things. This is why the recovery of the voice of the classroom teacher from the past is of such importance.[6] It offers us access to those issues and concerns which teachers themselves saw as standing at the heart of their professional identity.[7]

This does not mean, however, that the restitution of the teachers' voice offers a royal road towards understanding the construction of teacher identity in the past. This is a source which is always, to some degree, fashioned as it responds to the stylised teacher identities celebrated or deprecated by government reports, by newspapers, by unions and professional associations and by school inspectors.[8] The teachers' voice, like the historical experience on which it draws, cannot be properly understood without recognising that it is shaped by the expressions of each of these agencies just as, in its turn and in its time, it also shaped each of them.[9] This is a voice, in other words, that is always a record of change and adaption as well as continuity and

3 P. Cunningham 'Teachers' professional image and the press 1950-1990' *History of Education*, 21,1 (1992) pp. 37-56.

4 P.H.J.H. Gosden *The Evolution of a Profession* (London: Basil Blackwell, 1972); A.Tropp *The School Teachers* (London: Heinemann, 1957).

5 D.Lortie *Schoolteacher* (Chicago: University of Chicago Press, 1975) pp. 15, 22-4.

6 Interview extracts are taken from two interview series involving 144 former teachers. I am grateful for grants from the Nuffield Foundation and the Leverhulme Trust.

7 K. Rousmaniere *City Teachers: Teaching and School Reform in Historical Perspective* (New York:Teachers College Press, 1997) p. 8.

8 M. Wetherell 'Life histories/social histories' in M. Wetherell ed. *Identities and Social Groups* (Milton Keynes:Sage/Open University Press, 1996) pp. 299-342.

9 J. W. Scott 'The Evidence of Experience' *Critical Inquiry* 17 (1991) pp. 773-97; W. H Sewell Jr. 'How Classes are Made : critical reflections on E.P. Thompson's theory of working-class formation' in H. J.

Kaye and K.
McClelland, eds. *E.P.
Thompson: Critical
Perspectives* (Oxford:
Polity, 1990) pp. 50-77.

stability. Whilst expressing the internal regularities and patterns of daily classroom life, it is also a moving and critical commentary on those representations of teaching produced outside or away from the classroom.

Attention to the teachers' voice is indispensable for understanding the ways in which teacher identities were being reconstructed between 1904 and 1945. In listening to the voice however, we need to be aware that the stories it relates are in fact doubly reconstructed. In the first place, these are accounts which give us unique and direct evidence of the ways in which teachers in the first half of the century sought to manufacture a usable professional identity from many different and sometimes contradictory elements. In the second place, these accounts are themselves historical reconstructions of that identity across many decades, fashioned from the exercise of memory and enacted in dialogic exchange. This means that the voice might be simultaneously that of participant, reporter and analyst. In one breath, it revisits the immediacies of a single moment from the past; in the next it comprehends the entire sweep of a forty-year career.

Beneath the details of what it has to tell us, the voice of the classroom teacher has a particular and characteristic quality. This is difficult to describe adequately, but its principal constituents are twofold. On the one hand, there is a persistent inwardly-oriented concentration on those personalities and places which dominated everyday working life – principally classrooms, playgrounds, children and other teachers. Those beyond this group figure only occasionally and at a considerable remove – inspectors, trade union leaders, politicians and parents. On the other hand, there is an attempt to reconcile, or at least to recognise, classroom life as balanced between the pressure of change and the force of continuity. The voice acknowledges the inevitability of change, sometimes applauding or embracing its manifestations, sometimes decrying or ignoring them. Change is occasionally seen to emanate from the schools themselves but, more commonly, it is associated with concerns distant from theirs and which are usually interpreted as the exercise of political rather than educational interests. Whatever its provenance or its intent however, the tendency towards change is, for this generation, always accompanied by the recognition of elemental continuities. Change originated 'out there' and might be deflected, absorbed or defeated. Continuity could not be resisted in this way. It resided 'in here' and was symbolised by the classroom itself – that small, unchanging physical space in which, throughout his or her career, a single adult teacher stood daily before dozens of child learners – and by the endless circularity of the many generations of pupils who came, went and were replaced within that teacher's professional lifetime.

The changes which teachers of the 1903-45 generation identify as being of lasting importance are few but significant. The three most striking instances concern the professional preparation of teachers themselves, relationships with parents and the attitudes of teachers towards those they taught. The first of these issues occupied the earlier years of the period, impinging particularly upon teachers' perceptions of their social and professional status. The second effectively spanned the whole period and affected teachers' integration in local communities and the degree of their autonomy at the workplace. The third was concentrated in the later years and chiefly affected everyday classroom practice.

In the nineteenth century, elementary school teachers commonly endured low social status.[10] They were often isolated, marginal and misplaced figures, caught between their middle-class employers and

10 P. Gardner *The Lost Elementary Schools of Victorian England* (London: Croom Helm, 1984); M. Sturt *The Education of the People* (London: Routledge, 1967).

11 Board of Education
(1907) Circular 573;
B.P.P.[British
Parliamentary Papers]
1914, xxv, *Report of the
Board of Education for the
Year 1912-13* pp.3-69;
R.Roberts *The Classic
Slum* (Manchester,UK:
Manchester University
Press, 1971) p. 5.

12 Tropp (1957)
pp. 108-12.

13 B.P.P. 1888 xxxv, *Final
Report of the
Commissioners* (Cross
Commission); B.P.P.
1898 xxvi, Report of the
Dept. Committee on the
Pupil-Teacher System
vol.1; H.C. Dent *The
Training of Teachers in
England and Wales 1800-
1975* (London: Hodder
and Stoughton, 1977),
47; L.E.G. Jones
*The Training of Teachers
in England and Wales*
(Oxford:OUP, 1924)
p. 27.

14 B.P.P. 1914, xxv,
*Report of the Board of
Education for the Year
1912-13*, pp.148-53; F.
Widdowson, *Going Up
into the Next Class:
Women and Elementary
Teacher Training, 1840-
1919* (London:
Hutchinson, 1980) p. 39.
A departmental enquiry
into teacher training,
reporting in 1925, could
still observe that, 'up to
this point it would
seem to have been the
case that the teachers in
Public Elementary
Schools have been
recruited almost
entirely from the less
well-to-do classes.' The
authors of the report
were, 'in no doubt that
Public Elementary

their working-class clients. But in the early years of
the new century, this was changing. From its humble
working-class origins, elementary school teaching
was beginning to achieve a measure of social
respectability.[11] The origins of this achievement had
much to do with the establishment of the National
Union of Elementary Teachers in 1870, and with the
rapid expansion in the demand for elementary
teachers following the Education Act, passed in that
same watershed year.[12] But a yet more significant
factor was the drive, gathering force from the late
1880s and underwritten by successive governments,
towards progressive improvement in both the extent
and the quality of programmes of teacher training.[13]
A defining characteristic of this policy, refined and
carried to its highest point by Robert Morant,
Permanent Secretary at the Board of Education from
1903 to 1911, was the incremental driving up of the
age at which pupils could apply to be apprenticed as
pupil-teachers - from an initial thirteen in 1846, to
fourteen in 1877, to fifteen in 1900 and finally to
sixteen in 1903. In so doing, central government
began to dilute, though not effectively to exclude,
that traditional working class constituency which
had dominated teacher supply for half a century.[14]
This trend was further accentuated in 1907 by new
training regulations which aspired to the termination
of early apprenticeship as the characteristic route into
the profession.[15] In its place came scholarships for
full-time secondary schooling to the age of seventeen
or eighteen, and a corresponding relegation of
practical teaching experience merely to an optional
single year as a 'student-teacher' based in an
elementary school.[16] The majority of trainees were
also expected to go on to complete a two-year course
at a training college, institutions which, from 1902,
could be provided by the new Local Education
Authorities as well as the traditional voluntary
agencies. Together, these reforms represented a
historic shift in the pattern of preliminary education
for intending teachers. The result was that

elementary teaching as a career could now be seen as presenting a dual advantage. In the first place, it promised secure employment of an increasingly respectable character. In the second, in place of the old, narrowly vocational character of elementary teacher training, it offered a high quality subsidised academic education of a kind which, a few years before, had been beyond the means of all but the very wealthy.

Those entering the profession in the early decades of the twentieth century were ambivalent about these reforms, by which Morant hoped to transform elementary teachers into a corps equipped not merely to inculcate knowledge but to, 'foster a strong respect for duty and that consideration and respect for others which must be the foundation of unselfishness and the true basis of all good manners'.[17] Though the enhanced status and the extended academic education which Morant's ambitions called for were welcomed, the downgrading of traditional classroom skills and the loss of opportunities for an early apprenticeship in school-based craft knowledge were mourned.[18] By the late 1920s, even the optional student-teacher year was disappearing;

> They did away with that and went straight to college... Oh, the whole system was changed, but I still think it (the student-teacher year) was a good preparation, because there were some girls at college who hadn't done it and had never stood in front of a class... It helped a lot, and the people who hadn't done the year student-teaching wished they'd been able to do it.[19]

But for many teachers, regret for the loss of the old craft traditions of the nineteenth century was compensated by the sense of enhanced prestige which the new training regime brought. If, for their pupils, the elementary and secondary systems of

School teaching has little attraction at the present time for young people whose parents are well-to-do.' B.P.P. 1924-5 xii, *Report of the Dept. Committee on the Training of Teachers for Public Elementary Schools* pp. 33-34.

15 Jones (1924) p. 37.

16 Board of Education (1922) *Regulations for the Training of Teachers,* p.13; Board of Education (1908) Circular 597, *Student-Teachers,* pp.2-4; Board of Education *How to Become a Teacher in a Public Elementary School* (1907).

17 Morant quoted in B. M. Allen *Sir Robert Morant: A Great Public Servant* (London: Macmillan, 1934) pp. 214-15.

18 P. Gardner 'Teacher training and changing professional identity in early twentieth century England' *Journal of Education for Teaching* 21 (1995) pp. 191-217; P. Gardner 'Intending teachers and school-based teacher training, 1903-1939' *Oxford Review of Education* 21,4 (1995) pp. 425-45.

19 Edith Smart (elementary teacher), b.1904, Burnley; f. blacksmith; m. at home [Interview Transcript extract by author].

schooling were to remain separate until after 1944, at least the teachers from the elementary sector could feel that, in their own education, they had bridged this divide a generation earlier. Within the communities in which they worked, teachers could now feel that their local standing had been reformed.

20 Rose Duffy (infant teacher), b.1917, Birmingham; f. tool manufacturer; m. at home.

When I was teaching, you felt that you were somebody in society, and somebody important and responsible. And if there was anything to be done, teachers were turned to.[20]

21 Elizabeth Trafford (elementary teacher), b.1901, Co. Durham; f. colliery manager; m. at home.

There was more respect then than now. Because you were a teacher, a parent looked up to you.[21]

22 Martha Robertson (elementary teacher), b.1897, Stockport; f. foundry manager; m. at home.

If you were a teacher, people always seemed to think you were on a higher plane because you knew more and they knew less.[22]

For those young teachers – probably still the majority – recruited to teaching from the working class, the erection of new distinctions between themselves and their local communities was particularly striking and seldom unwelcome.

23 Edith Smart.

People always looked on teachers as being superior. They didn't realise that a lot of them were of their own class – that had qualified, you see. And they all thought teachers were from the better-off class. There was a barrier between them... They always expected teachers to be better dressed and everything, you know. And speak proper – that was a big barrier.[23]

The language of barriers is appropriate but in one sense misleading. It suggests that teachers perceived the widening gap between themselves and the users of their schools as an impediment, as a difficulty to be overcome. This was not so. The majority of teachers

Reconstructing the Classroom Teacher

recognised the practical utility of this distance in the degree of professional autonomy it afforded. Since the emergence of mass schooling in the later nineteenth century, there have been three identifiable phases in the relationship between teacher and parent. The first, dominating the school board years from 1870 to 1902, was framed by endemic conflict. Teacher's principal objective during this phase was to master the perceived fecklessness of working-class parents in conspiring with their offspring to avoid regular attendance at school. By the end of the century, teachers – in concert with school boards, school attendance committees and school attendance officers – had won this battle, with the principle of regular, sustained and universal elementary schooling passing from policy into popular culture. The third period, occupying the second half of the twentieth century, has seen the progressive establishment of idealised mutual relationships between parent and teacher based either upon the logic of the marketplace or upon the common concerns of partnership. Both have celebrated the principle and the practice of close, consensual contact between a child's teacher and his or her parents as a prerequisite for successful education. In the years intervening between these two periods – the years corresponding with the careers of the generation of teachers with which we are concerned – parents scarcely figured at all.

Having conceded the right of the state to enforce the attendance of their children at school, they had achieved no reciprocal right to a say in the content or the character of their schooling. For teachers, this opened the way to a degree of professional classroom autonomy unknown in either the preceding or succeeding periods and which seemed naturally to complement the status gains which the Morant reforms had brought. Both changes worked towards the exclusion of the parent.

In the early days, the parents used to leave the education to us. I think they sort of trusted us and felt that we knew what we were doing. Parents didn't interfere so much as they do now. Of course they're in and out of school all the time now. You really can't compare it.[24]

24 Amy Grant (infant teacher), b.1904, Newcastle-on- Tyne; f. cabinet maker; m. at home.

They weren't interested. They only came up if they had a grouch. But I didn't see much of the parents.[25]

25 Edith Smart.

No, they never came to school. They kept us at a distance, sort of thing. I don't mean it in a nasty way but, you know, they never bothered.[26]

26 Mary Boston (elementary teacher), b.1899, Glamorgan; f. colliery engine driver; m. at home.

I felt that I was running the school and I didn't want parents to run the school. That's how I felt about it. I knew more about it, I felt, than they did.[27]

27 Ray Stenfield (elementary teacher), b.1902, Southampton; f. school teacher; m. at home.

After the Second World War, the secret garden cultivated by teachers in the early decades of the century would be exposed, gradually, to a widening public gaze. Those who experienced teaching both before and after the War recognised the loss and struggled to understand the reasons why it had come about.

28 John Grills (elementary teacher), b.1914, Gravesend; f. clerk; m. at home.

We lost the mystique, the expertise. We allowed everybody to say they could do it.[28]

The language here is significant. In constructing a workable professional identity, elementary teachers in the first half of the twentieth century were able to draw upon both the rational and the magical to claim an exclusive right to shape the education of the children in their charge. Ultimately, the claim would prove to be a fragile one, but in the prewar years, it was substantially successful. Distanced from, and effectively untroubled by, the parents of the children whom they taught, elementary teachers maintained their classroom strongholds where the only constraints on practice might come from an overbearing headteacher or from the intrusion of the occasional inspector. The price of this relative autonomy, however, was often relative isolation within the local community. Teachers' claims to higher status and exclusive classroom expertise were sufficient to divide them from the parental constituency but inadequate to bring them recognition by, or social intercourse with, local professional groupings and particularly with their apparently natural allies, the secondary school teachers.

The elementary teacher certainly held sway in the territory bounded by the school railings. It was, however, a small space.

> They had their own little kingdoms and they were the kings... The school was their world and a lot of them were very narrow – a lot of them. I found that so particularly with the men, because I used to feel they were not equipped – they hadn't enough knowledge of the world.[29]

29 Edith Smart.

> I think teachers were so – enclosed, some-how... I mean, teaching to me wasn't the be-all and end-all of life, which it was for a lot of people because of course they were so – I don't know – they wouldn't go out with men because they'd perhaps have to choose between a love affair and a school affair and they'd choose a school affair. A lot of teachers were ignorant about what was going on in life.[30]

30 Marion Mortimer (elementary teacher), b.1905, Derby; f. master plumber; m. dressmaker.

Teachers often lived in the local community but they were seldom part of it. Just as they were remote from local parents, the life lived within that community by the pupils whom they taught was often largely unknown to them.

> One of my little boys I really liked was ill – very ill with pneumonia. So I went to his house and I went upstairs into the bedroom to see him, and I heard this rasping. It was just whitewashed, no carpets on the floor, two old crones sitting there, watching this poor lad die. It was a revelation to me. I'd never met poverty like that. It was terrible, really. He died of course – malnutrition and one thing and another.[31]

31 Edith Smart.

It was rare for teachers to be able to feel close to those they taught. This was in part a result of social and cultural distinction, but also a consequence of pedagogical precepts formed in response to teaching over-large classes in small spaces crammed with heavy or fixed classroom furniture. Under such conditions, teachers could be impatient of the criticisms of occasional visitors enjoining them to change their ways.

> I can remember asking an HMI [a national school inspector] how he expected me to have individual handwork for 60 boys. He said, 'They're all doing alike, too much alike. It should be more individual.' I said, 'Well, will you tell me how I can do it?'And he couldn't.[32]

32. Martha Robertson.

Paradoxically, the teachers' voice is relatively silent about daily life in classrooms in the first half of the century. It is in such activity that teachers spent most of their professional lives, but their collective recollection typifies the school day as routine, ordered and predominantly unchanging, despite the reorganisation of elementary schooling into primary and secondary levels.[33] There is little to say about it.

33 S. Meacham *A Life Apart: The English Working Class 1890-1914* (London: Thames and Hudson, 1977) pp.169-75.

Children are recalled as they were taught, en masse and with little sentimentality. Teachers seldom had the time, opportunity or inclination to try to engage their pupils as individual personalities.[34] The occasions when teachers did catch glimpses of their charges in this wider spirit were sufficiently rare to be still remembered very closely.

> I sent each of the (pupils) just a little Christmas card. Well, the elder brother of one of them came to me; he said, 'Miss, you sent our Tone a Christmas card?' I said, 'Yes, why?' He said, 'That's the only Christmas card we've ever had in the house.' You know, it shakes you.[35]

> There was a boy at the school, his name was MB, and he was a pathetic boy. I mean, his father was in prison, his mother had left them and he lived with his grandmother. And he was terribly, terribly dim. And he was always losing his pen and he was always coming to me to say, 'Miss, I can't find me pen.'... And one day he said to me, 'I wish you were my mother.' I'll never forget that. I could have cried... It was something special really.[36]

It would be unjust to suggest that the general attitude of teachers towards children showed no signs of change in the forty years or so that we are examining. Change was certainly far slower in this area than it would be in the next forty, but it was discernible, most obviously in relation to teachers' perceptions and practices of corporal punishment. Few were prepared to relinquish altogether the symbolic authority of the cane, but many – perhaps most, certainly among women teachers – were increasingly uncomfortable in its use.[37] Nevertheless, the characteristic pattern and practice of teacher-pupil relationships at the outbreak of the Second World

34 P. Gardner 'The giant at the front: young teachers and corporal punishment in inter-war elementary schools' *History of Education* 25 (1996) pp. 141-63, 156.

35 Venee Blatch (elementary teacher), b.1909, Liverpool; f. clerk; m. governess.

36 Marion Mortimer.

37 Gardner (1996).

War would have been recognisable to the teacher approaching retirement as being broadly similar to those which had prevailed at the start of his or her teaching career. Dramatic changes, however, were at hand. In the coming few years, the bases upon which teachers had for a generation constructed their perceptions of appropriate pedagogical relationships would be transformed. If, as has recently been asserted, 'Effective change in a field as dependent on human interaction as education requires millions of people to change their behaviour'[38], no stimulus on such a scale had impacted upon the dominant pattern of teacher-pupil class room relations in the pre-war period.

The teachers' voice suggests, however, that with the outbreak of war, such a generalised stimulus may have begun to have a rapid and far-reaching effect on the ways in which school teachers perceived the nature of their responsibilities to their pupils. The source of this movement was the process of mass evacuation enacted in the face of the anticipated enemy bombing of major towns and cities. There are many suggestions in teacher recollection that as a result of evacuation, teachers came to see the lives and personalities of those they taught in far more intimate ways.[39]

> It wasn't 'til the War. There wasn't a lot of change before then, because a number of people didn't know how the other half lived...They had these terrible slums...They wouldn't go back to that. They'd seen other places where things were different...From then on, changes started.[40]

Here then are those issues to which the teachers' voice in the years between 1903 and 1945 directs us in seeking the elements of perceived change within whose parameters the profession was reconstructing itself; improved social and professional status at the

38 Department for Education and Employment *Excellence in Schools* (London:The Stationery Office, 1997) p. 12.

39 The significance of such suggestions is currently being investigated as part of a major three year research programme, 'The impact of wartime evacuation upon teacher attitude and practice' funded by the Economic and Social Research Council and co-directed by P. Cunningham and P. Gardner.

40 Venee Blatch.

start of the period; the relegation and confinement of the parental interest in popular education throughout; and the reformulation of the relationship between teacher and pupil as the period drew to its close.

These were not, however, the only elements from which teacher identity was reconstructed in these years. Alongside the issues which teachers understood principally through the language of change were others, no less significant in the overall formation of identity, which teachers comprehended more readily in terms of fundamental continuities. The first and perhaps the most powerful of these, as we have seen, turned on the persistent and familiar regularities and routines of everyday life in schools and classrooms. Beyond this came a succession of significant others against whom elementary teachers could locate their distinctive identity. Two of these were relatively straightforward – the secondary teachers and the government. And two were enormously complex – the unions and the men (or the women).

Throughout the first half of the twentieth century, the gulf between elementary and secondary teachers, rooted in long-standing social, educational and professional separation remained unbridged.

> I think a large number of primary school teachers were always rather jealous of our status... In local jargon, the schools were either elementary schools or grammar. And an elementary school teacher was, you know, was a different status altogether – 'She's only an elementary school teacher.'[41]

41 Gwyneth Tomlinson (secondary teacher), b.1903, Swansea; f. businessman; m. at home.

> There was very little connection between teachers of the elementary schools and the secondary schools. There was almost anathema between them... A secondary

Reconstructing the Classroom Teacher

42 Herbert Gaymer
(secondary teacher),
b.1888; f. soldier;
m. seamstress.

school man, he'd probably have a degree, and the elementary, well he wouldn't, you see...You were left on your own in secondary school teaching. You were left quite entirely alone, you see, to do it. It was quite a different atmosphere. You felt that you were master of your job.[42]

However successfully elementary teachers might feel that they had augmented their social and professional status and their autonomy at the workplace, such achievements were always overshadowed by the figure of the secondary teacher. The claim of the latter – more powerful for being so understated – to embody teaching in a form that was not only higher but somehow more intellectually authentic, was one that the elementary teachers could not match. Their characteristic strategy was to ignore their secondary counterparts. For different reasons, this was also their most common attitude towards the ultimate architect of the structures within which they worked – central government. Throughout the first half of the twentieth century, elementary teachers often professed no interest and little knowledge of governmental educational policy. There was undoubtedly an element of professional bravado in this, a demonstration of autonomy through studied ignorance. But there was also the maintenance of a real tradition of localism in elementary teaching in which the Director of the Local Education Authority was regarded as the truly determining political authority. Such figures, if they were perceived as competent and fair, could be held in great esteem by classroom teachers.

43 Olive Walsh
(elementary teacher),
b.1907, Wigan; f.
postman; m. at home.

I didn't know who was the Minister of Education at the time. I knew who the Lancashire people were.[43]

No (not the government). It was County Durham and a very, very good Education

Officer, AJ Dawson... They looked after their teachers in AJ Dawson's time.[44]

44 Elizabeth Trafford.

We weren't interested, not really. We did various courses, but I can't remember what they were about... We weren't interested in what was happening in London.[45]

45 Amy Grant.

I remember the name (Hadow Report) but I don't remember anything about it.[46]

46 Mary Boston.

I don't think I ever thought about it. No, no, no. All I thought about was getting on with my job, you know, and hoping that if an inspector came he'd be satisfied with it. Once, nearly all the teachers in Worcestershire went to Hadley Hall and Mr Trevelyan – I think he was somebody big from the Board of Education – came to talk to us. Now don't ask what he came to talk about, because I can't remember.[47]

47 Mary Donaldson (elementary teacher), b. 1904, Glos.; f. butcher; m. at home.

I think that (government education policy) would have interested those teachers who were active in their union, who went to union meetings and so on, but I don't recall them having much impact in the ordinary school. But there again, there wasn't a lot of lingering around to talk to other teachers in the school in those days. At the end of the day you went home.[48]

48 Edith Norton (elementary teacher), b.1906, Kent; f. draper's manager; m. draper.

Union membership was axiomatic among elementary teachers and identification with a union – usually, of course, the NUT [National Union of Teachers] – was often very strong. An influential minority saw the union as a lever for securing sustained educational advance and improvements in conditions of service, particularly in relation to the removal of the marriage bar and the importance of salaries. Most teachers shared the grievances of activists, and often very strongly, yet what was evidently a highly persistent undercurrent of collective dissatisfaction was extremely difficult to mobilise in any sustained way. Any prospect of industrial action was eschewed by the majority, for whom the union was seen either in terms of practical security and support, or, in a much deeper sense as an emblem of elementary teachers' traditions, history, and shared interests.

> We more or less had to be in the NUT. I joined for peace and quietness, I suppose, because, well, everybody did... I didn't want to be mixed up with teachers and so I never went to union meetings and I never, sort of, got involved with arguments. They must have gone on, I suppose, but I fought shy of that sort of thing.[49]

49 Marion Mortimer.

> The salary issue was the worst. The men got more than the women... The conflicts were right through the NUT. The NUWT [National Union of Women Teachers] were all strongly for equal salaries. But the NUT – there were such a lot of men in the union. It was a very difficult business. I got fed up with unions altogether. In the end I stopped going.[50]

50 Amy Grant.

> I do remember the women broke away didn't they? Then, of course, somebody tried to persuade me, you know, 'Oh, this women's thing.' But I decided not to join – better to stay in the NUT.[51]

51 Mary Boston.

> I belonged to the NUT, which I was proud to belong to... And there was a women's union, the NUWT as well. They fought hard. I represented all the teachers of South Derbyshire on the Education Committee... There were fierce arguments, you know... between our point of view, those of us who were for equal pay, and the men. A lot of the

men were dead against it. They said they had the responsibility of the home and all the rest of it... I thought we should all be in one union. I didn't believe in the split.[52]

The struggle of women teachers for professional equity in the inter-war years achieved much.[53] But it seems likely that, in the construction of professional identity, the pattern of gender relations in this period spoke to most teachers more of continuity than progress. This is not just a matter of the entrenched opposition and often hostility of many male teachers to the women's case. More fundamentally it was a problem rooted in the difficulty of building a common professionalism from a workforce historically divided by sex.[54] Just as it had been in the old inner-city 'three-decker' board schools of Victorian Britain, it was possible for men and women in the inter-war elementary schools, increasing numbers of mixed schools notwithstanding, to work virtually side by side yet with little or no contact or communication.

> Well, there were differences, but I'm not certain that we were so aware of them in the sense that if you were in a normal all-woman set-up, you didn't realise always what the differences were until later on, and then I began to take an interest in the National Union of Teachers, and began to compare things, you know. You realised then that the pay was so different.[55]

> We always felt the men got more than we did. Their salaries were always higher than the women teachers. We used to grumble about that on the quiet....That was the accepted thing, you see, until people got militant and women started to fight for equality. You took it for granted that men would get more. It didn't please you,

52 Ivy Denning (elementary teacher), b.1902, Derbys.; f. miner; m. at home.

53 A. Oram *Women Teachers and Feminist Politics 1900-1939* (Manchester, UK: Manchester University Press, 1997).

54 Oram is right to stress the relative lack of segregation in the formal institutional structures of the teaching profession. In daily practice, however, divisions between men and women were keenly felt. Oram (1997) pp. 4-7.

55 Edith Norton.

56 Edith Smart.

especially when I used to think that a lot of the men teachers were darned idle.[56]

(The men) were resentful towards the women. Well, most schools, you see, were separate boys and separate girls, and the staff in the girls' school were women and the staff in the boys' schools were men. Didn't mix.[57]

57 Norman Wilson (elementary teacher), b.1908, Liverpool; f. shipping clerk; m. at home.

In the first half of the twentieth century, the professional identity of British elementary school teachers was reconstructed from a complex combination of elements which drew both upon currents of change and continuity. To illuminate this process, much further work remains to be done. But to the extent that such work fails to listen to the voice of the classroom teachers themselves, its outcomes will be incomplete and it will never ring fully true.

An Open-ended Education

Littlefield

An Open-ended Education: problems in reconstructing the history of an African-American classroom

Valinda Littlefield

> On one side of this road were long low warehouses where huge barrels of tobacco shavings and tobacco dust were stored. All day long our nostrils sucked in the brown silt like fine snuff in the air. West End looked more like a warehouse than a school. It was a dilapidated, rickety, two-story wooden building which creaked and swayed in the wind as if it might collapse... Outside it was scarred with peeling paint from many winters of rain and snow. At recess we [were] herded in to a yard of cracked clay, barren of tree or bush, and played what games we could improvise like hopscotch or springboard, which we contrived by pulling rotted palings off the wooden fence and placing them on brickbats.[1]

> ...the floors were bare and splintery, the plumbing was leaky, the drinking fountains broken and the toilets in the basement smelly and constantly out of order. We'd have to wade through pools of foul water to get to them...[2]

Historically, African-Americans and whites held different views of education. African-Americans viewed education as a means of progress—a way out of manual labor and poor, unhealthy living conditions—but also as an antidote to cure all the ills caused by racism. Throughout much of the twentieth century, 'classrooms' did not mean rows of uniform seating, a blackboard, desks, a globe and a collection of books and papers for the majority of African-American teachers in the southern United States. The description given by Pauli Murray – Episcopal priest,

1 P. Murray, *Proud Shoes: The Story of an American Family* (New York: Harper & Row, 1956), p. 269.

2 *Ibid.*

educator, civil rights activist, and lawyer – of her elementary school in the early 1900s provides a vivid picture of the condition of schools for African-Americans.

Most whites believed that African-Americans needed little, if any, education to prepare them for their prescribed role as manual laborers. As the debates and movements for public education in the South intensified during the late nineteenth and twentieth centuries, so did the determination of some whites to keep African-Americans out of the state-funded educational system. The white viewpoint distinctively bore out in funding and educational access patterns. In 1916, Georgia had 122 four-year white public high schools and none for its African-American population, which constituted 46 per cent of its secondary school population. Similarly, North and South Carolina had no four-year African-American public high schools. Virginia supported six, mainly in the northern section of the state.[3] As late as 1957, Sunflower, Mississippi, provided no public high school for its African-American population. Historian James D. Anderson notes that after 1900 the proportion of funding to black schools dropped significantly. From 1900 to 1920 in every southern state, tax appropriations for building schoolhouses increased; however, virtually no funding went to the building of black schools.[4] A 1930 survey revealed, at a time when the average expenditure for the nation was $99.00 per child, 11 southern states spent an average of $12.57 to educate an African-American child as opposed to $44.31 to educate a white child. In 1937, 64 per cent of schools for southern African-Americans were one-teacher, and 19 per cent were two-teacher schools.[5] As late as 1941, it was reported by the State Superintendent of Negro Education in North Carolina that the schools for African-Americans were 'small, poorly built, dilapidated, unfurnished, insanitary.' He considered many to be in such a 'bad state of repair that they are

3 J. D. Anderson, *Education of Blacks in the South, 1860-1935* (Chapel Hill: University of North Carolina Press, 1988) pp. 196, 199.

4 Anderson (1988) p.156.

5 'Survey, 1930,' Box 115, Folder 1045, General Education Board Records. Rockefeller Foundation Archives, Tarrytown, New York.

both a menace to health and dangerous to life and limb.'[6] At this time, North Carolina was considered a progressive southern state as far as educational facilities and access for its African-American citizens went.

6 Letter of N.C. Newbold, North Carolina Superintendent for Negro Rural Schools, to Dr. Fred McCuistion March 12, 1941 (GEB, Rockefeller Files, Box 115, 1041).

Left with few alternatives, African-American communities created their own institutions depending primarily on women to provide the basic instruction. Southern African-American families encouraged their daughters to attend school and to become teachers. This was preferable to working as maids in southern homes where African-American women were more subject to sexual harrassment. Education was therefore a way of protecting females. In return for 'saving' or 'advancing' the race, these women not only avoided a life of drudgery in domestic servitude but also received praise, respect, status, and salvation.

Improving the status of African-Americans through education required that these women labor in classrooms with fluid walls. They often worked long hours; established and maintained personal contact with the African-American community, the white community and health and agriculture officials; and actively participated in churches of different denominations. Thus, the reconstruction of the classroom of African-American teachers forces historians to realize that the classroom cannot be studied as an island. Through the windows of the classroom, one must view the values of a society in a particular time and locality and political, religious, cultural, gender and racial issues must be addressed to portray an accurate analysis. Reconstruction also requires usage of a multitude of sources and an examination of the public, private, and secret lives of teachers.

Analyzing the teaching career of Pauli Murray's aunt, and later adopted mother, Mary Pauline Fitzgerald

7 Murray, (1956) p. 239. St. Augustine's in 1880 was a teacher training school in Raleigh, North Carolina but offered 'little more than high school training,' p. 64. According to GEB Records at the Rockefeller, 'St. Augustine's School, original chartered as St. Augustine's Normal School and Collegiate Institute, has been and is the institution of the Episcopal Church especially designed to train Negro leaders and teachers. . . . (GEB Records, 'Resolutions adopted by the Executive Committee of the Board of Trustees of St. Augustine School, March 26, 1926' Rockefeller Foundation, Box 108, Folder #981). St. Agnes Hospital, also a part of the school, was established on the campus in 1896 to train African-American nurses. See H.V. Brown, *A History of the Education of Negroes in North Carolina* (Raleigh: Irving Swain Press, 1961).

8 Murray (1956) pp. 231-33 and 239. At the age of six or seven, Mary Pauline lived with white family members and was tutored by a Miss Maria Spear described as a 'warm, loving Yankee,' who lived with the Smith family. Harriet, a mulatto, owned by a slave-holding Smith family in Chapel Hill, North Carolina, was the

Dame (1870-1955), who taught for sixty-one years, allows for the recovery of the social history of the classroom for African-Americans. A number of sources (correspondence, poems, an autobiography, oral interviews, as well as secondary sources) allow me to recreate classrooms and address the aforementioned issues. For example, Mary Pauline's father was almost blind by 1880 and Pauline's mother attempted to send her to St. Augustine's School, a high school for African-Americans, in Raleigh, North Carolina.[7] She was asked to spell, to solve arithmetic problems, to answer questions in history and literature, to give the parts of speech and to recite poetry.

> They said that I knew the work all right but I was too young to stay. They sent me home again and told me I could come back when I was ten. My tenth birthday came that September, so Mother put me on the train again and I entered St. Aug's.[8]

Specific questions need to be addressed to illuminate certain issues and to recreate the classroom. Why was Mary Pauline required to leave her community for additional education? Why was a ten-year-old allowed to attend this institution? What kind of education did this institution provide? What was its purpose, and who supported it financially? Mary Pauline's short autobiography provides insight into her schooling and her reason for attending St. Augustine's. By the time she was ten, she had completed all the public elementary grades in her community available to her race. In order to get additional education, she had to leave her community. Many families, circumventing the lack of public education access, sent their children to live on campuses, with relatives, friends, and sometimes friends of friends in order to attend schools such as St. Augustine's. Historians such as James Anderson and Linda Perkins state that higher education institutions for the majority of African-Americans in the South after the Civil War and throughout the two decades of the twentieth century were privately owned and oftentimes by religious institutions.[9] Reports and school histories allow me to understand that the main purpose of St. Augustine's and similar schools was to educate teachers, ministers and later nurses. And, Mary Pauline's description of her first visit to St. Augustine's reveals that this classroom provided a liberal education—spelling, arithmetic, history, literature—as opposed to an industrial one.

Mary Pauline's first teaching position in 1886 in Durham County, North Carolina was in 'the first 3 grades in an ungraded district school.'[10] She described the school as a one-room building with two teachers and more than seventy pupils, six to twenty years old. Her short autobiography also offers an image of her first classroom:

> One room log cabin with only benches made from a split log with holes bored in the end and small trees sawed so as to make legs, — no backs and no desks. The children had to sit on them and swing their legs over the side, leaving their books and lunch pails on the floor.[11]

Oral interviews, her autobiography, poetry and secondary sources offer a portrait of what Mary Pauline taught as well as her interpretations of gender roles, race uplift ideology, and religious beliefs. Pauli describes the classroom of elementary children during the month of February as engrossed with activities such as cutting out log cabins, hatchets and bunches of cherries in celebration of the birthdays of George Washington and Abraham Lincoln: 'Aunt Pauline's classroom walls were full of American flags, pictures of American Presidents, and a print of the famous Spirit of '76'.[12] What lessons were provided to Mary Pauline's students in

servant of Miss Mary Smith. Harriet was raped by Mary's brother Sid and bore him a daughter, Cornelia, who was Mary Pauline's mother. Harriet also bore three daughters for Frank (Sid and Mary's brother). All four girls were raised in the Smith house with considerable pain because of the feud between Frank and Sid over Harriet and the stigma of miscegenation. Mary Pauline was also educationally advanced at an early age because her father taught school and often took her with him to school when she was between the ages of three and five. She could read and write at the age of four. She was also sent to a private school in Durham when she was eight or nine, Murray (1956) p.237. Also, see *An Autobiography of My Life* by P. F. Dame, Summer, 1944. Pauli Murray Papers. Boston: Radcliffe College, Schlesinger Library.

9 See Chapter 7 in Anderson (1988).

10 Dame (1944) p.9.

11 *Ibid*, p.13.

12 *Ibid*, pp.271-72.

February? Certainly, she provided historical and popular images or context for Washington and Lincoln. Students possibly assembled a collage of their cut images to portray a portrait of the experiences of the two former presidents. Mary Pauline viewed these two men as important contributors to American history and passed on such a view to her students by the activities that she assigned.

An undated poem, *The School Mistress*, written by Mary Pauline provides another avenue for examining her classroom experience. Two lines are the most revealing:

13 Murray Papers, Schlesinger Library, Cambridge, Massachusetts.

> I Teach Morality and truth
> To the maiden and the youth[13]

These snippets of information require interpretations of race, class and gender issues during the late nineteenth and early twentieth centuries. Such questions have to be addressed as: What was the significance of morality to the African-American community, to the white community? How did such views affect the students' education? What, if any, tensions did this create for the African-American female teacher?

In describing the teaching duties of her mother/aunt, Pauli Murray permits a reader to examine expectations of the teacher from the school system and the African-American community:

> Up at five every morning and usually at school before seven-thirty. Got home late in the afternoon, prepared supper, and then returned to night school to conduct literacy classes for the hardworking parents and grandparents of her day school pupils. If a child was absent, she visited the child's home after school to discover the reason. She was

expected to attend all community gatherings in addition to teachers' meetings and parents' meetings. On Sundays she usually went to church twice: morning service at her own St. Titus Episcopal Church and evening service at the neighborhood Second Baptist Church, which many of her students and parents attended.[14]

This information also provides for interpretation of values and attitudes of the African-American community. Teachers were expected to be active community members, even attending churches of their students of a different denomination. Such interactions allowed for the development of personal relationships between student and teacher. Teachers' interaction and availability provided students with powerful and positive role models. Such expectations could also deprive teachers of any semblance of a personal life, as collective needs were valued more than individual needs. Mary Pauline's teaching of class during the day and at night reveals the importance of education for young and old. Her returning home in the evenings to prepare supper sheds light on gender and familial responsibilities. Both her parents were aged; she was the primary caretaker of them as well as of Pauli from age three.

For the Jim Crow South, few, if any, educational efforts provide a better framework for reconstructing the silenced voices of female teachers and their classrooms than that of industrial education. Philanthropists such as Anna T. Jeanes, a white Quaker woman, contributed to the education of African-Americans in southern rural areas through the Jeanes Fund which hired Jeanes Teachers.[15] Julius Rosenwald, president of Sears, Roebuck and Company, established the Rosenwald Fund which provided seed funding for the building of rural school houses in the South from 1913 to 1922.[16] Both programs stressed industrial education.

14 P. Murray. *The Autobiography of a Black Activist, Feminist, Lawyer, Priest, and Poet* (Knoxville: The University of Tennessee Press, 1989) p. 15.

15 The Jeanes Fund, established in 1907 by Anna T. Jeanes, encouraged industrial education and community involvement. It provided funding to hire mainly African-American females to serve as Jeanes Supervisors for rural schools. In addition to teaching and supervising, this group was charged with improving the 'living conditions among the colored people.' Jeanes Teachers, mainly active throughout the South from 1908 to 1968, also worked in the U.S. Southwest, Africa, Asia and Latin America. See L. E. Jones, *The Jeanes Teacher in the United States, 1908-1933* (Chapel Hill: University of North Carolina Press, 1937).

16 Rosenwald contracts stipulated that African-American community members match or exceed the amount requested from the Fund; required the approval and cooperation of the state and county school officials; required that all land and equipment for such schools be deeded to the local school system. See E. R. Embree and J. Waxman, *Investment in People: The Story of the*

Julius Rosenwald Fund (New York: Harper, 1949); C. V. Woodward, *Origins of the New South, 1877-1913* (Baton Rouge: Louisiana State University Press, 1951), 396-406; and G. B. Tindall, *The Emergence of the New South, 1913-1945* (Baton Rouge: Louisiana State University Press, 1967), pp. 268-72.

17 Minutes of the Gates County School Board, 1909-26, June 1, 1914 (Gates County Schools Administration Office, Gates County, North Carolina).

18 The Jeanes Foundation was established with a donation of $1,000,000 to 'encourage the rudimentary education of Colored people residing in rural districts of the following southern states: Delaware, Maryland, Virginia, W. Virginia, North Carolina, South Carolina, Georgia, Florida, Alabama, Mississippi, Louisiana, Texas, Arkansas, Missouri, Kentucky, and Tennessee. 'Minutes of the Meeting of the Jeanes Funds, 1907.' (Hampton Archives, Hampton Institute: Hampton, Va.)

19 North Carolina Archives, Department of Public Instruction, Division of Negro Education. N.C. Newbold correspondence, 1913-1914. See also the report of N.C.

The experiences of Annie Holland allow me to examine another aspect of rural black school teachers and further demonstrates the fluidity of their classrooms. In 1911 Holland became the Jeanes Fund supervisor in Gates County, North Carolina for an annual salary of $385.00.[17] The Jeanes Teacher Program was modeled after the work of Virginia Randolph, an African-American teacher in Honrico County, Virginia. Randolph became the first Jeanes teacher to be paid from the fund.[18] Sometimes referred to as Jeanes Supervisors and sometimes simply as Jeanes Teachers, their official title was Jeanes Supervising Industrial Teacher. They encouraged industrial education and community involvement. Holland's duties were to visit schools; to help and encourage teachers to teach sanitation, sewing, cooking, basket making, chair caning, and mat making; to meet men and women and form Improvement Leagues or Betterment Associations, whose purpose was to improve the 'living conditions among the colored people'; to paint or whitewash school houses, homes, and outhouses; to raise money to build better school houses and to lengthen the school terms; to encourage and organize home and school gardens, tomato clubs, and corn clubs; and to 'promote higher standards of living, integrity of character, honesty, and thrift among all people.' In addition to those duties, she was directed by N.C. Newbold, North Carolina State Supervisor of Negro Education, to improve the quality of instruction in county group meetings, reading circles, study groups, extension courses, libraries, and summer school; and to organize programs dealing with health and industrial arts.[19] Jeanes supervisors were obliged to work around-the-clock and much of their labor fell in the category of noncompensatory for salary allocation. They were responsible for creating public school sentiment by encouraging African-Americans to give money and time to improve their educational system; organizing moonlight schools in which many also taught; and, organizing county commencement and exhibit events.

An Open-ended Education

A major contribution to the southern educational system of Jeanes supervisors was fundraising. Supervisors in a 1914 Progress Report to Newbold stated, 'In January $65 was raised and used to add a porch and paint one school.' 'Another $85 for improvements, a table and chair were bought in each of the other schools for the teacher,' Mrs. L.B. Yancy of Vance County wrote.[20] A school under Holland's direction 'had an entertainment' to raise money for school materials. The money was used to purchase a bamboo curtain for use in the place of a door, to whitewash a room, and to put in a sanitary drinking keg.[21] In 1927, Jeanes Teachers raised $41,121.20 and by February 1929 they had raised $14,171.46 for improving rural education. These reports also reveal the non-wage work of these women. 'We organized a Betterment Association... They are going to work for a better school, churches, and looking after the poor of the neighborhood. After seeing our yard so clean, they [parents and students] decided to clean church yard, cemetery, and scrub church,' stated Bessie L. Fogg of Beaufort County.[22] While another supervisor stated that, 'In at least 25 districts school houses were cleaned and fumigated according to the rules given by the County Health Officer.'[23]

Jeanes Teachers were also responsible for raising funds for and coordinating the development of Rosenwald schools. The Rosenwald program stressed industrial education and community members agreed to promote industrial education. Most schools had an industrial room for the boys and a kitchen for the girls. The first Rosenwald school was built in 1913 in Alabama. By the 1930s, more than 5,300 buildings had been constructed in fifteen southern states; North Carolina erected more Rosenwald schools than any other state and by this time more than one-third of all its schools for African-Americans were Rosenwald schools.

An analysis of records dealing with Rosenwald

Newbold for November, 1913.

20 NCA/DPI/DNE, N.C. Newbold papers, January 1914 'Monthly Progress Report.'

21 NCA/DPI/DNE, N.C. Newbold papers, November 1914 'Monthly Progress Report.'

22 NCA/DPI/DNE, N.C. Newbold Papers, January 1914 'Monthly Progress Report.'

23 NCA/DPI/DNE, N.C. Newbold 'Monthly Progress Reports,' November, 1913. Statement of Mrs. Sadie Battle, Jeanes Supervisor for Monroe County, North Carolina.

24 Rockefeller
Archives, GEB,
ED.27X- 'Techniques in
the Teaching of
Reading, Language,
and Arithmetic in the
Small Rural School'.

schools permit a glimpse at such factors as type and
school size, classroom make-up, and conditions
under which teachers labored. For example, a 1937
course outline notes that 64 per cent of schools for
African-Americans were one-teacher and 19 per cent
were two-teacher. Under the heading of 'Problems of
rural teachers' was listed attendance and building
and equipment.[24] By examining this document and
using statistical data, several classroom makeups are
evident. Resources allow me to look at this from both
a state level and a county level. An example of how a
county level analysis can provide such a
reconstruction follows.

In analyzing data for Durham County, North
Carolina, where Mary Pauline taught, certain
classroom images are vivid. Black elementary school
teachers were more likely than white teachers to
teach in one- and two-teacher schools. This
arrangement could mean that white teachers had
better opportunity to develop relationships with
other teachers in the school, to share on a daily basis
curriculum and instructional ideas, and to receive
and give moral and physical support to colleagues.
However, the one- and two-teacher situation for
blacks need not be viewed only as negative. Such an
arrangement allowed these teachers to develop
characteristics of independence and self-reliance.
These were qualifications most of them would need
to continue in the profession. Teacher/student ratios
reveal that prior to 1926, African-American teachers
had two to three times the number of students that
white teachers did. Between 1926 and 1934, the ratio
revealed a similar number of students for both black
and white teachers. The analysis of attendance/census
and average age per grade by race revealed that black
males attended school less than any other group. Data
on the average age of students by grades showed that
black teachers taught children of a wide range of ages
and cognitive skill capabilities. The mean for blacks
in the first grade was 8.27 compared with the mean

age for whites of 6.88. The mean age for blacks in the second grade was 10.19 compared with the mean age of whites of 8.23. A comparison of types of buildings reveal that most schools for African-Americans were wood frame with several log buildings. There were no brick buildings reported. White school buildings consisted of 55 per cent wood frame and 45 per cent brick structures. No log buildings were reported.

Another example of the fluidity of the classroom can be seen in clubs organized by teachers. By April 1916, Newbold had convinced Holland's immediate supervisor, the superintendent of Gates County schools, to loan her to the state to supervise forty-four county supervisors. In a letter dated April 10, 1916, Newbold requested that Holland 'visit some of the supervisors and give them aid in organizing Home-Makers' Clubs.' Home-Makers' Clubs were student and parent organizations which grew and preserved foods, such as peaches, apples, and tomatoes, and raised mainly poultry and pork. The teachers under Holland's supervision in Gates County maintained one of the highest production rates in North Carolina. An October 1914 report shows that under Holland's direction more than 4,500 jars of vegetables and fruit were canned.[25] Those canned goods were used to provide food for the poor, to raise funds for school improvements, and to help pay tuition for normal school or college training for students.

The Home-Makers' Clubs were far-reaching agencies in terms of social change. During this period, rural southerners often lived in unhealthy conditions. Slop jars and a few outhouses or privies were the norm. Houses were often dilapidated structures. Doctors were scarce, if at all available. Hookworm disease, tuberculosis, and syphilis were prevalent. Unlike in the city, there were few institutions organized to care for the poor and the ill. Such care was primarily the responsibility of the community. African-American teachers often took on such responsibilities through

25 Holland to Sherman, January 3, 1916 stated, 'As to my work in the country the outlook is very hopeful. The people are becoming more interested in all phases of educational work. ...For the past two years I have been making hard to interest the people in improvement of school buildings. As a result we have erected a nice school building that we feel will be a credit to the community and the county. It is to cost $1,000. When completed we think it will cost a little more than that. We have just completed a room that was added to one of our school buildings, that will cost a little over $300. The people gave $114 in cash, labor and material. The county $112, and we have the promise of the balance from the Rosenwald Fund. Other schools are becoming aroused and we are planning to erect new buildings. We have several leagues, known as clubs and betterment associations' (Annie W. Holland File, Hampton Institute, Hampton Va.)

An Open-ended Education

agencies such as the Home-Makers' Clubs which allowed them to stay in direct touch with the home life of the students in the communities. To get the children to attend schools regularly, they often had to make sure that they addressed issues in the home, such as helping parents provide health care, food, clothing, shoes and other basic necessities. While teaching in Franklin, Virginia, Holland spent five dollars given to her by a Boston woman, and 'bought shoes for three children who had gone barefoot until this time, which was in the freezing month of January.' Holland saw to it that these same three received flannel material to make each a dress, 'since none of the three had a change of dress for the entire fall.'[26]

26 N.C. Newbold ed., *Five North Carolina Negro Educators* (Chapel Hill: University of North Carolina Press, 1939), p. 71.

In addition to caring for the poor and ill, the Home-Makers' Clubs provided financial support to the community. The rise in the fund-raising activity of North Carolina Clubs is an example of such support. The 1914 annual report of the Clubs shows that a total of $1,396.26 was raised by selling vegetables, fruit, canned goods, and poultry. The 1916 report indicates that $9,778.92 was raised.[27] All of the funding went into the improvement or construction of school buildings and financial support for the poor. Preserved products also saved community members money by providing a source of food that was less expensive than in stores.

27 Rockefeller Foundation Archives, GEB. 'Home-Makers Clubs Summary,' Box 16, NC 236.2 Folder.

As noted, Jeanes Teachers were responsible for organizing and often teaching in moonlight schools. These teaching responsibilities normally did not increase their salaries. Moonlight schools were established to teach illiterate adults how to read and write and were normally conducted at night for two to four months. A report for 1916 to Newbold from Holland for Gates County reveals that she organized two schools in that county. Six adults, between the ages of forty-five and seventy, were enrolled for three months. A supervisor in Durham reported to

Newbold that seven schools were organized and that 65 adults between the ages of thirty-five and sixty were enrolled for terms of two to four months. The reports also reveal that sewing and food preservation skills were taught in addition to reading and writing.[28] After working during the day, Holland, Mary Pauline and others labored tirelessly at night to educate the parents and grandparents of their day students.

There are at least two questions to consider for researching the classroom of African-Americans. Why is the social history of the classroom important and why are the experiences of African-American women important in reconstructing the silence of the classroom? In addition to the information provided previously, oral interviews also shed light on these two questions. The majority of African-American teachers in the South were expected to teach reading, writing, and arithmetic; however, they were also expected to provide a wholistic education to their students and community. Classroom boundaries extended into the home, which often served as an extension of the school. Members of these classrooms were therefore required to visualize the classroom as open-ended, as teachers considered their duty to range from educating the students to providing racial uplift for the masses. Because of inadequate or non-existent funding, members of these classrooms were also required to support their education both financially and materially. Thus, the experience of Annie Holland illustrates the agency of schoolteachers during the Jim Crow era.

It was also necessary that teachers instill in their students moral values as well as survival skills for members of an oppressed group. Examples of information obtained from a secondary source and two interviews allow elaboration. Pauli Murray described a classroom learning game that reveals the complexity of reconstructing the African-American

28 April 11, 1916 Report of Jeanes Teachers. Correspondence of N.C. Newbold (NCA/DPI/DNE).

29 Murray, (1956)
p. 18.

classroom.[29] Children recited readings and spelling lessons standing in line side by side. If a mistake was made, the next child, on success, took his or her place. The objective was to reach the head of the class. Murray remembered it as a harsh game for slow learners but fun for fast learners. A discussion with historian Deborah Gray White, who grew up in the North, revealed that she remembered a similar spelling game. As a child visiting relatives in the South during the summer, she attended school with her cousins. She noted that when students made a mistake they received a 'lick with a leather strap' causing her to rethink her opinion of being 'smarter than country kids' while awaiting her turn.

At first glance, such a game can be viewed as encouraging competition. Placing the game in historical and spacial context however, allows for another interpretation. The game deals with issues of control, discipline, collective versus individual values, northern versus southern attitudes, child rearing practices and the importance of education.

Recollections of fundraising events for schools include a box bidding event and a shoe dinner event. 'Attractive' girls and teachers decorated boxes. The boys were allowed to bid on the boxes and were awarded a date with the girl who had made the box. Similarities are evident in the 'shoe dinner' contest described by a former rural teacher. Female students stood behind a partition and showed only their shoes. A male student paid for an opportunity to pick a shoe. He was then granted dinner with the person wearing the shoe. Girls often changed shoes amongst one other or brought a different pair to change into after going behind the partition.

Teachers and principals were constantly involved in fundraising, and the kinds of events that they came up with allow us to discern the prevailing values and attitudes about gender. The girls were expected to make things pretty, as evident in their box-making. The boys were encouraged to value certain female attributes, that is the ability to make things pretty. An even more problematic aspect of the box-making event is that of the category 'attractive' that was used to select the girls. Fundraising did rely on traditional gendered roles.

Researching the classroom in all its complexities provides a view of the values of a society in a particular time and locality. The silences allow larger issues of politics, religion, race, gender and social and cultural values to be developed within a more complex and nuanced analysis.

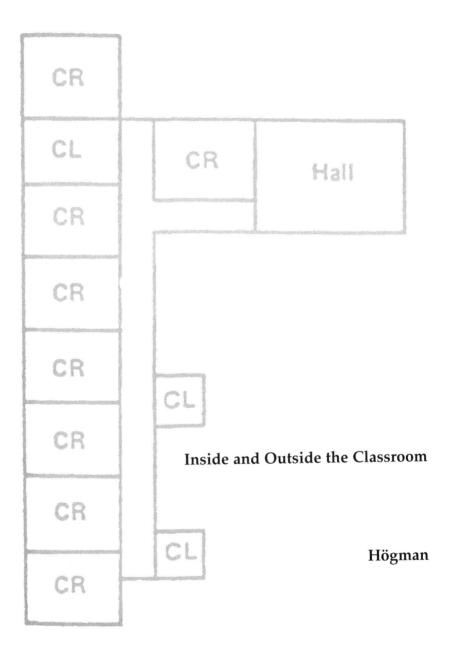

Inside and Outside the Classroom

Högman

Living the Life: inside and outside the classroom

Lars-Göran Högman

This chapter is based upon two long interviews with a Swedish teacher, 'Eva' (undertaken in 1995) and is an exploration of her relationship to the classroom. For Eva, to be in the classroom is to live the learning life and to be undivided, and when she is promoted out of the classroom she feels displaced and almost powerless. The chapter looks at the relation between the teacher, pedagogy (and its language) and educational reform and restructuring through Eva's life. Throughout she remains in the same geographical space but not in the same public space. The new reforms emphasise structures and relations for teaching that alter her work and relation to the classroom. From this analysis, we can raise comparative questions about teachers and classrooms. For example, using Eva's view of herself as the learner and the classroom as a practical democracy, we can open out new questions about teachers and classrooms.

The classroom can be seen as a space and an organizational and structural form. Its significance as a feature of education might often be overplayed because of its familiarity and ubiquity. However, the meaning of the classroom in the life and work of the teacher has to be examined by historians as if its visibility was not clear.

This chapter has two functions. It is an exploration of part of one teacher's occupational life, from 1982 to 1995, as she moves into a specialist support role in the Swedish system and away from her earlier classroom role. In 1982, Eva was a classroom teacher (grades 5-6) in a small village in the north of Sweden. By 1990, Eva was a remedial teacher at the upper level in the compulsory school (grades 7-9). Finally, Eva tells us about 1995, when she is employed as a manager for

Silences and Images

1. After the 1991
general elections a
four-party coalition
government headed by
the Conservative party
came into power.
Concepts like
'privatisation',
'marketisation', and
'freedom of choice'
were established in the
public debate about the
national school system.
The municipality and
particularly the local
school system where
Eva worked in 1995
characterised the 'new'
trends.

pedagogical development in the same municipality where she has been working as a classroom teacher and a remedial teacher since the beginning of the 1970s. Now she has an all-encompassing responsibility for pedagogical development among the compulsory schools (grades 1-9) in the municipality.[1]

So this chapter is concerned with the effect the earlier classroom life had on Eva, as the place in which her identity as a teacher was constructed; the later problem of teaching without a classroom and the power of the classroom in determining change.

The second function of the paper is to explore the ways in which school reforms affect the teacher and her actions, language and opportunities. In particular, the reforms of the 1980s, in common with other European national reforms, sought to decentralize and deregulate schooling, which meant changing the work of the teacher. This chapter tries to show what effects these reforms had upon one teacher, especially in relation to her work and the classroom.

As will be seen, the teacher tells us about her experiences from three different positions in a local school system and we can observe Swedish school reforms over a certain period (1982-1995) from the perspective of one teacher. Kallós and Nilsson summarise the development of reforms in this way:

> Decentralisation measures were gradually introduced and local school development work was given an increased emphasis. An increase in local political governance meant that State intervention gradually moved towards control through evaluation and an introduction of the concept of a goal- and result-oriented school. Teacher responsibilty, cooperation and planning were dictated not

only by State authorities but also by local authorities.[2]

2. D. Kallós and I. Nilsson, 'Defining and Re-defining the Teacher in the Swedish Comprehensive School', *Educational Review*, 47 (1995) pp. 173-88.

In addition, concepts such as 'teachers' cooperation', 'teachers' professionalism' and 'the new head', and became the focus in the national documents. At the end of the second interview, Eva was requested to comment on those terms. One feature of Sweden's contemporary school reform was 'a more flexible personnel policy'. The government proposes that:

> Skilled and ambitious teachers should be able to take on greater responsibility than just their own activity when it comes to, for example, the development of education and student care, without, for that reason, having to leave their assignments.[3]

3. Prop. (1988). *Skolans utveckling och styrning. Regeringens proposition 1988/89:4. (The Development and Governance of the School.* Government bill presented to Parliament). Stockholm. pp. 33-34. (my translation).

Eva's career could be seen as a manifestation of this policy, except that she left her classroom teaching step-by-step (bodily if not in spirit).

Eva was asked about (a) her work-related ambitions before and during a particular year, (b) her relationship to colleagues and the headteacher, (c) some conflicts (if any) in which she had been involved, and (d) what she regards as her fundamental understandings as a teacher.

At the end of the chapter, I discuss the teacher's and (the teacher as) manager's narrative, and some features of the school reforms, in relation to the classroom in terms of power, knowledge and control.

1982 : Living a Learning Life

When this school year started, Eva had been working for two years in the little school (grades 1-6) in the village where she lived. Eva was a classroom teacher for grades 5-6. One of her first impressions, when she joined the school two years before, was an oppressive atmosphere among the pupils; the older pupils terrorised the younger ones. During the preceding period in the school, many teachers had worked there for only one year before leaving. Eva said that 'the pupils had no idea about what a school should be like'. She meant that a school should be the 'pupils' school'. She wanted to 'democratise' the school in different ways so that the pupils should decide themselves what they wanted to learn and not just turn responsibility over to the teacher.

Eva said that she arranged the pupils into small groups (each included pupils from grades 5 and 6). Each group planned some activities for the coming week. What she remembers from this year is the class planning a journey to Norway where they had pen friends in a Norwegian class:

> what I also wanted them to do was to write to their pen pals in Norway... and to describe their village, because these village children did not have a very positive self-image, and I had the idea that if they start to know what they want to learn, start describing their reality, then they would experience that there was a curiosity among others concerning their lives.

Eva is not only a classroom teacher but a certified remedial teacher as well (educated for one year at the end of the 1970s). As a classroom teacher, she focused on the children who had different kinds of social and cognitive problems: 'my heart belonged to them'. Eva felt herself to be both a remedial teacher and a classroom teacher.

The concept of 'democracy' seemed to be important to Eva, and I asked her to explain her meaning of the word. The class had previously had a very authoritarian (male) teacher, who often took free time away from school (he was a local politician), and the class had had several supply (substitute) teachers.

Inside and Outside the Classroom

Because of these circumstances, small, strong groups of pupils directed the class activities.

Eva's first step for her 'strategy for democracy' was to let the children initiate, discuss and decide some parts of the class activities in the class council meetings. In the beginning, pupils were very confused and angry. They expected the teacher to initiate the schoolwork. Eva noticed a change after three weeks. The children suggested a visit to an old, unoccupied, presumably haunted vicarage for one night. Eva did not reject the suggestion, and the pupils started to plan the visit carefully.

When I asked Eva for her meaning of 'democracy' I did not get a theoretical exposition, but a concrete one. According to Eva, the pupils themselves were allowed to decide the content of the learning but they were not allowed to decide ' where in the classroom each of them would sit working. I chose certain literature, certain goals...'.

During this school year, there were two other classroom teachers, one male and one female. The female teacher, who was new to the school that year, became very interested in Eva's teaching and especially the idea of classroom democracy:

> She had not believed that pupils could take on that much responsibility if you let them loose. She believed that if you asked what they wanted to do, they would use the situation. Now she has completely changed her teaching and you could say that the pupils are planning the work. She is now 62 years, and she has really been influenced by what happened at the school.

The male teacher did not share the same ambitions about pupil participation and democracy:

He had class councils, but he didn't give them a free reign... I think that he thought that he had enough, that is that he followed the teaching plan... I think that he thought that it was rather chaotic in my class that the children did such an incredible amount of things at the same time.

There also was an older female remedial teacher in the school that year. She tried to take some of the pupils (for example, those with specific reading disabilities) out of Eva's classroom for lessons during the week to train these children in reading and writing. Eva did not allow her to do that; her pupils would not be subjected to such 'a boring kind of work'. Eva won the struggle. The remedial teacher was welcomed into the classroom where she could help the children with different kinds of problems.

Eva can't remember developing any contacts with the school supervisor (there was no head in the school). The four teachers at the little school minded their own business. Perhaps the supervisor visited the school three or four times per year.

Except for the conflict with the remedial teacher, Eva does not remember any conflict with her colleagues or the pupils. She does remember a very strong conflict with one of the parents. This mother and her family took care of children with troubled home conditions. Because of the big farm where the family lived, the social authorities allowed several children to live there at the same time:

> She was good at cooking, but I saw that it was terrible for the children in that home, because the mother played them out against each other, forbid the biological mother to come there, trying to make her look bad, even though she was fantastic in my eyes. I had a lot of work with that parent and I

couldn't... I became part of that game to play out the children against each other and me. It was a really tough time.

When Eva remembers her life as a classroom teacher in 1982, she interprets a teacher's job as a way 'to live the life itself in some respect'. She said that the activities which other people did during their spare time, such as learning new things, going to the theatre, reading books or walking in the mountains, are all things a teacher is allowed to do in his or her job:

> to live a learning life in general... to have the opportunity to do that with kids that change and that also live a learning life, that, I thought, was a great adventure... and that was rather egoistic actually.

1990: A Divided Life

During this year, Eva worked as a remedial teacher in the upper level of the compulsory school (grades 7-9). When I asked her to tell me about her expectations and ambitions when she started the school year, she started to describe the traditional role of a remedial teacher. A remedial teacher would concentrate on a few pupils with certain social and cognitive problems and pull those children from the classroom, the main reason being to establish a peaceful environment for the at-risk pupils. As we have seen above, Eva did not accept this way of working. The children would not be separated from their friends in the classroom! It was a fundamental right that every child be given the opportunity to develop his or her learning together with other children in the classroom. When the subject teachers asked Eva to 'help' them by removing pupils from the classroom, she responded:

> I always said that if I am to help then I want time with you and then we sit down and plan what you would be able to do to change

things, so that everyone can work with their
respective qualifications as a starting point.

Eva told me that many teachers viewed her as
something new and threatening because another
teacher would be in 'their' classroom. In 1990, after
two years as a remedial teacher in this school, Eva
had developed a fruitful collaboration together with
three subject teachers (in Swedish and Social Science).
Eva's reputation as a child-orientated teacher spread
among the pupils, and Eva's ambition to get the
under-achieving and under-motivated children 'to
love learning, love writing and reading, and to be
curious' became a reality, step-by-step.

There were fifteen teachers in the whole school. The
teachers were organised into so-called 'work-units'
(wu's). By management decree, each work unit had
one stipulated wu-conference a week. Eva's
impression was that these conferences were mainly a
kind of pupil case review. Questions about teaching,
learning in the classroom, and the content of the
education rarely appeared on the agenda.

The school had a headmaster and director of studies.
From Eva's point of view, they were mainly planners,
co-ordinators and schedulers.The school conferences,
which included all teachers at the school, were
characterised by 'information, information and
information' passed from the school leaders to the
teachers. For a period, the teachers refused to take
part in these school conferences. Eva remembers only
one hidden but important conflict from this year. The
conflict dealt with two groups of teachers: on one
side, Eva and the teachers in Swedish and Social
Science, and on the other, the other subject teachers,
especially the language teachers, who were very
worried about the new child-centered and
'democratic' teaching and learning among some
pupil groups:

They got very worried when we tried to change their way of teaching because they were of course used to, sort of, teaching in language patterns, and now the pupils were to speak English themselves or write freely and then it became... you felt like you weren't teaching anything

When Eva compared her former life as a classroom teacher with her life as a remedial teacher, she noticed that her work as a remedial teacher had been more 'divided'. She had shorter but more frequent contact with individual pupils. As a classroom teacher, she lived in the classroom together with all her pupils, and different questions arose in such a context. Yet, this year, she saw her job as a remedial teacher:

As an equally big adventure because here we had teenagers that shared their lives with me and my colleagues... when we made them think that it was meaningful so we assumed that they had interesting things to tell about themselves... and that meant that they shared their own lives with us.

1995: A Life of Uncertainty
In July 1994 Eva started her work as a manager for pedagogical development in the municipality where she has been employed since the beginning of the 1970s. During 1991-1994, a coalition of the Conservative party and some liberal parties held the majority in the local government council. During this period, a quasi-market local school system was established. Eva had the responsibility for pedagogical development of the comprehensive schools (grades 1-9), and the school management areas received economic resources to 'buy' different pedagogical duties from Eva. Eva herself had no money to spend and she had now definitively left the classroom.

For the first time in the interview, I noticed a

remarkable uncertainty and hesitance. When I asked her about her ambitions, she said:

> Actually, I want to do the same with these people or I want to have the same... contact... or I want to have the same opening... I don't know how to say it... what I am hoping is that I will experience the same kind of change, that is, here we actually know that if children are to learn anything and if teachers are to handle their work, then we need to change the roles, we can't go on and sort of believe that we should teach, that we should do it in a certain way, but here we have to let out what is coming from the pupils.

An important question is who are 'we'? Eva includes 'those who are thinking about the curriculum'; 'those who are thinking about how children are learning'; 'some researchers who had to go further'; and 'we, the teachers, as a group [who] perhaps have something to learn'. Obviously she is considering herself as a teacher and:

> In school I was more involved with the people around me, since there were children and young people and colleagues in some kind of creative mess. What I am good at is to be in this mess, in something that is development. There I didn't know exactly where I was going. Now I am in a grown-up world and not so many unexpected things happen there, everything is planned, it's thought-out, slow and all that.

Eva is aware of her new position in the local school system, 'but what is interesting is that when I, as a teacher, criticised something coming from above, then I thought that criticism was okay'.

She has a few contacts with other officials at the

central office, but when I asked her about any contact with former colleagues, she got very happy:

> Yes, I have quite a lot of contact with them... What it is that has happened now is that the whole of my area use me as a tutor/instructor in a big project that is about changing the way of working with six-year-olds and upwards... There they are working with making an analysis of the whole situation; the teachers will say what they need to develop. They use me quite a bit and I ask them questions and it feels really fun.

Contacts with people in other school management areas have not yet been established. Eva hopes to implement the working methods of a certain project she is involved with in her former school management area into other areas, but she is not sure that these areas are interested in 'buying' it.

This project also includes the heads. These 'new heads' are those who work half-time as teachers and half-time as heads. These heads have been extremely positive about Eva's participation in the project. I asked her if the heads have delegated their formal pedagogical responsibility in any way:

> I think the situation now of the principals here, in the whole municipality, is such that they have grasped that we're living in a new time... They have difficulties making their staff want to change or want to think in new ways, so I have seen that they are rather positive... well, they haven't directly delegated to me, but they run their heads into the wall when they try; they are out looking for co-operation partners that might not be as threatening as they are as principal.

Before Eva was employed as a manager and

consultant for pedagogical affairs, the local school board had established a local centre for dyslexia. The centre and its employees are convinced that the causes of some children's problems with reading and writing are hidden in the brain in certain neurological information processes. Eva is convinced that the problems are fundamentally social and emotional ones. In different ways in different local contexts, she had made her opinion clear. After a few weeks at her new job, she received a serious reprimand from the local board of education and its officials. The board had ordered a dyslexia centre, and the new manager for pedagogical development was not allowed to question such a decision! That was Eva's first conflict in her new position, but it may be not the last.

When I asked Eva about the fundamental meaning of her new life 'outside the classroom' she answered:

> Well, it doesn't feel as evident, meaningful, I must say. I'm thinking quite a bit on that and it can be because I don't know the job yet, that I'm not involved in any course of events, in any development. It feels considerably more difficult; it doesn't feel as developing for me as a person as it is to be together with kids or young people.

The Struggle for the Classroom

In this final section I want to deal with the professional identity of the teacher that Eva created in her first classroom. A paradox developed in Eva's career in that her strength as a teacher enabled her to leave the classroom and move into specialist teaching and advisory roles, but, in doing so, she lost some of her power, her sense of worth and the closeness of colleagues and pupils. Gaining promotion and status, she actually lost power and control. The classroom is central to this paradox.

Eva's relation to the classroom begins with her pedagogical ideas. In 1982 she dealt with democracy in schools and pupil participation and focused on under-achieving and under-motivated children ('my heart belongs to them'). She believed that pupils should learn to co-operate, and a teacher should counteract different kinds of oppression. The school should be 'the pupils' school'. Yet she had power over the pupils' bodies; she moved them and she forced them to co-operate.

Eva's heart belonged to the under-achieving children. Shouldn't the female remedial teacher's heart have belonged to those children as well? The remedial teacher wanted to move some children into a small, peaceful room to help them, but she was not allowed to do so. As a classroom teacher, Eva had the power to prevent that; she had the power over the classroom and the pupils who were there. We don't know exactly which pedagogical ideas this conflict concerned. Eva was convinced of the considerable value of letting all the children work together in the classroom. Even the remedial teacher would be there. Was it because of the overwhelming value of co-operation or because of the classroom teacher's ambition to control the under-achieving children and the remedial teacher as well? If co-operation is important to positive learning processes, to what extent did the teachers co-operate? In 1982 Eva co-operated with the new female teacher who appreciated Eva's pedagogical ideas. The remedial teacher was forced to co-operate, and the male teacher refused.

We have glimpsed some power relations from a rather isolated social context in 1982. Four teachers on the periphery of a municipality fight for power over the students' activities. Probably the main part of the daily activities is ruled by regulations in the syllabi. When Eva talks about her pedagogical ambitions, the syllabi seem to be invisible. The supervisor visited the school three or four times a year, but the teachers worked independently for the most part.

The circumstances changed in 1990. Eva is a remedial teacher in the upper level of the comprehensive school in the centre of the municipality. Democracy and pupil participation are in focus again, but the organisational and social circumstances are different. She had no class and no classroom. Because of that, she had to enter the classrooms to make contact with the pupils, especially the under-achieving and under-motivated teenagers. The subject teachers wanted to get rid of these pupils and they wanted the remedial teacher to take care of them. As we saw, Eva refused; she wanted to come into the classrooms. She began 'teaching' the distrustful subject teachers and she told them how to work. Only three teachers co-operated by letting her into their classrooms.

This year Eva was apprehensive about her job being 'divided', probably because the education at the upper level is divided in different subjects. Each class has ten to twelve subject teachers per week. The remedial teacher had no chance of obtaining control over one single class.

The former classroom teacher had lost her little school; she had lost her classroom. Because of that, she lost the control over a larger group of children. As a remedial teacher, while she was better paid than the other teachers and was more educated in some respects, the power and the possibilities for control had been reduced under the new educational reforms.

Four years later in July 1994, Eva entered her new job as a manager for pedagogical development. When she talked about her ambitions and ideas, the fundamental ones were unchanged, but the teachers (as a professional group) became the focus of her thinking. She felt that they should read the National Curriculum and should learn from researchers. Her position in the local school system was now very different. She had no real power over either the classrooms or the schools. She had no formal or economic power over the teachers, but she did have something that they could 'buy' if they wanted to: expert knowledge. When she realised she had no school, no class, and no children to go to every morning, she got sad and confused. She tried to get contacts with (and control of) the pedagogical development in any way possible. Then she began to talk about teachers, the curriculum, and research, and talk of the children disappeared. Is it possible that such keys as 'in service-training', 'curriculum', and 'research' could unlock the classroom doors? What did Eva do in her new position? With her former colleagues and the new heads in her former school management area, she continued her work as a 'teacher' in a project that allows her contact with children.

We have seen how an ambitious and enthusiastic female teacher has moved up toward the 'pedagogical top' of the hierarchy and, at the same time, lost the contact with and the power over a pedagogical development.

As mentioned previously, one of the features in contemporary school reforms in Sweden is 'a more flexible personnel policy'. The appearance in Eva's career of a new phenomenon — the employment of specialists and consultant teachers — suggests that pedagogical development, the space of the teacher, is now spread out. Lawn has pointed out variations in the meanings of 'the good teacher' and 'teaching quality' during four distinct periods in the twentieth century. These concepts are social constructions and imply contradictions that, in turn, influence the teaching staff:

> However, the social construction of teacher quality is a contested process; initiatives are

taken in response to shortages or emerge out of particular political and social conjunctions which are then responded to by teachers. Generations of teachers are themselves divided, containing as they do, competing practices, favoured 'good teacher' models and biographical-ordered work experiences around which teachers organize or group.[4]

4. M. Lawn. 'The social construction of quality in teaching' in M. Lawn and G. Grace eds., *Teacher Supply and Teacher Quality.* (Clevedon, U.K.: Multilingual Matters, 1991) p. 65.

The power relations which shape these social constructions are complex, and the complexity appears in the day-to-day practice among teachers. Former notions of 'the good teacher' coexist side-by-side with new meanings of what a good or a professional teacher should be. When we consider Eva's career, we have some idea about such circumstances.

Eva said that the professional teacher had to 'organise', 'comment on' and 'document' his or her work. Of course, that can imply positive things for teachers and pupils as well. I suppose now that Eva is mainly isolated from the practice, however she needs to know something about those practices. She wants to know what they are doing and she wants to participate in the documentation and the oral comments as well. She is losing control of the practice.

Eva is mainly positive about teacher co-operation and pupil co-operation. She thinks that an individual teacher dares to 'challenge' pupils when another adult is present at the classroom. The individual teacher also has a stronger sense of 'responsibility' to realise what has been decided by a group of teachers. When teachers co-operate, they have the opportunity to reach consensus about working methods.

Eva's career is a reflection of the new flexible work practices happening in teaching; she has become an expert consultant. Yet the space of the classroom is crucial to her identity and power and she is unable to recover her undivided life. Her language has altered. She values cooperation with teachers whereas once she could exclude them. The classroom is not just a space; it is a defining sign of her identity as a teacher, and even in its absence it shapes her purpose and actions as a teacher.

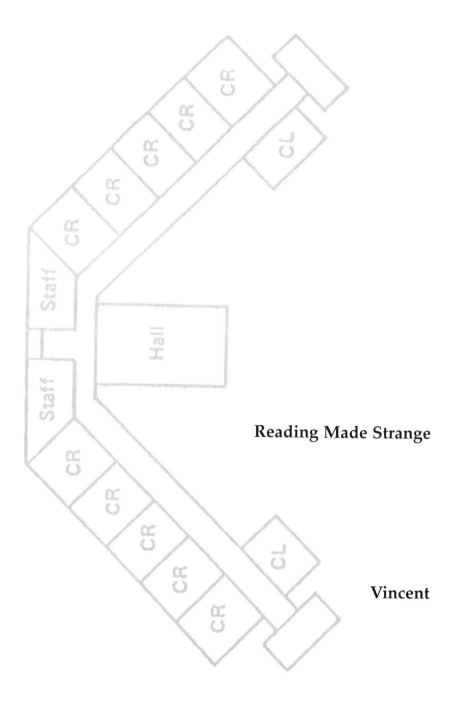

Reading Made Strange

Vincent

Reading Made Strange: context and method in becoming literate in eighteenth and nineteenth-century England

David Vincent

At first sight, the history of learning to read seems insulated from time. In 1707, Thomas Dyche published a *Guide to the English Tongue*. Chapter 1 presented the pupil with a list of disconnected syllables: 'ba be bi bo bu ca ce ci co cu'.[1] A generation later, William Markham's *An Introduction to Spelling and Reading English* began: 'ab eb ib ob ub ap ep ip op up'.[2] The 1793 edition of Thomas Dilworth's *A New Guide to the English Tongue*, one of the most popular primers on both sides of the Atlantic in the second half of the eighteenth century, commenced 'ba be bi bo bu ab eb ib ob ub'.[3] Finally we arrive at 1835, and the first page of Henry Innes' *The British Child's Spelling Book*: 'ba be bi bo bu by ab eb ib ob ub yb'. Through decades of wars and threats of wars, revolutions and threats of revolutions, through a transformation in society and the economy, all that happens at this most fundamental level of encountering the printed word is a transition from 'ba be bi bo bu' to 'ba be bi bo bu by'. Even in the narrower field of institutional teaching, these years witnessed epochal developments, with Dyche appearing just as the Charity School movement of the Society for the Promotion of Christian Knowledge was getting under way, and Innes just as the state was beginning to subsidise the mass instruction of children. But when it comes to the gateway to reading, we are reduced to hunting for tiny alterations in the typeface and layout of the most widely used guides.

This chapter addresses the apparent absence of movement in the process of learning to read. It argues that the sense of stasis is both real and artificial, and that the key to the relation between continuity and

1 T. Dyche *Guide to the English Tongue* 2nd ed., 1710.

2 W. Markham *An Introduction to Spelling and Reading English* 5th ed. 1738, first published 1728.

3 T. Dilworth *A New Guide to the English Tongue* First published in London in 1740, North America in 1747.

THE BRITISH CHILD'S
THE ALPHABET.

With the simple Sound of each Letter explained. *

A	a as in day	N	en
B	bee	O	as in no
C	see	P	pee
D	dee	Q	cue
E	as in thee, me	R	ar
F	eff	S	ess
G	jee	T	tee
H	aitch	U	you
I	i or eye	V	vee
J	jay	W	double u
K	kay	X	eks
L	el	Y	wy
M	em	Z	zed

NOTE.—C and G are hard before a o u l and r:—as cat, game, cord, gold, cup, gun, cloth, gloss, cramp, grass. C and G are soft before e i and y;—as cellar, gender, civil, ginger, cypress, elegy; except in get, give, girl, gear, geese, &c., and before er at the end of a word, as finger.

THE VOWELS,
With their various Sounds shown and distinguished.

a as in fate	i as in pine	u as in pure
a — cat	i — pin	u — rule
a — far	i — virgin	u — full
a — what	i — bird	u — busy
a — wall	i — machine	u — sun
e — theme	o — note	y — by
e — her	o — move	y — ably
e — met	o — woman	
e — clerk	o — love	
e — where	o — on, not	
	o — nor, gone	

* The above is principally intended to meet the eye of the Teacher rather than the Learner. Sometimes a young person superintends the initiation of a child, and it is important that the sounds should be distinctly conveyed.

Syllables of Two Letters.

ba	ga	la	ra	wa	eb
be	ge	le	re	we	ec
bi	gi	li	ri	wi	ed
bo	go	lo	ro	wo	ef
bu	gu	lu	ru	wu	eg
by	gy	ly	ry	wy	el
ca	ha	ma	sa	ya	ib
ce	he	me	se	ye	ic
ci	hi	mi	si	yi	id
co	ho	mo	so	yo	if
cu	hu	mu	su	yu	ig
cy	hy	my	sy	za	il
da	ja	na	ta	ze	ob
de	je	ne	te	zi	oc
di	ji	ni	ti	zo	od
do	jo	no	to	zu	of
du	ju	nu	tu	zy	og
dy	jy	ny	ty	ab	ol
fa	ka	pa	va	ac	ub
fe	ke	pe	ve	ad	uc
fi	ki	pi	vi	af	ud
fo	ko	po	vo	ag	uf
fu	ku	pu	vu	al	ug
fy	ky	py	vy	an	ul

change lies in the shifting balance between the strange and the familiar, particularly as it was experienced by the consumers of this literature. The search for the meaning of these curious fragments of language throws into sharp relief the impact of the inspected classroom. It raises three connected questions: the relation between the teaching methods of the official school and those employed in the home and in the unofficial schools located in the homes of un-certificated teachers; the interaction between the physical and social space of the official school and the methods and literature of instruction; finally, the consequence for the child of the system of instruction, and the consequence for the system of the child's experience.

It was a firm convention for primers to lay claim to novelty. William Mavor launched his immensely successful *English Spelling Book* of 1802 by routinely assaulting his predecessors:

> Notwithstanding the vast number of initiatory books for children in the Nursery, which have been written these few years by persons of distinguished abilities, and sanctioned with their names, it must still be allowed that there has not appeared an Introduction to Reading for the general use of *Schools*, that rises above the level of the vulgar, though popular, compilations of Dyche, Dilworth and Fenning',[4]

4 W. Mavor, *The English Spelling Book* (London: np 1804 edn.) p. 3.

and then he proceeded to replicate their work exactly, beginning with the alphabet, two-letter syllables and lists of complete words of escalating length. In reality, almost everything had been tried before. The first printed aid to acquiring literacy (an illustrated alphabet) appeared within thirty years of the invention of printing, and thereafter large sums were available to those who found a niche in the market. Standard works sold in version after version: Dyche was in print from 1707 to 1830; Markham from 1728 to 1885; Dilworth from 1740 to about 1850; and Mavor, which claimed a 332nd edition by 1826 and a 446th by 1840, outlasted Victoria's reign, finally expiring in 1902. At the very least, the continuity rendered the books very unsurprising. However odd, artificial and dislocated they may now seem, they were what the customer expected to find. The most basic teaching aids of all, the hornbooks, contained on their single cruciform surface the initial elements of the primers, the alphabet, basic syllabic combinations and perhaps a simple religious text. The three-leaved battledores which came onto the market in the later eighteenth century were based on the same pattern.

The breadth of diffusion of this material imparted a second dimension of familiarity. As Ian Michael has established, a wide range of teaching material was bought for use in the home in the centuries before church and state launched their campaign to monopolise the process of instruction.[5] The growth in school textbooks after 1830 only doubled the appearance of new titles (from seventeen to thirty-five a year). The scale of the private market makes it particularly difficult to confine these books to a specific institutional setting. Many of the authors were themselves teachers – Dyche taught at Stratford Bow, Dilworth described himself as a schoolmaster – and addressed their work to fellow professionals. But the SPCK's charity school system was much too small to sustain the volume of sales. In general, writers and publishers were unconcerned about the distinctions which inform the standard histories of education. Markham explained that the purpose of his primer was 'to render this first and principal Part of Education as easy as possible, both to the Teachers and Learners'.[6] His teachers were variously ordained ministers, untrained proprietors of day and dame schools, and domestic instructors of both sexes and all ages. By the same measure, his learners were to be

5 I. Michael, *Early Textbooks of English* (Reading,UK : Colloquium on Textbooks, Schools and Society 1993) p. 2.

6 W. Markham, *An Introduction to Spelling and Reading English* (5th ed. London, 1738) p. vii.

found in any educational structure and none at all.

If professional experience was required to compose and validate the textbooks, there was no accompanying claim that their effective use depended on a particular physical context or specialist skill. We still need more work on price, print-runs and market, but there is evidence of a relatively broad diffusion through all ranks of society.[7] 'I am very sensible', wrote Sarah Trimmer in 1801, 'that there is already a great variety of *Spelling-Books*, by means of which children have been taught to read and spell successfully.'[8] Alongside the traditional practice of adapting literature written for adults, there are indications that by the early nineteenth century, primers and spelling books were being used in the homes of the common people. Many of the texts were intended for a rapidly expanding middle class market, but they were so cheap and published in such numbers that it was not difficult for a working class parent to get hold of something like Mavor's *English Spelling Book*.[9] The local newspapers in the Potteries, for instance, regularly carried bookseller's advertisements in the 1830s and 1840s for manuals on reading and writing at prices from sixpence to two shillings.[10] One of the reasons why it was so easy to start a dame or private adventure school was the availability of cheap spelling books. Ian Michael quotes Crabbe writing of elementary textbooks, 'Soil'd, tatter'd, worn and thrown in various heaps'.[11] The widespread foraging on these heaps may help to explain the comparatively high levels of literacy which the nineteenth century inherited from the eighteenth.[12]

We are, with good reason, accustomed to placing the acquisition of reading skills in the context of a deeply divided system of learning. If however, we approach the first encounter with the printed word through the textbooks, we can identify a kind of common heritage. The combination of longevity and dispersal

7 See W. J. Gilmore's detailed study of learning to read in contemporary New England: *Reading Becomes a Necessity of Life* (Knoxville: University of Tennessee Press, 1989) pp. 122-24, 219.

8 S. Trimmer, *The Oeconomy of Charity* (London: T. Longman, 1801) p. 55.

9 For the wide availability of Mavor and other cheap primers on mid-nineteenth-century bookstalls, C.M. Smith, 'The Press of the Seven Dials', in *Little World of London* (London: np 1957) p. 261.

10 See for instance, *The Staffordshire Mercury* (Jan 2, 1830); *The Potters' Examiner*, vol. 1, no. 7 (Jan. 13, 1844) p. 48.

11 Michael (1993) p. 7.

12 For advent of mass literacy in this period, see D. Vincent, *Literacy and Popular Culture. England 1750-1914* (Cambridge: Cambridge University Press, 1989).

13 E.M. Field, *The Child
and his Book* (2nd edn.,
London: Wells,
Gardner and Darton,
1892) pp. 113-225;
M.F. Thwaite, *From
Primer to Pleasure in
Reading* (2nd edn.
London: Libary
Association, 1972) pp.
4-7; A. Ellis, *Educating
our Masters*
(Aldershot,UK: Gower,
1985) pp. 87-102.

14 This remains a
lesson to be learnt. The
leading authority on
teaching literacy in
Britain today has
recently written, 'The
most serious myth
about reading is that it
has to be taught in
school'. M. Meek,
'Literacy: redescribing
reading' in, K.
Kimberley, M. Meek
and J. Miller, *New
Readings. Contributions
to an Understanding of
Literacy* (London: A &
C Black, 1992) p. 227.

15 T. Lye, *A New
Spelling Book* (2nd ed.,
London: np 1677)
Preface.

meant that the Tudor schoolboy would have quickly recognised the books bought for his early Victorian counterpart, just as the schooled poor man's son in the new industrial settlements could have swapped primers with the home-educated heir of a landed gentleman.[13] After so broad a distribution over so many years, the disconnected syllables had lost their connection with time and social status.

The long and varied history of aids to instruction in reading puts into proper perspective the late and contested arrival of state education. Textbooks teach us to be less preoccupied with the work of official schools and their trained teachers. Adults from a wide range of backgrounds had for centuries accepted a responsibility for instruction in basic literacy.[14] As Thomas Lye wrote in his *New Spelling Book* of 1677, 'that *Parents* generally throughout this whole Kingdom are at constant, vast expenses for the ingenious education of the dear Children, is a Truth written with a Sun-beam.'[15] Many others found ways of achieving a workable end without such cost, and they continued to play a role alongside the growth of state-funded and controlled education. At the same time they instruct us to think much more sharply about the meaning of the physical organisation of teaching. Whereas teachers were influenced by their materials, those materials themselves changed their function and eventually their substance during their transition from the home to the classroom. What emptied the process of learning to read of its element of familiarity was not the reading matter itself, but rather the way it was deployed. It was the context which made the content strange, and eventually it was this strangeness which forced a change in the literature of instruction.

The initial impression of the first years of the British and National Schools Societies is the sheer antiquity of their basic classroom literature. They inherited a method of teaching children their letters which predated printing.[16] The system embodied in the first primer published in 1538 had been in use for several centuries and was in turn based on what were thought to be classical techniques of instruction. This tradition of teaching to read was founded on two principles: firstly that spelling should be mastered alongside rather than subsequent to reading; secondly that learning proceeded from the particular to the whole.[17] The decomposition and reconstitution of language was at the heart of these teaching books. It was believed that a child's learning processes naturally operated by combining fragments of knowledge into larger wholes, and it seemed logical to begin with the smallest units of language and work upwards.[18] The pupil was to begin with the alphabet, then combine letters into syllables which were succeeded by simple monosyllabic words.[19] In the more ambitious primers of the early nineteenth century, the subsequent word lists were carefully arranged in ascending length, with the curriculum ending with seven-syllable tongue-twisters which the child might never again encounter in any passage of prose or poetry.[20]

The syllabic method of instruction had not, however, enjoyed a monopoly in the market place. The discovery that serious money could be made from disseminating the skills necessary to exploit the new technology of communication brought into the field a host of pedagogic entrepreneurs. As with the parallel trade of medicine, the claim to professional authority was in essence a commercial strategy. Each new device promised to revolutionise the teaching of reading, but in practice it merely added to the array of techniques. Innovations in England and Germany by the beginning of the seventeenth century included: 'the use of graded and familiar vocabulary in a realistic setting; the reinforcement of pictorial illustrations; the variety of the Look-and-Say and Sentence approaches; the emergence of phonics as a viable teaching method; the quasi-linguistic systems

16 For the antiquity of teaching methods embodied in printed materials see I. Michael, *The Teaching of English* (Cambridge: CUP 1987); H. Graff, *The Legacies of Literacy* (Bloomington, Indiana, 1987) p. 72.

17 Michael (1987) p. 14.

18 *Ibid* pp. 56, 91, 117.

19 W. B. Hodgson, 'Exaggerated estimates of Reading and Writing', *Transactions of the National Association for the Promotion of Social Science* (1867) p. 400. See also, Rev. F. Fox, *An Introduction to Spelling and Reading* (17th ed., London: F. and C. Rivington, 1805); J. M. M'Culloch, *A First Reading-Book for the Use of Schools* (Edinburgh: Oliver and Boyd, 1837); L. Murray, *A First Book for Children* (17th ed., York: np 1825); S. Trimmer, *The Charity School Spelling Book* (9th ed., London: F. and C. Rivington, 1805); W. M'Leod, *A First Reading Book, for the Use of Families and Schools* (London: np 1848); *Reading Made Easy in a Variety of Useful Lessons* (4th ed., Berwick, UK:1835).

20 M. Matthews, *Teaching to Read, Historically Considered* (Chicago: University of Chicago Press, 1966) pp. 19-74.

21 W.J. Frank Davies,
*Teaching Reading in
Early England* (London:
Pitman,1973) p. 151.

22 In 'Thoughts
Concerning Education'.
See, Darton and
Harvey, *Children's
Books in England*
(London: np 1805)
p. 127.

of the shape-of-the letter and patterns of sounds in a
coherent story; the regularisation of spelling codes;
and hint of the use of colour'.[21] This much had been
achieved by the Glorious Revolution rather than the
industrial revolution. Locke referred to the use of
alphabetic dice in 1693.[22] During the succeeding
century, the market continued to diversify. Alongside
the alphabets and primers, anthologies of leading
writers were compiled to entice the young reader. For
novices, non-literary devices such as card and board
games were devised to ease the pain of instruction.

23 Essays from the
1996 Conference on the
Jane Johnson
Collection have been
published as, M.
Hilton, M. Styles and
V. Watson eds.,
*Opening the Nursery
Door. Reading, Writing
and Childhood, 1600-
1900* (London:
Routledge, 1997).

This flow of innovation meant that energetic teachers,
professional or amateur, inside or outside a
classroom, were faced with an essential plurality of
methods embodied in a multiplicity of formats. The
Jane Johnson Collection, a particularly rich variety of
teaching aids assembled by an eighteenth-century
mother in order to instruct her children, embraced
the kinds of primer discussed above, a number of
other specialist publications, and a range of hand-
made devices such as carefully-fashioned flash
cards.[23] Although the Collection can be categorised
into different forms, in practice mother and child
integrated the various devices as they proceeded
towards a command of the written word. Beyond this
particular example, it is difficult to generate a precise
account of the journey to literacy in the wide range of
households in which it took place in the eighteenth
century. Whilst methods were prescribed in the
primers, their users were free to adapt and combine
them with other home-made learning aids and non-
specialist printed material as availability, aptitude
and inclination dictated. In the home, and in the host
of un-regulated schoolrooms, the pace, the direction
and the means of progress were open to continual
adjustment and variation.

24 K. Jones and K.
Williamson, 'The Birth
of the Schoolroom',
*Ideology and
Consciousness*, 6 (1979)
pp. 73-8.

It was otherwise in the monitorial system which was
at the heart of the early nineteenth-century church
schools.[24]The drive to universal literacy was founded

on a deliberate narrowing of the range of pedagogic options. Faced with the task of conducting simultaneous instruction in a single, undivided classroom, it was only possible to select one method from the rich menu now on offer. As a result, the deconstruction of language was embraced as a theory of organisation as well as of learning.[25] The sequence of rebuilding words in the primers of Dyche and Markham and their imitators provided a ready-made solution to the problem of mass instruction. Method and structure met at the point of classification. The division of labour in the new schoolroom, which was itself an agent of discipline,[26] found its analogue in the dismantling of sentences in the old textbooks. The pupil's measured advance through the curriculum was calibrated by the climb from monosyllables to lengthening polysyllables.

In 1816, there were eight classes in the schools of the British and Foreign Schools Society. The first four progressed from the alphabet to four-letter syllables; the next two mastered one- and two-syllable words; the final two encountered simple religious passages and then some anthologies carefully vetted for their improving content.[27] By 1831, the Bible had been postponed, and the ladder from the alphabet reached four syllable words by the seventh lesson, with the eighth reserved for mixed sentences.[28] The primers, which once had served only to prepare children for continuous prose, were now exclusive and self-sufficient courses of learning. Where the mass purchase of complete texts proved too expensive, their contents were simplified into seventeen by ten inch 'reading sheets', containing the alphabet, the basic syllables and lists of simple monosyllabic words.[29] The study of spiritual texts became the primary objective of the instruction: 'it has been the compiler's aim', wrote Henry Innes, 'to make learning the hand-maid of religion'.[30] Only the most advanced children were introduced to consecutive sentences, which did not include any of the

25 Michael (1987) p. 124.

26 Jones and Williamson (1979) p. 21.

27 *Manual of the System of Teaching Reading, Writing, Arithmetick, and Needle-Work in the Elementary-Schools of the British and Foreign Schools Society* (London: np 1816).

28 *Manual for the System of Primary Instruction, Pursued in the Model Schools of the B.F.S.S.* (London: np 1831).

29 J. M. Goldstrom, *The Social Content of Education, 1808-1870* (Shannon: Irish University Press, 1972) pp. 36-37.

30 Innes (1835) Preface.

comparatively rich literary anthologies of the late-eighteenth century.

The official and unofficial structures of learning became separated by the differing function of the same textbooks. In the home, and in the myriad of private adventure schools which were inculcating more reading skills into more children than the monitorial experiments which have attracted such attention from educational historians, the standard primers in old and new versions were still widely used. But the range of other printed materials with which they could be combined was increasing exponentially. It may be argued that the most effective device of the period for assisting the key transition from a hesitant knowledge of letters to a fluent command is to be found not in the body of pedagogic literature but rather in streets where the penny broadsides were sung and sold. During the heyday of the monitorial system, popular items of this form of literary entertainment achieved seven-figure sales. The typical production of Catnach or Pitts presented three versions of a single dramatic event, a formulaic prose account for practised readers, a sequence of verses set to music which could be learned by heart by those more immersed in the oral tradition, and a crude woodcut of the murder or execution for the non-literate.[31] These broadsides were the exact opposite of learning by division-of-labour. The single document embraced all levels of learning, providing both the incentive and the opportunity to improve a command of reading.

The changing function of the primers severely aggravated the long-standing problem of context. It had never been very clear how the child was to connect the syllables and word-lists either to its oral vocabulary or to the tasks of reading and writing joined-up paragraphs. But where domestic tutors might make do and muddle through, the new generation of trained schoolteachers ran on a narrow,

31 C. Hindley, *Curiosities of Street Literature* (London: np 1871) p. ii; C. M. Smith, 'The Press of the Seven Dials' in *The Little World of London* (London: np 1857) p. 261; L. James, *Print and the People*, (Harmondsworth: Penguin, 1978) p. 25.

prescribed track. They were not permitted to use invention or improvisation in teaching any more than the pupils were to employ imagination or play in the process of learning.[32] They could not vary the speed, or start in the middle, or double back, or integrate other methods and material. In their hands, the artificiality of this technique of instruction was exposed with forbidding clarity. As the teaching methods became more intense, learning to read became increasingly divorced from the child's encounters with language in the home. The fragments of words and sentences which it faced in the classroom bore no visible relation to the complex linguistic skills which had been mastered in infancy and early childhood.[33]

In the context of the monitorial classroom, the inevitable strangeness of print became unnecessarily absolute. Learning to read could never be as non-reflexive an activity as learning to talk. Whether or not the activity was mediated by an identifiable teacher, there would be some awareness of a transition from incapacity via deliberate application to independent practice. In the monitorial system the artificiality of the process became not merely the means to an end but essential to the end itself. The new schools set out with the deliberate ambition of dismantling the mental resources which children had previously acquired from their family and the neighbourhood, and replacing them with a new structure of moral and intellectual discipline. It was held that putting children through the eight-class progression to reading 'forms them to habits of virtue, and habituates them to subordination and control'.[34] The deconstruction of language in the syllabic method embodied the ambition of teaching children that at the point of entry to the classroom, they possessed no skills of moral or intellectual value. 'Ba, be bi, bo bu' was baby talk. It symbolised the need to wipe the slate clean, to recommence the process of cognitive development from the beginning.

32 The tension between the new humanist ambition of developing the potential of the child, and the institutional requirement to develop a rigid, disciplined system of teaching is discussed in M. J. Maynes, *Schooling in Western Europe* (Albany: State University of New York Press, 1985) pp. 61-62, 76.

33 For a survey of the complexity of this period of learning see M. Jackson, *Literacy* (London: David Fulton 1993) p. 58.

34 Manual of the System of teaching Reading (1816) p. vii.

The initial function of learning to read was not to extend but rather to demolish the child's existing stock of knowledge. The lessons were meant to seem strange, because what was familiar was the enemy of true learning.

The Revised Code of 1862 brought forth a new generation of textbooks. One of the most influential was written by a former school inspector, J. S. Laurie. *First Steps to Reading* began by attacking the method of instruction which had informed the works of Dyche and Innes and all their rivals:

> The confusion caused by this altogether imperfect and illusory analysis, renders the teaching of reading on the old plan an extremely slow and difficult operation throughout the whole of the first stages; and it is no wonder that teachers have found by experience, that is infinitely better to dispense with analysis entirely, and to teach reading by what is termed the 'Look and Say Method'. According to this method the pupil learns to read words at sight by mechanically associating certain sounds with certain appearances. He is not embarrassed by any intermediate process but goes straight from the printed form of the word to its enunciation.'[35]

'Look and Say' was not, of course, as novel a method as Laurie implied. It was also under discussion in Germany and the United States,[36] and we have seen that it is possible to identify its forerunner as much as two centuries earlier. Jane Johnson certainly deployed a version in her cornucopia of texts and games.

It may indeed be argued that in the field of learning to read, as perhaps more broadly in education, the search for the origin of particular methods is an

35 J. S. Laurie, *First Steps to Reading* (London: np 1862) Preface. See also the contemporary publication, London: W. J. Unwin *Infant School Reader* (London: np 1861).

36 Mathews (1966) pp. 49-50, 75-101. Horace Mann was a notable advocate.

exercise of limited value. The question is not when a certain device was first invented, but rather what circumstances caused the foregrounding of one amongst an established menu of devices. The conventional historiography of education presents a linear progression punctuated by key dates.[37] A better model is a series of conflicts resulting in the temporary ascendancy of one approach rather than another, or as often, a new configuration of a number of different techniques.

In the case of the second third of the nineteenth century, the exclusive reliance on the syllabic method turned out to be as short-lived as the monitorial system in which it was embedded. By the time the state started to subsidise and then inspect the work of the church schools, doubts were surfacing about the value of the tables of syllables and 'unmeaning combinations'.[38] The professionals themselves began to ask questions about the connection between the lessons and the language skills the child had acquired before the written word was encountered and about the relation between polysyllabic mastery and a genuine competence in independent reading.[39] 'Look and Say' began to be discussed in official circles in the late 1840s and received formal sanction in the 1852 Minutes.[40] The method was brought in from the margins of pedagogic theory as the limitations of the particularistic method were exposed by its use to structure the first generation of elementary schools. Under the new approach the pupil was to be introduced to complete, monosyllabic words, preferably in the context of short sentences. The way in which the words were spelled would be taught after, not before the pupil had learned to recognise them.[41]

The speed and scale of the transformation are difficult to gauge. The better inspectors recommended some combination of the holist and particularist routes. The alphabet still needed to be

37 See most recently, N. J. Smelser, *Social Paralysis and Social Change* (Berkeley: University of California Press, 1991).

38 *Manual of the System of Primary Instruction Pursued in the Model Schools of the British and Foreign Schools Society* (London, 1831); H. Dunn, *Popular Education; or, The Normal School Manual* (London: np 1837) p. 69.

39 See the evidence of Henry Dunn to the 1834 *Select Committee on Education*, Parliamentary Papers 1834, IX, p. 25.

40 *Minutes of the Committee of Council on Education, 1851-2* (London, 1852) II, p. 48. C.W. Connon, *A First Spelling Book* (London: Oliver and Boyd, 1851) p. 4; A. Ellis, *History of Children's Reading and Literature* (Oxford: Pergamon Press, 1968) pp. 51-53.

41 W.F. Richards, *Manual of Method for the Use of Teachers in Elementary Schools* (London: np 1854) p. 66. For the parallel development of this theory in the United States see Matthews (1966) pp. 75-101; and in Russia, J. Brooks, *When Russians Learned to Read* (Princeton: Princeton University Press, 1985) p. 50.

42 Mathews (1966)
p. 101.

43 C.W. Johnson, The
*English Rural Spelling-
Book* (London: np 1846)
p. 111.

44 Jackson (1993)
p. 50.

45 J. Gill, *Introductory
Text-Book to School
Management* (2nd edn.,
London: np 1857).

46 For a survey of the
expansion of this
literature, see A. Ellis,
*Books in Victorian
Elementary Schools*
(London: Gower, 1971)
pp. 21-32.

learned, and the syllabic method retained a superficial logic and simplicity. Editions of Markham, Mavor and their rivals continued to be churned out in the succeeding decades. In the United States, a similar shift towards the new technique failed to put the more old-fashioned spellers out of business.[42] However the change in emphasis was of genuine importance. The new approach required the teacher to make an accommodation with the knowledge and skills that pupils acquired before or outside their schooling. As recently as 1846, Cuthbert Johnson's *English Rural Spelling-Book* had enjoined the pupil to 'avoid guessing' when encountering a new sentence.[43] Now for the first time the child was permitted to take a chance on a word. Where the child learned to talk by imitation and only later became conscious of the rules which controlled spoken language, now the child was permitted by the schoolmaster to read first and work out the reasons later.

With much hesitation, textbook writers began to glimpse a fact that is much emphasised in recent research; as Margaret Jackson puts it, 'young children learn to deal with print by "having a go"... early childhood is a continual process of experimentation, risk-taking and negotiation, in purposeful, intentional ways.'[44] And where the oral vocabulary had been discounted, it was now recommended that, 'the first lessons should consist entirely of words with which the ear of children is familiar.'[45] Whatever damage the Revised Code caused to wider areas of the curriculum, the newly defined standards in the field of reading brought forth a generation of textbooks which represented a clear advance over their immediate predecessors.[46] The tradition of literary anthologies which had flourished in the later eighteenth century was revived in publications such as Laurie's *Graduated Series of Reading Lesson Books*, which began with complete sentences and culminated with extracts from Macaulay, Spenser,

Reading Made Strange

Milton, Goldsmith, Cowper, Byron and Longfellow. When it evoked a response, this reading challenged the acquired knowledge and expectations of the school child in the proper sense. There is a critical difference between the strange which renders the commonplace unfamiliar, and the strange which renders the commonplace meaningless. Context was everything, in the sense of the organisation and control of the teaching, the physical environment, and perhaps above all, the conception of purpose. William Cobbett's immensely successful intervention in the pedagogy of reading through his *Grammar* and his later *Spelling Book* deployed exactly the same technique as Dyche, with even longer word-lists – the two-syllable columns in the *Spelling Book*, for instance, run to 5,320 words – but the method was embedded in a cheerfully iconoclastic assault on the pretensions of the learned and a patient exposition of the value of reading to the unlearned. All sorts of useful skills for living and working could be acquired by the illiterate, he argued, and were no less valuable for that: 'But, though we may be taught much without ever looking into books, that is no reason that books should be of no use; on the contrary, more is to be learned, and learned in less time, from books, than can possibly be learned in any other way'.[47]

47 W. Cobbett, *A Spelling-Book with Appropriate Lessons in Reading and with A Stepping-Stone to English Grammar* (London, 1831) p. 103.

Cobbett was writing for an audience which had yet to accept the inevitability of the inspected classroom. The journey toward the schooled society could not be completed while the first encounter with reading remained so alienating an experience. The textbook was not an autonomous agent of change in this period, but an integral element in the complex process of negotiation between the official and domestic curriculum which characterised the history of English elementary education in the nineteenth century. Once the initial fascination with the mechanical perfection of the monitorial system had worn off, it was gradually recognised that if the churches and then the state were to realise their new goal of a society in which reading was a universal skill, they would have to secure some level of active consent by both parents outside the school and children inside it.

Lip service had long been given to the need to adjust the method to the child. Back in 1734 William Markham stated that, 'I have purposely used the lowest language, as the best adapted to a Child's Understanding.'[48] By the middle decades of the century, however, with costs spiralling and attendance inconsistent, the issue of the child's response to the textbook assumed a much greater urgency. The increasingly self-conscious profession had to grapple with a dilemma which remains unresolved to this day. On the one hand the profession was committed to making the classroom as self-sufficient an arena of teaching as possible,[49] with the deficiencies of one method to be met by the development of yet more sophisticated pedagogic systems embodied in still more elaborate printed teaching aids. On the other it was coming to realise that effective education required continuity as well as discontinuity between the rich structure of learning outside the school and the narrow pattern of instruction within it.

The sequence of changes did nothing to reduce the gulf between the professional and the amateur teacher. Because 'Look and Say' permitted more activity by the pupil, it required yet more expertise on the part of those who compiled and applied the teaching materials. Laurie had no intention of putting his trade out of business. He advised that, 'the technical difficulties of written speech must be met and overcome by lessons, arranged on a graduated and uniformly progressive plan, which need not be the less systematic because it discounts the minute classification of orthographic method'.[50] It was all the more important that the right words were selected for the young reader to encounter, and that a trained

48 Markham (1738) p. viii.

49 Maynes (1985) pp. 62, 72.

50 Laurie (1862) Preface.

adult was on hand to control the progression of learning. The implementation of the new method coincided with the final attack on the realm of the un-inspected school and its un-certificated proprietor, whose work continued to be stigmatised by the absence of system.[51]

In the social history of the classroom, the construction of the trained expert was and remained critical to the development of the official pedagogy of literacy. As reading performance became a central unit of exchange between the school and the state and between the teacher and the parents, so the capacity to apply a technology of instruction and to calibrate its progress gained added significance. In this sense, any method of teaching reading was strange. Whether syllabic, phonic or whole-word, whether embodied in word-lists, object lessons or flash-cards, it implied a subordination not just of the pupil to the organisation of the lesson and the space of the room, but of the child's sense of purpose to that of the expert teacher.

The vigorous contemporary debate about reading standards and systems of instruction can be divided into two camps. There are those who are still conducting the disputes about appropriate techniques which have been raging since at least the seventeenth century, and those who no longer attach that much importance to method wars, whatever their outcome. The latter group would point to recent ethnographic studies which have established the immense variety of journeys which children take towards the variable destination of functional literacy.[52] And they would stress that the successful completion of those journeys is founded on the pupil's evolving sense of the point of the exercise. In the classroom, more time has to be spent listening to the child's account of what he or she is doing and why, and less to the expert's narrative of practice and purpose. For an effective process of learning to commence, the meaning of reading has to be defined by those who cannot read.

51 See, for instance, Kay-Shuttleworth's dismissal of their activities for this reason, in *Four Periods of Public Education* (London: np 1862) p. 104.

52 Meek (1992) pp. 226-32.

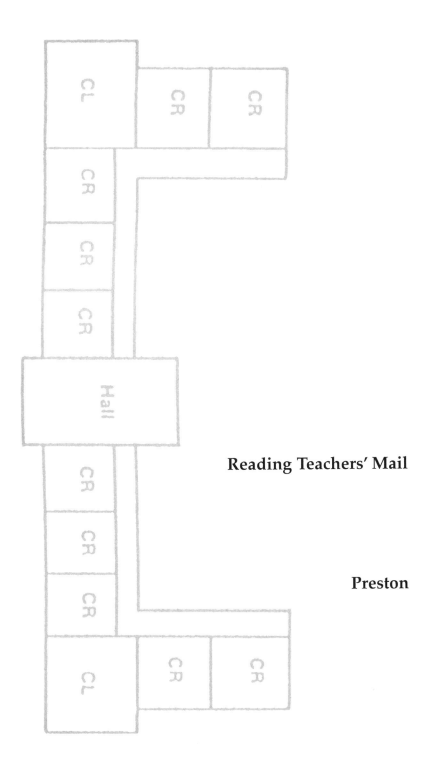

Reading Teachers' Mail

Preston

Reading Teachers' Mail: using women's correspondence to reconstruct the nineteenth-century classroom

Jo Anne Preston

Only recently have scholars attempted to recover the social dynamics of the nineteenth-century classroom through the use of primary documents. Barbara Finkelstein's ground-breaking book, *Governing the Young*, was the first to examine the classroom by consulting accounts of nineteenth-century teachers, students, foreign observers, school reformers, and public officials.[1] From this array of evidence, she reconstructs classroom behavior, student-teacher interaction, and classroom practice. Richard Altenbach, too, stresses the importance of teachers' experience and perspectives to understanding both nineteenth and twentieth-century schooling. In *The Teacher's Voice*, he argues for a 'detailed, historical analysis of the actual conditions of teaching as experienced by the teachers themselves'.[2] Recognizing the importance of teachers' experiences, Sari Biklen, in her book, *School Work*, extensively employs the writings of women teachers to illuminate the conditions of nineteenth-century American schoolrooms.[3]

Central to these and other recent studies of the classroom is the significance of primary sources in determining the constellation of social interactions in the classroom. Yet no assessment of the relative value of different sources has been done, and not all accounts of the classroom are the same. In the case of conflicting accounts, how and why should the researcher privilege one or another? In what follows, I make a case for the advantages of using female teachers' correspondence and the need to locate more of these valuable sources of data. By examining correspondence, I show how essential female teachers' accounts are to determining the social dynamics of the classroom. The accounts used are from mid-nineteenth-century New England, a period

1 B. Finkelstein, *Governing the Young: Teacher Behavior in Popular Primary Schools in Nineteenth-Century United States* (New York: Falmer Press, 1989).

2 R. Altenbaugh, ed., *The Teacher's Voice: A Social History of Teaching in Twentieth-Century America* (London: The Falmer Press, 1992) p. 1.

3 S. K. Biklen, *School Work: Gender and the Cultural Construction of Teaching* (New York: Teachers College Press, 1995).

of school reform that can also reveal how changes outside the classroom might have affected what occurred inside.

First I present two descriptions of nineteenth–century classroom — one by a public official and one by a teacher — and then compare the two in terms of their relative value in revealing the social dynamics of the classroom. In the second section I discuss method-ological issues such as validity and reliability in using correspondence as evidence. In the third and final section, I demonstrate how our knowledge of the nineteenth-century classroom is advanced by using female teachers' correspondence.

A comparison of two accounts of the nineteenth-century classroom

In its 1856 report, the Marshfield, Massachusetts, school committee gave the following account of examination day in the local school:

> On examination day, a certain pupil was making a disturbance, which attracted the attention of the teacher, she beckoned him to her side and administered a reproof that carried with it a most salutary effect. He came to her side, and she spoke no words of censure, but gently smoothed his hair while she continued to hear the recitation of the class before her. The attention of the other pupils was not withdrawn from their books, as is often the case when corporal punishment is administered — no inter-ruption of the exercise was occasioned, and everything went on as before... the teacher asked the little boy, if he could take his seat and be a good boy... The kind spirit manifested in this gentle reproof was felt by the offender, and was more efficacious than a severe chastisement would have been.[4]

4 *Marshfield Annual School Report for 1856,* Marshfield, Massachusetts, 1856, p.11.

Also writing in the 1850s, Lynn, Massachusetts school teacher Mary Mudge gave a different depiction of examination day in her classroom:

> Today is my examination day. Oh Dear! How I hope & fear this morning. Several scholars present who were absent yesterday, but not all in. A. B. Stone one of my smartest boys is sick but I will try to do my best... I heard the arithmetic class 'round once. They did well. Hope they will do as well this P.M. Half past I brought Mr. Richards and a number of ladies into the classroom. We commenced by singing Siloam and then the 4th classes in reading read 'Dialogue on Attention' 'Thoughts on Death' 'The Wintry Night' and a part of 'Love of Order', defined and spelt well. 1st class read 'Pennsylvania Truly' 'Shepherd and Philosopher Mercy.' Did not speak well enough in defining but did much credit in reading. They sang 'Swear Not' then the 3rd and 4th in Geography recited. Mr. Richardson questioned them. Mistakenly the Arithmetic class recited after the reading. The 4th class had from the 70 pages they picked questions for them and they did well. And then the 3rd Class did the same. They had ninety pages. 2nd class did well except Division of mixed numbers. Did questions of mixed numbers on page 121 and did well. Sang 'Better Land.' Then 'Geography & History.' Classes in Geography then 2nd class in History.... then we sang 'Lord dismiss us' and then the Company left. They seemed well satisfied. There were 52 scholars there... there were about 75 visitors... I had a feeling as though a load had rolled off my shoulders.[5]

5 Mary Mudge Diary, 7 February 1854, Schlesinger Library, Cambridge, Massachusetts, U.S.A.

Despite differences in locale and size of school, one can easily conclude that the teacher's description offers a better historical account of examination day in a mid-nineteenth century New England school than traditional studies of nineteenth-century schooling which rely on school officials' published reports. The writings of those not part of the educational leadership, namely the female teachers, provide a superior source of evidence for the reconstruction of the nineteenth-century classroom.

Nineteenth-century school officials provide overly sentimentalized descriptions of classroom dynamics stemming from their allegiance to the school reform movement. For instance, the Marshfield school committee included the preceding description in a report promoting the increased hiring of female teachers.[6] Its appearance in an essay designed to persuade local citizens of the superior disciplinary methods of female teachers, collectively referred to as 'moral suasion', challenges its claim to objectivity. The school committeemen's views of women teachers, in turn, were influenced by nineteenth-century school reformers who had launched an extensive propaganda campaign extolling the virtues of female teachers. Moreover, female teachers' depictions of classroom interactions contradict this sentimental account. In their correspondence, ninety-two female teachers wrote of resorting to the same method of controlling the classroom used by male teachers - physical coercion.[7]

Female teachers' writings also provide fuller and richer descriptions of the classroom. The greater detail in Mary Mudge's personal narrative — the reporting of the components of the exam, the performance of the students, the number and role of the participants, and the ordering of events — furnishes more evidence concerning examination day in schooling than does the imprecise rendering of the same activity by the Marshfield school officials. From the teacher's account, scholars can begin to reconstruct the academic program of common schools and their pedagogy. The published school

6 *Marshfield, Annual School Report for 1856,* Marshfield Massachusetts.

7 J. A. Preston, 'Domestic ideology, school reformers and female teachers: School teaching becomes women's work in nineteenth-century New England', *The New England Quarterly,* LXII (December 1993).

reports are replete with essays on how and what should be taught, but only reports from the classroom will inform us of what was actually taught and how it was taught.

Female teachers' personal writings also provide a more complex picture of the relationships among those who occupy the classroom. Mary Mudge, for example, in the preceding account revealed her fear of her supervisors' evaluation of her teaching and her dependence on her students' performance. In subsequent writings, she expressed her annoyance at the frequency of the school officials' impromptu exams. On January 5th of the same year, she wrote, 'Dr. Callaupe and Mr. Ambler into the school this P.M... heard the 1st class... asked many questions not in their lesson. Harriet Brown got confused and could not spell Alcohol.' In regard to her relations with her students, Mary Mudge made it amply clear that she did not employ moral suasion to keep order, contrary to the Marshfield school committee report. On June nineteenth she wrote that she 'went to school this morning determined to stop the noise with the lips, have punished several, had quite a quiet school'.[8]

8 Mary Mudge Diary, 5 January, 20 April 1854, Schlesinger Library, Boston.

Female teachers' more graphic and elaborate reporting pertains to their third advantage over school officials accounts as a source of data on nineteenth-century schooling: these women were full-time adult participant-observers of the classroom and one could argue that they were in the best position to record what transpired. Although not trained as social scientists, they convey such rich and specific descriptions of their experiences in school that social scientists can make extensive use of them. And unlike the school officials, they write not for public consumption but rather for their private communication and record-keeping. They write from the perspective of ordinary people, as workers, whose livelihood depends on their accurate assessment of their situation. Their candor allows for a more unbiased reporting of the emotional atmosphere, social and interpersonal relationships, and effects of types of disciplines than that of school committees and other school administrators.

The advantages of using women's personal writings suggest that researchers should look beyond school administrators' published records and other forms of evidence when seeking evidence on nineteenth-century schooling. Privileging the perceptions of those whose observations of the classroom are limited and whose political stake in advancing school reform, with its emphasis on greater centralization of power, is all too apparent, and leads to a portrayal of the classroom as consistent with school reformers' wishful thinking, a result not helpful to a faithful reconstruction of nineteenth-century educational history — except to better understand the mind of school reformers.

Instead, historians of education should make a more concerted effort to locate and consult female teachers' correspondence. The personal writings of non-elite people, especially their correspondence, has gained popularity among historians with the advent of social history in the 1960s. The growing use of these documents demands a consideration of methodology. How can correspondence be used to answer important questions about history? What methods can be employed to select and analyze personal documents? And why use female teachers' letters? These questions require a closer examination of the use of such documents.

Methodological issues in using female teachers' correspondence as evidence

The use of letters and other personal documents as social science data is not a new proposal. In 1918, William Isaac Thomas and Florian Znanieski published *The Polish Peasant in Europe and America,* a sociological study of the correspondence of Polish emigrants. It was enthusiastically received and became 'a monumental work' in the profession for the next two decades.[9] Despite the success of *The Polish Peasant*, few social scientists embraced the use of personal documents of ordinary people until the recent interest in social history and historical sociology. Even in these new fields, scholars too often use these manuscripts to illustrate or supplement other forms of evidence rather than as the central focus of their research. Or, in their haste to find what they presume to be important, they neglect to systematically examine personal documents for crucial evidence. Such was the case of the diary of a Maine midwife, Martha Ballard. After enumerable other researchers dismissed it as unrevealing, Laurel Urlich discovered its importance to understanding the lives of colonial women and produced an award-winning book.[10] Recognizing the importance of personal documents, then, is just as critical as uncovering them.

In failing to understand the importance of personal documents, such as correspondence and diaries, scholars frequently criticize their high dross rate.[11] Obviously, the relationship between the content of the correspondence and the researchers' goals determines whether the writings are of value. The growing interest in teacher-student relations, female teachers' working conditions, and the execution of theories of pedagogy in the nineteenth century creates a need for different sources of historical evidence. Because detailed description of events in the classroom furnish the best and, in some cases, the only valid evidence for exploring these topics, the substance of female teachers' letters, once considered insignificant, become essential to these research endeavors.

Why stress *women's* correspondence? Social scientists should made a special effort to consult female teachers' correspondence and other private writings

9 W.I. Thomas and F. Znaniecki, *The Polish Peasant in Europe and America* (New York: Dover, 1958. Original editions published in 1918-20); K. Plummer, *Documents of Life: An Introduction to the Problems and Literature of the Humanistic Method* (London: George Allen & Unwin, 1983) p.40.

10 L. T. Ulrich, *The Life of Martha Ballard, Based on Her Diary* (New York: Vintage Books, 1991).

11 Plummer (1983) pp. 23-24.

for a variety of reasons, although the gender bias in preserving manuscripts might make them difficult to locate. First and most important, women comprised the vast majority of female teachers in New England by the mid-nineteenth century. Furthermore, teaching became an accepted female vocation, with male teachers viewed as the exception. Men who entered teaching in this period did so only on a temporary basis and felt little commitment to the profession, whereas women welcomed this new employment opportunity.[12] Second, as a consequence of their relatively recent entry into teaching, women made a concerted effort to record their perceptions of an experience not only new to them but to women as a group. The audience for their letters included an extensive network of women friends to whom they had formed intense life-long emotional attachments despite their geographic mobility.[13] Letter-writing furnished the only means of sharing the quality of their employment experiences with these friends once they had left home. In the typology used by Thomas and Znaniecki in *The Polish Peasant* these women's letters fall under the category of 'informing letters' — those that give 'a detailed narration of the life of the absent member.'[14] Thus the quantity and quality of personal correspondence emanating from female teachers gives researchers a third reason to concentrate on women's correspondence.

As social science data, female teachers' personal writings can be analyzed by using the methods of qualitative research. Employing the techniques of grounded theory proposed by Glaser and Strauss, researchers can apply the same coding conventions and analysis applied to interview transcripts.[15] After reading each letter, the investigator can make tentative hypotheses that are modified with further analysis. Clearly, a collection of female teachers' correspondence cannot be acquired through any random sampling procedure. A more appropriate approach, formulated by Daniel Bertaux, recommends

12 J. A. Preston, 'Feminization of an Occupation: Teaching Becomes Women's Work,' Ph.D. Dissertation, Brandeis University, 1982.

13 C. Smith-Rosenberg, "The Female World of Love and Ritual: Relations between Women in Nineteenth Century America," *Signs* 1 (1975) pp. 1-29.

14 Typology and quote of Thomas and Znaniecki presented in Plummer (1983) p. 21.

15 B. Glaser and A. Strauss, *The Discovery of Grounded Theory* (Chicago: Aldine Publishing Co., 1967).

a 'process of saturation of knowledge'.[16] As each case substantiates the findings of the one before it, certain social processes become identified. Once confirmed, the social scientist can stop collecting additional data.

What crucial questions in nineteenth-century educational history can female teachers' personal writings assist us in answering? Despite the claims of school reformers, little is known about teacher-student relations. Horace Mann, Henry Barnard and other school reformers discuss at length the 'natural affection' female teachers display toward their charges without describing how this attribute translates into actual classroom behavior.[17] Female teachers' letters and journals, on the other hand, consist of extensive descriptions of their day-to-day interactions with students. Moreover, teachers' accounts describe the social and physical characteristics of the students, allowing the researcher to explore what groups were served by public education in terms of class, race, sex, and ethnicity. Even less is known about the authority relations between female teachers and their supervisors — a critical element to understanding teachers' working conditions. Teachers discuss their relations with administrators and their emotional reactions to this supervision. In addition to descriptions of these conditions of their employment, the teachers disclose their various tasks in teaching giving invaluable data on nineteenth-century teaching methods — those that were actually used, not just prescribed. Vivid and concrete descriptions of the classroom also inform researchers of the special layout and physical conditions endured by nineteenth-century teachers.

The classroom as revealed in female teachers' correspondence

To reconstruct the characteristics of the nineteenth-century classroom, the following text analyzes the correspondence of ninety-eight female teachers who taught in New England public schools between 1820

16 D. Bertaux, "From the Life-History Approach to the Transformation of Sociological Practice," in D. Bertaux (ed.), *Biography and Society* (London: Sage, 1981) p. 37.

17 Preston (1993) pp. 537-42.

and 1880. Their strong motivations towards letter writing that would inform their friends and families of their employment experiences furthers our knowledge of the social dynamics within nineteenth-century schools. Accounts of teacher-student interactions comprise much of the correspondence. Female teachers eschewed 'moral suasion' and used corporal punishment as needed. Some references to punishment were as off-hand as Mary Mudge's 'determined to stop the noise with the lips, have punished several', whereas others elaborate on methods of punishment. Annie Lane, teaching in Greenland, New Hampshire, in 1856, refers to her 'wooden assistant' that she used 'for punishment'. Later she gave two students 'something of a shaking'. Dixville, Maine school teacher Chancel Norcross wrote her mother in 1855 that she 'pinched one boys' neck'. In 1870 Mary Aldridge wrote her friend that she had whipped a student in her Hinsdale, New Hampshire, school:

> At the end of the fourth week I provided myself with a weapon in case I should need it. A leather strap one yard long and two inches wide... I lighted on a fellow of fifteen summers... I gave him about twenty strokes with it doubled up as hard as I could put it on.[18]

In addition to these deliberate and conventional uses of corporal punishment, female teachers reported other forms of discipline. Adeline Reed, a teacher in a 1836 Roxbury, Vermont, school, wrote that she sometimes punished a child 'by putting a string around his neck attached to a nail behind him'.[19] Certainly none of these accounts supports the school reformers' claims of women's 'natural' desire to use moral suasion. More important, these female teachers' writings provide researchers with detailed and graphic descriptions of how teachers strove to maintain order in the classroom.

18 Mary Mudge Diary 20 April, Schlesinger Library; Annie Lane Diary, 2 June, College Library Archives, Mount Holyoke College; Chancel Norcross to Nancy Norcross, 13 May 1855, Cargill-Knight-Norcross Families Papers, Maine Historical Society; Mary Aldridge to Kate Foster 18 December 1870, Kate Foster Papers, private.

19 Adeline Reed to Ann Eliza Brainherd, 12 January 1836, Smith Family Papers, Special Collections, Manchester Historical Association.

The nature of affective relations between students and teachers also emerges from female teachers' letters. Instead of the school reformers' cliched, sentimentalized portrayal of student-teacher emotional relationships, female teachers reveal the complexity and variety of feelings that were exchanged between them and their students. Candia, New Hampshire, school teacher Susan Moore, for example, wrote the following to her friend Mary Bell on June 14, 1851:

> They tell me my scholars like me very much. One little boy told me he liked me very much but liked his mother best and another told me he liked me best of anyone and he was going to save all of his <u>kisses</u> for me... I told you I had but one dull scholar and that one I fairly hate. You might as well think of learning the ABCs to a dog as learn him to read or spell.[20]

20 Susan Moore to Mary W. Bell, 14 June 1851, Mary W. Bell Collection, Manchester Historical Association.

Female teachers often expressed some apprehension concerning students who are physically larger, particularly the 'big boys'. In the following passage, Agnes Walker, a Springfield, Vermont, teacher, assesses her 1864 class:

> Have had twenty-one different scholars which might be divided into three classes small large & big. The largest number being in the last class. I have four boys older than I am & as many as seven, that are about mangrown. But thus far they have been respectful, & I sincerely hope they continue to be - I have five large girls smart and pretty.[21]

21 Agnes Walker to Kate Foster, 21 December 1864, Kate Foster Collection, private.

Still others confessed to caring for their students and lamented the end of the term when their class dispersed.

Although many teachers wrote of their affection for their students and forecasted missing them after the school term had ended, a preponderance of evidence from their writings showed that they also grew impatient with their ill-prepared and often unmotivated students and recoiled at their physical appearance and personal hygiene. Because many teachers came from modest but respectable rural families, they were totally unprepared for such close association with the poor, who increasingly inhabited the growing cities and mill towns of New England. Mary Aldridge wrote her hometown friend in 1870 that her Hinsdale, New Hampshire, class was comprised of '34 of the most uncouth specimens'. Her following elaborate description of her students reveals the sources of her negative assessment:

> The girls do pretty well but the boys are tough ones smoke and thieve like pirates and are terribly profane. The biggest one drinks. The right foot of him is about an inch shorter than the other. The next one has belonged to a circus, and has had a cancer cut from under his lip which often times has caused his mouth to assume a [strange] curved appearance. The next one is nearsighted and squint-eyed. One has had a sunstroke which has caused an eternal grin to rest upon his face which is maimed by freckles about an inch in diameter. One has a wink over his left eye. One is deaf. Of the girls one is cross-eyed, one is near-sighted and one has a harelip which draws the muscles down on one side so that her eye is drawn with them. She has only half a palate poor thing. I am going to have a blind boy soon. He can see to get around but cannot study. He learns by having the others recite.[22]

22 Mary Aldridge to Kate Foster, 18 December, 1870, Kate Foster Collection, private.

Her report on the individual children who comprise her class makes more understandable her disparaging remarks. Hers, like the correspondence of other female teachers, shows that they did not naturally love or hate their students; their emotional responses emanated from their experiences with their charges and the social expectations that they brought with them.

Furthermore, female teachers' comprehensive descriptions of the members of their classes aid scholars in determining the social characteristics of students who attended nineteenth-century schools. Clearly, Mary Aldridge's Hindsdale students came from impoverished families who most likely worked in the Hinsdale factories. Researchers might also uncover the ethnic composition of classes, as teachers sometimes reported on the ethnicity of their pupils. For example, when the next year Mary Aldridge moved to Northampton, Massachusetts, she reported that her class, 'as poor as poverty and a thousand times as dirty as Felche's folks were', consisted of 'twenty scholars' and 'all are Irish but two; a German and a Yankee'.[23]

23 Mary Aldridge to Kate Foster, 17 September 1871, Kate Foster Collection, private.

Female teachers also wrote detailed and frequently agonizing accounts of interactions with supervisors — an important issue in nineteenth-century schooling that is all too often ignored. Their first and most crucial encounter with school committeemen occurred at their initial hiring, when they underwent an examination. From their writings, one can trace the evolution and formalization of these exams. Hannah Adams in 1831 took her examination at a hastily called meeting in her Sandown, New Hampshire, school. She wrote her sister:

> At four I closed the school. The rest not coming Mr. P. examined me. Before examining me he made many excuses saying he was not fit to examine, etc. etc. After he was done said Squire Hunt would examine me and write the certificate and if necessary he would sign

it. I showed him Mr. Porter's and requested he copy that and sign it. He did... Mr. Pillsbury owing to some misunderstanding, had just come... to examine me. He examined me and signed the certificate Mr. P. had written, though not without a smile at the chirography and punctuation.[24]

24 Hannah Adams to Mary Adams, 9 June 1831, Adams Family Papers, private.

In 1851, Candia, New Hampshire, teacher Susan Moore's examiner appeared better prepared. She wrote the following to her friend Mary Bell:

One of the examining committee has been in today to see my school... I dread it dreadfully but was set for doing it. First he made me read then parse two lines then he asked me two questions in Grammar — How many modes are there and what they were. Then he asked me a few questions in Arithmetic and Geography and gave me a certificate and four regulation papers.[25]

25 Susan Moore to Mary W. Bell, 14 June 1851, Mary W. Bell Collection, Manchester Historical Association.

When Chancel Norcross was examined in 1854, she attended a formal meeting at the superintendent's office, where the Dixfield school committeemen assembled to administer a set of questions to a group of newly hired teachers. She wrote:

School did not keep but half a day and said the teachers were requested to meet in his office at 4:00 o'clock in the afternoon. I could not think what it could be for, but soon I found out it was to examine us there... there a Mr. Richards, Mr. Sheel, Mr. Baker examined us... Some of the questions were What is the difference between a river and a creek, the difference between a girl and a boy, and another Why was the river on the eastern side of South America larger? Another. Imagine yourself in a canoe in a lake in the middle of the woods. What waters would you pass through to get to the ocean.[26]

26 Chancel Norcross Correspondence, 28 January 1854 Cargill-Knight-Norcross Family Papers 1807-1866, Maine Historical Society, Portland, Maine, U.S.A.

By mid-century many school committees began administering written exams. A female school teacher in Northampton, Massachusetts, reported that her 1868 exam 'was conducted by written answers to printed questions'.[27] With this increasing formalization, school committees asserted more power over the hiring of teachers.

27 Anon. Female Teacher's Diary, 17 September 1868, Connecticut Historical Society, Hartford, Connecticut.

Female teachers recognized the growing authority that supervisors assumed over their work as their more frequent complaints in their writings demonstrate. And their concern extended beyond the initial exam. While Susan Moore reported that she did 'dread it dreadfully', Mary Mudge expressed her consternation about the constant incursions into her classroom by school officials. In her 1854 Lynn school, supervisors used these observations to produce regular written evaluations of teachers, a practice that she acknowledged and resented.[28]

28 Susan Moore to Mary W. Bell, 14 June 1851, Mary W. Bell Collection, Manchester Historical Association, Mary Mudge Diary, Schlesinger Library.

Besides giving valuable information concerning the social relations in the classroom, female teachers' writings provide the only valid account of how pedagogical methods were deployed in nineteenth-century schools. Much was written by school reformers and even by local school officials regarding what subjects should be taught and what methods teacher should use. Only the teachers, however, possess the knowledge of what actually transpired in the classroom. Their personal accounts reveal the vast variety of subjects taught to students on several different levels. A Northampton schoolteacher describes how she devised a course of study for her district school class in 1868:

By Thursday and Friday, I got settled with a programe, which I endeavor to carry out. There are three classes in Spelling. One of these are from the Primer, which I hear when I can — The other two are heard regularly twice a day. Two classes in <u>Reading</u>. The <u>1st</u> I hear twice. The second but once. The Primers are heard at the beginning of the sessions. There are two classes at present in <u>Arith</u>. One recites the tables, etc. and the other performs examples in Reduction of United States money. Two also in <u>Geography</u>. One of these draws maps and are just commencing while the others are half way through the large Geog.[29]

29 Anon. Female Teacher's Diary, 27 September 1868, Conneticut Historical Society.

In addition to reading, spelling, arithmetic and geography, the primary school teacher also taught rhetoric, history, literature, biology, astronomy and singing. With this extensive array of subjects, (each taught at three or four levels within a single classroom), the women experienced difficulty covering all required lessons in a day. From her Lynn, Massachusetts, school, Mary Mudge complained on April 22, 1854 that 'I don't have half the time in school to learn them what I want'. Nor did they have much opportunity to explore a subject in depth to the disappointment of the more intellectually inclined teachers. Chelsea, Massachusetts, teacher Mary Louise Browning expressed her discontent in a letter to her brother in 1853. She wrote that 'a teacher of a Primary School is not improved by what she teaches: on the contrary, having the mind so occupied with the rudiments of knowledge drives from it what one may have learned of higher branches'.[30]

30 Mary Mudge Diary, 22 April 1854, Schlesinger Library; Mary Louise Browning to Charles Browning, 10 September 1853, Mary Louise Browning Collection, College Library Archives, Mount Holyoke College, South Hadley, Massachusetts.

Female teachers' duties extended beyond teaching. The numerous other tasks included sweeping floors, collecting fees, piling firewood, tending stoves, and taking attendance. Margaret Tait, teaching in Reading, Vermont, in 1865, reports that 'after recitations were all through, I sweep and dusted my school room'. Other teachers' letters, however, show that custodial work became taken over by others. Readfield school teacher Augusta Sewell gave evidence to this trend when she wrote the following in 1865: 'One of the boys takes care of the house, and thus pays his tuition. This is as it should be, it is very unpleasant to ask Misses who are nicely dressed to stay and sweep a dirty, dusty schoolhouse, and I could not do it'. On the other hand, the task of recording the daily attendance of every student increasingly took up more of teachers' time and effort. Teachers were not only required to take attendance but to enforce regular attendance. When, in 1854, Mary Mudge found out that 'David Gardner staid from school Saturday" she gave him "a severe punishment'. Anne Stoddard, while teaching in a North Ridge, Vermont, school in 1865, was unable to teach because of a severe snow storm. She wrote, in jest, 'Did not get up early enough to go to school in Storm so I had to have a tardy mark'.[31] Her comment acknowledges that teachers recognized that their attendance also became more rigidly enforced. Such accounts contribute much valuable data on the nature of teachers' work in the nineteenth century.

31 Margaret Tait Diary, 13 October 1865, Vermont Historical Society, Montpelier, Vermont; Augusta Sewell to Abby Sewell, 9 September 1865, Sewell Family Collection, Schlesinger Library; Mary Mudge Diary, 19 June 1854, Schlesinger Library; Anne Stoddard Diary, 5 November 1866, Schlesinger Library.

Conclusions

Consulting female teachers' correspondence and other personal writings such as diaries and journals allows for scholars of nineteenth-century schooling to reconstruct important social dynamics and practices in the classroom that in the history of education has traditionally been undervalued. Using the first-hand observations of female teachers, researchers can better determine the consequences of nineteenth-century school reform: the changes in relations between teachers and students, the transformations in authority relations between school officials, and the deployment of new curricula. How did the radical new prescriptions for schooling affect the classroom? The best source, I have argued, are the personal writings, penned at the time of observation, of female teachers.

School officials, of course, make some contribution to the historical record. They, however, have two disadvantages as recorders of the nineteenth-century classroom. First, most had immersed themselves in the politics of school reform, some for its implementation and others against it, to the extent that it biased their perceptions as shown in the beginning of this chapter. Second, school officials spent little time in the classroom, a serious disadvantage for an observer. Clearly, female teachers' perceptions had some bias but never to the degree of those engaged in political battle. Teachers' most important advantage, however, comes from their perspective in the classroom and their propensity to write about their experiences.

Given the importance of these documents, scholars should seek them out in archives. Nineteenth-century family collections frequently contain the letters of daughters who left home to teach. With the renewed interest in women's history, especially working women's history, university archivists actively sought female teachers' manuscript writings. The additional effort used to consult these documents will immeasurably aid in determining the social context of nineteenth-century schooling. And the reconstruction of the nineteenth-century classroom can best be done by relying on women's own words.

Staff R CL CR CR CR

CR

B.CL

CR

lav

Courtyard

CR

RR

CR

HM

CR

Sec

Hall

CR

CR

HM

Courtyard

CR

G.CL

lav

CR

Staff R CL CR CR CR

Carrying the Torch

Chirhart

Carrying the Torch: African-American and white female teachers and professional culture in the Georgia Upcountry, 1920-1950

Ann Short Chirhart

Eudora Welty's *Losing Battles* portrays a family reunion in Mississippi during the 1930s. Members of the Vaughn-Beecham-Renfro families recall the ways in which their teacher, Miss Julia Mortimer, shaped their lives and values. 'You'd never forget the name of Miss Julia Mortimer,' says Aunt Beck. 'Or ever hope Miss Julia Mortimer would forget yours.' 'She had designs on everybody', says Uncle Percy. 'She put an end to good fishing.'[1] As the afternoon wanes, family members continue to evoke Mortimer's designs as interventionist and instructive, for Mortimer's teachings included not only academic fundamentals but morals and cultural values—the 'designs' to which Uncle Percy refers. And because her teaching style frequently undermined traditional rural values by urging students to remain in school and learn a trade or profession rather than continue to grow cotton and remain in the local community, Mortimer's former students recast her identity as a formidable, often frightening, and yet unquestionably significant person in their lives.

Welty's portrait of Miss Julia Mortimer captures the complex and elusive ways in which teachers affect a culture and community. For approximately half the year, children's days are guided, managed, and directed by educators, most of whom are women. In some instances, notably in rural schoolhouses, teachers taught generations of families. Mortimer, like other fictional teachers, remained at the same one-room school for decades, and her labor carved a swath through the community by reshaping notions of leisure, work, family, and productivity. Little wonder that teachers became such dominant figures in family tales, individual remembrances, and national culture.

1 Eudora Welty, *Losing Battles* (New York: Vintage Books, 1970) pp. 226-27.

2 Beulah Rucker Oliver, *The Rugged Pathway* (Np,1953) p. 3.

3 For southern women and the metaphor of light, see for example S. Shaw, *What a Woman Ought to Be and to Do: Black Professional Women Workers in the Jim Crow Era*. (Chicago: University of Chicago Press,1996) V. R. Littlefield, 'Moving Quietly but Forceably: Annie W. Holland and Education in North Carolina, 1911-1934,' unpublished paper in author's possession. Many Georgia normal and industrial schools called their campus newspapers *The Light* or *The Torch*. The Georgia chapter of the Women's Christian Temperance Union referred to the torch of light in *The Christian Index*, the Georgia Baptist newspaper. See *The Christian Index*, February 12, 1925, vol. 105, no. 7, p. 17.

4 For the meaning of racial uplift, see L. R. Harlan, *Booker T. Washington: The Wizard of Tuskegee, 1901-1915* (New York: Oxford University Press, 1983); D. L. Lewis, *W. E. B. DuBois: A Biography of a Race, 1868-1919* (New York: Holt, 1993); W. E. Montgomery, *Under Their Own Vine and Fig Tree: The African-American Church in the South 1865-1900* (Baton Rouge: Louisiana State University Press, 1993).

Like Miss Julia Mortimer, southern African-American and white women carried complex motivations and beliefs from their rural households to teacher training to their classrooms, beliefs that drew students into the webs of education and wage labor. As Beulah Rucker, an African-American teacher who founded an industrial school for blacks in Gainesville, Georgia wrote, 'I have sacrificed both night and day to light a torch of instruction for my race'.[2] Rucker's metaphor of light, one that black and white teachers mention repeatedly in their personal narratives, church meetings, and teacher training institutes, functions in three ways in the South. In its most fundamental meaning, light infuses the meaning of education with evangelical Protestantism—witnessing for the promise of Christ's redemption for sinners. As Baptists and Methodists, teachers believed that their duty to God encompassed service to him. Part of their evangelical duties included individual conversion and spreading the gospel to others.[3]

At another level, carrying the torch of light consisted of uplifting both races and recreating the wage labor and cultural values for black and white southerners. In cultural sites like schools, churches, households, and communities, black and white women resisted modernization's push toward atomization and social dissolution—the prioritization of bourgeois individualism that de-emphasized interdependent household and church links.[4] Teachers concomitantly embraced aspects of modernity that rejected the social and economic relations of an agricultural society that relied on unstable crop prices, uncertain living standards, and often unbearable poverty. To women like Beulah Rucker, wage labor was far more reliable than working someone else's land, usually a white family's, because it offered a dependable wage and the potential of self-help.

Finally, the torch of light meant acquiring an education. From the days of Reconstruction, African-

Americans insisted that freedom included literacy as well as property ownership and voting rights. Across the late nineteenth century South, African-American churches and schools appeared, often funded by northern philanthropy and always supported by the local black community. By the turn of the century, many Georgia white families and educational reformers agreed that children required new skills and knowledge for establishing industries and enhancing cotton production. In truth, some reformers' motivations derived from concern about African-American schools' growth compared with the paucity of rural white schools. Class and racial motives nonetheless served to build and improve a white public education system by 1910.[5]

Taken together, southern black and white teachers reconstructed their rural household educational duties into the public domain from cultural and economic patterns as well as personal goals. Unlike northern black and white women, southern women, because of the permeable walls of their rural households, experienced few of the sharp distinctions between private and public domains. As Welty's portrait of Miss Julia Mortimer suggests, southern women, black and white, redefined professional autonomy by linking their vocation with their communities that included churches, households, neighborhoods, class, and race. In this respect, communities describe interlocking human groups as well as discursive communities—the prisms and concepts on which teachers drew and through which they learned to see themselves as professional women.

Families, churches, and settlement residents shared an essential role in ensuring the continuity of cultural values as well as contributing to various changes. By 1900 Upcountry culture had regrouped and realigned social, economic, and political life.[6] Now governed by the agricultural market and cotton production,

5 For African American educational history in the South, see J. D. Anderson, *The Education of Blacks in the South, 1860-1935* (Chapel Hill: University of North Carolina Press, 1988); R. E. Butchart, *Northern Schools, Southern Blacks, and Reconstruction: Freedmen's Education, 1862-1875* (Westport: Greenwood Press, 1980); J. Jones, *Soldiers of Light and Love: Northern Teachers and Georgia Blacks, 1865-1873* (Chapel Hill: UNC Press, 1980). For studies on southern states, see J. L. Leloudis, *Schooling the New South: Pedagogy, Self, and Society in North Carolina, 1880-1920* (Chapel Hill: UNC Press, 1996); W. A. Link, *A Hard Country and a Lonely Place: Schooling, Society, and Reform in Rural Virginia, 1870-1920* (Chapel Hill: UNC Press, 1986); L. Harlan, *Separate and Unequal: Southern School Campaigns and Racism in the Southern Seaboard States, 1901-1915* (New York: Atheneum Press, 1968); A. S. Chirhart, 'Torches of Light: African-American and White Female Teachers in the Georgia Upcountry, 1910-1950,' Ph.D.Diss. Emory University, 1997.

6 C. V. Woodward, *Origins of the New South; 1877-1913 ,* (Baton Rouge: Louisiana State Univ Press, 1951) S. Hahn, *The Roots of Southern Populism: Yeoman*

*Farmers and the
Transformation of the
Georgia Upcountry,
1850-1890* (NY: Oxford
University Press, 1983);
N.V. Bartley, *The
Creation of Modern
Georgia* (Athens:
University of Georgia
Press, 1990).

7 Anderson (1988),
Chirhart (1997),
Leloudis, (1996)
Littlefield, (nd) G. E.
Gilmore, *Gender and
Jim Crow: Women and
the Politics of White
Supremacy in North
Carolina, 1896-1920*
(Chapel Hill: UNC
Press, 1996); Shaw,
(1996).
For the impact of the
national market on
women's rural labor,
see E. Fox-Genovese,
'Women and
Agriculture in the
Nineteenth Century,' in
*Agriculture and National
Development: Views on
the Nineteenth Century,*
ed. by L. Ferleger
(Ames: Iowa State
University Press, 1990)
pp. 267-302.

8 Teacher certification
in Georgia required a
county or state exam
until 1948. In 1948, the
state passed legislation
mandating a bachelor's
degree for certification.

9 For the
historiography on
separate spheres, see
L. K. Kerber, 'Separate
Spheres, Female
Worlds, Woman's
Place: the Rhetoric of
Women's History,'
*Journal of American
History* 75 (June 1988)
pp. 9-39. Among the
many works on
southern women, see

smaller, self-sufficient farms gave way to larger farms that relied on commercial markets for crop sales and some consumer items such as cloth, white flour, and seed. Upcountry households, churches, and other communities developed the language through which women defined themselves, but the congruence among these communities in the antebellum years began to diverge, occasionally straining and frequently pulling gender constructions to adapt to the national modern market. Rural education, for example, rapidly shifted from a woman's household duty to a state-operated system that relied on women's wage labor and partially replicated the North's established public school system. While few families could spare sons from agricultural tasks like plowing, black and white women's rural chores gradually decreased as fabrics, running water, and canned goods became accessible, even though most women continued to pick cotton and raise a garden.

At the same time, educational opportunities for many rural women increased as industrial and agricultural schools, normal schools, and high schools offered teacher certification.[7] The early decades of the twentieth century promised women respectable wage labor as teachers as Georgia's educational system ballooned. Created by and for Georgia teachers, teaching assumed characteristics of a craft and vocation. As women added to their traditional household education duties by attending normal or high schools, agricultural and industrial schools, or colleges, they positioned themselves above most community residents.[8] And by circumscribing this academic authority with their conversion experience and knowledge of their salvation, black and white teachers understood teaching to be a profession to which they had been selectively called and divinely instructed to fulfill.[9]

Yet because upcountry teachers linked their professional labor with renegotiated values and respective communities, their work has remained inexplicable to American historians. Relying on local board of education minutes or state education records veils the work that teachers did, because few teachers kept diaries, and Georgia superintendents and reformers expressed their own opinions rather than those of teachers'. Unless historians rely on the dubious proposition that teachers simply did what they were told, what women taught and why they taught must be discovered from other sources.

E. Fox-Genovese, *Within the Plantation Household: Black and White Women of the Old South* (Chapel Hill: UNC Press, 1988).

To analyze how African-American and white women reappropriated cultural beliefs and became agents of change and continuity in their classrooms, this study relies on personal interviews with former teachers. Then, by contextualizing these interviews within Georgia Upcountry history, teachers' stories and practices are refracted and retraced into the past. While individual memories may be shaped by nostalgia or class and race beliefs, the combination of personal remembrances with state and national archives and northern philanthropic records reveals a richer portrait of culture.[10] Former teachers' narratives articulate themes of evangelical Protestantism, caretaking, work habits, family ties, and academic fundamentals. Agents of modernity and tradition, early twentieth century southern teachers promoted and contradicted their official role as academic instructors by sifting through cultural values and reinterpreting them as their rural world became part of the American industrial economy.

10 On the problems of using personal narratives, see D.Thelan (ed.) *Memory and American History* (Bloomington: Indiana University Press, 1989); Shaw (1996); E. Hobsbawm and T. Ranger (eds.) *The Invention of Tradition* (Cambridge: University Press, 1984); E. Fox-Genovese, 'My Statue, My Self: Autobiographical Writings of Afro-American Women,' in *The Private Self: Theory and Practice of Women's Autobiographical Writings*, ed. S. Benstock (Chapel Hill: UNC Press, 1988). Among the best examples of personal narratives in American History are J. D. Hall, *et al., Like a Family; The Making of a Southern Cotton Mill World* (Chapel Hill: UNC Press, 1987).

By the 1940s, upcountry women, while clinging to traditional rural beliefs in evangelical Protestantism, hard work, and self-sufficiency, elaborated new cultural views on female autonomy by claiming a specific cultural and professional realm in their classroom. As Leona Clark Williams asserted, 'You don't become a teacher to get rich. You do it for the children. Teachers find out your problems and help solve them. It's not about reading writing and

11 Leona Clark Williams, tape recorded interview by author, Buford, Georgia, June 13, 1991.

arithmetic all the time'.[11] As they borrowed from traditional values, they negotiated new cultural views on female autonomy. In a congruence of mothering and teaching, community and household needs, African-American and white women teachers merged racial and class solidarity and autonomy in their female identities, presenting a distinct grasp of what it meant to be a professional woman in the early twentieth century.

Future African-American teachers came from rural families who owned approximately fifty acres of cleared land or from families in towns who worked day labor jobs or taught school. Household production relied on children's labor from sun-up to sundown, the endless tasks of caring for crops and farm animals, chopping wood, sewing, and housekeeping. In most families, mothers earned wages, predominantly as teachers, to supplement their families' income. Part of each family's task was to teach appropriate work habits and values. Daughters who eventually became teachers recall their families' rules regarding proper behavior. 'Mama', states Dorothy Oliver Rucker, 'only spanked one time a week. That was on Tuesday. And I was in every whipping line. Because when she'd whip you, she always said, "I'm whipping you because I love you, and I don't want somebody else to have to do it". She'd get you for rocking the boat and doing things that were undesirable'.[12] To Beulah Rucker, 'rocking the boat' ranged from behaviors such as drinking alcohol and gambling to dancing, talking back to adults, or swearing. Most daughters claim that their upbringing followed similar rules. Laura Mosely Whelchel remembers her parents enforcing strict obedience to their rules, which included respect for adults, property and one another.[13] Rosa Penson Anderson recalls,

12 Dorothy Oliver Rucker and Carrie Oliver Bailey, tape recorded interview by author, Gainesville, Georgia, May 19, 1993; Dr. Nancy Stephens, Dorothy Oliver Rucker, and Carrie Oliver Bailey, tape recorded interview by author, Gainesville, Georgia, June 10, 1993.

13 Laura Mosely Whelchel, tape recorded interview by author, Gainesville, Georgia, June 16, 1993.

We did not do any cursing; we did not talk like that. And my mother, she didn't allow us to talk about other people either because she said God made everything. You didn't talk back to your parents. [My mother] would get after you about that. We got spankings.[14]

14 Rosa Penson Anderson, tape recorded interview by author, Fayetteville, Georgia, March 24, 1992.

Most African-American household rules enforced settlement and evangelical Protestant values concerning how neighbors and parents should be treated and how dignified people acted. Those who were respected shunned foul language, alcohol, and gambling. They listened to adults quietly and avoided arguing with them. Yet the rules carried additional meanings for black youths. Living in Upcountry towns and settlements where a misplaced comment or a misinterpreted glance could cost a black individual her livelihood or even his life—proper behaviors to whites and blacks had to be inculcated at an early age. 'Rocking the boat' to Beulah Rucker and other upcountry blacks meant how blacks acted toward local whites in addition to one another. The survival of the black settlement was at stake. 'We used to go down the road everyday', recalls Dorothy Oliver Rucker about life in Gainesville from the 1920s to the 1940s, 'We'd get out to sell those rugs we used to make. We were trained to go around to the back. And sometimes an old dog would jump out. They'd stick the dogs on you'.[15]

15 Stephens, Rucker, and Bailey, tape recorded interview by author, June 10, 1993.

Born to former slaves and raised in rural families, rural teachers like Beulah Rucker knew the consequences of alcohol or gambling. Each nickel often meant the difference between survival and entry into the black middle class. An extra twenty-five cents allowed Dorothy Oliver Rucker to take piano lessons for one year, permitted Annie Ruth Moseley Martin to attend Beulah Rucker's school, or bought pencils for Rucker's students. Rucker even mentions having paid a bill in postage stamps.[16]

16 Rucker (1953) p. 10.

White former teachers came from rural families who in early decades of the twentieth century owned at least fifty acres of cleared farm land or from urban families who were part of the emerging middle class professions such as law, insurance, and small businesses. Ruth Smith Waters, Leona Clark Williams, and Jimmie Kate Sams Cole, for example, came from rural landowning families. Waters' father, Charlie Eugene Smith, bought sixty-three acres of land at Chestnut Mountain in Hall County and raised cotton on this land in addition to his job as bookkeeper and postmaster at the Thompson Mill cotton gin and grist mill in Jackson County.[17] Leona Clark Williams' family worked one hundred acres of land that had been in the Clark family for generations at the head of Ellijay Creek in North Carolina. Relying on family labor, the Clarks were self-sufficient and lacked a cash crop.[18] While each family differed in its ability to hire outside labor and the size of its holdings, they owned land, and they depended on mothers for childcare, sewing, cooking, and housekeeping.

Like African-American future teachers, each white former teacher recalled specific rules that their parents rigidly enforced. As the oldest child, one of Leona Clark Williams' duties was to prepare some of her ten siblings for school. One of her brothers, 'the twistiest little old thing I ever saw', refused to stand still while she checked behind his ears for dirt. At school Williams had heard other children command one another to do certain tasks by saying, 'Damn it! Do so and so'! Exasperated with her brother's refusal and pressed to get to school on time, Williams said,

> Damn it, Andrew, stand still till I get your neck washed. Boy, I hadn't more than said that till my daddy came on me with a broom handle. He'd like to have beat me to death. We didn't use ugly words, no, not in our home... He said, "There's three things you don't do in my house. If you're a woman, you don't whore hop. If you're a man, you

[17] Ruth Smith Waters, tape recorded interview by author, Flowery Branch, Georgia, June 10, 1993 and December 7, 1993.

[18] Williams, tape-recorded interview by author, June 13, 1991; Leona Clark Williams, *We Remember* (np, 1976), pp. 5, 11.

don't come in drinking. You don't use ugly words". And we never did.[19]

19 Williams, tape-recorded interview by author, June 13, 1991.

In the Smith household, Nancy Smith did most of the disciplining. Ruth Smith Waters states that 'Mother would send us out to get good peach tree hickories, and we knew better than not to get a good one or we'd be sent back'.[20] To parents, teaching children values such as listening and respecting adults protected the structure of their settlements. Parental discipline also served as a means to order what farmers perceived as a harsh and often arbitrary world. Households relied on parents to enforce behaviors concerning household property. In a world in which personal possessions were costly and sometimes irreplaceable, theft could offset a family's economic status and affect the interdependence of a settlement.

20 Waters, tape-recorded interview by author, June 10, 1993.

No doubt some rules were established in black and white households because of the precarious nature of rural life. A flash flood, a drought or a hail storm often meant economic ruin. Farm accidents often maimed individuals. Disease and death portended even worse consequences for African-Americans than for whites. With medical care almost impossible for blacks to obtain in rural areas, tooth decay, broken bones, or illness often had to be cared for in households. In this respect, whipping a child out of love carried various meanings. Beulah Rucker sincerely meant this as a warning to students about what could happen to them if they did not obey her. More than following parent's or God's rules, obedience meant the difference between survival and imprisonment or even death. And to learn this lesson from Rucker was far preferable to learning it from a white man or woman.

In most respects, African-American and white household rules enforced Baptist and Methodist prescriptives concerning appropriate behavior to other settlement members and parents. God's laws framed the ways in which people lived their daily lives. Although each household enforced rules differently, some more severely than others, household members learned what were considered respectable behaviors in the early twentieth century Upcountry. Rules against dancing, playing cards, and drinking alcohol had less to do with Biblical imperatives than with moral beliefs of southern rural regions.

Upcountry respectability, increasingly assailed by the consumer culture of the Sears catalog, hair styles, and fashion, framed the ways in which future teachers redefined appropriate styles and behaviors. Waters mentions a time when a classmate at Chestnut Mountain School bobbed her hair. 'It was just scandalous to be bare-legged and have bobbed hair. She was talked about... no one would have anything to do with her'.[21] Such styles of the 1920s as bobbed hair, shorter dresses, or bare legs, designated the incursions of commercialism and modernity in addition to wanton displays of sexuality.[22] To rural Upcountry households, bobbed hair signaled the mannerisms of the New Woman with attendant loose morals of the city.[23] The 'flapper' of the 1920s denoted acquiescence to modern values of disintegrating families, fractured households, and the collapse of the evangelical church's authority.

The impact of consumer culture with its values of acquisitiveness and materialism was nonetheless limited by poor rural roads, lack of cash, and the poverty of cotton culture. Many Upcountry households continued to rely on women's trade with itinerant pedlars. Indeed, while the country store may have provided rural men with socialization, the pedlar represented nascent consumer culture to rural women, bringing modern commercial goods such as fabric, spices, kitchen wares, and medicines in exchange for eggs and butter. Rural women, black

21 Ruth Smith Waters, tape-recorded interview by author, Flowery Branch, Georgia, November 18, 1994.

22 Hall (1987); Jacquelyn Dowd Hall, 'Disorderly Women: gender and labor militancy in the Appalachian South' *Journal of American History* 73 (September 1986) pp. 354-83.

23 W. A. Link, *Paradox of Southern Progressivism; 1880-1930* (Chapel Hill: UNC Press, 1992); Woodward, (1951); E. L. Ayers, *The Promise of the New South: Life After Reconstruction* (New York: Oxford University Press, 1992).

and white, modeled behaviors of exchange and barter to their daughters by acquiring only what was necessary. Frequently, women's contributions to the household, butter or eggs, provided the extra cash needed for the family's survival or the children's education.

As the daughters grew older, wage labor opportunities opened for women, and one of the most respectable positions was teaching. If daughters remained in school through the tenth or eleventh grade, they could take the county teachers' exam and earn a salary. As the Georgia public education system expanded during the early decades of the twentieth century, black and white women's ambitions to leave agricultural work coincided with the state's call for teachers, a situation that manifested the push and pull between southern women's goals and the national market. And by the 1930s, these Upcountry women, while clinging to traditional rural beliefs in evangelical Protestantism, hard work, and self-sufficiency, elaborated cultural attitudes on female autonomy by claiming a specific cultural and professional realm in their classrooms. As black and white women borrowed from gendered household values of labor, religion, and self-sufficiency in their move to wage labor, the realms of classroom and household values often merged to create a perception of professional labor grounded in traditional rural values yet reemerging in cultural constructions of teaching.[24] While they rarely saw themselves as separate from their churches, households, or settlements, they nonetheless presented themselves as respectable, middle-class, educated women who knew, often better than parents, what their students required in the modern industrial world. Their goals, which included improvement and continuity of the family, church, and rural values, present an alternative perspective on autonomy and professionalism.

24 P. Bourdieu, *Distinction: A Social Critique of the Judgement of Taste* (Cambdige: Harvard University Press, 1984); R. Williams, *Marxism and Literature;* (New York: Oxford University Press, 1977); E. Fox-Genovese, *Feminism without Illusions: A Critique of Individualism* (Chapel Hill: UNC Press, 1991).

According to most African-American future teachers, either their mothers or other female teachers in their region provided models of teaching from which they borrowed and to which they added. Laura Mosely Whelchel and her sister Annie Mosely Martin initially attended an elementary school taught by their mother in their black settlement, as did Rosa Penson Anderson and Dorothy Oliver Rucker. Their observations on how to speak correctly, to walk, to correct children, and to teach served several purposes. On the one hand, it taught them to assume a mask—a way in which to present themselves to the world thereby demonstrating that blacks could don attributes that whites counted as evidence of decency and respect. On the other hand, by assuming these characteristics, blacks like Rucker were able to accomplish some of their goals of racial uplift within their communities. The basic problem was that when blacks assumed these masks, they failed significantly to alter the economic and political hierarchy that designated them as inferiors.

Beulah Rucker lacked the specific expertise that most northern women professionals acquired from colleges or universities. And as an African-American woman, she failed to achieve the sort of independent agency that other professionals enjoyed. Yet to her racial community, Rucker clearly embodied their professional ideal. As one who knew the world beyond the Gainesville area, who learned how to achieve what she wanted from whites, who was more educated than the majority of local blacks, and who could shrewdly define, communicate, and articulate a comprehension of what blacks could accomplish in the Jim Crow South, Rucker earned prominence in her region. To Upcountry blacks, she became the person on whom they relied for suggestions and advice on what they should do, how they should act, and what their goals should become.[25]

25 Shaw (1996).

Rucker challenged her students to be self-sufficient and work for the benefit of the race. By presenting a mask of her labor to whites, she enhanced her labors for her people, ultimately increasing the number of teachers, ministers, and wage laborers in her region. White female future teachers also drew on Upcountry cultural values to frame the ways in which they understood their positions as teachers and they, like black teachers, were motivated by constructions of respectability and self-sufficiency. They saw teaching as a way to earn respect in their region although they knew it lacked the prestige of law or medicine. At no time did any of these women consider working in the mills nor did they contemplate returning to the family farm. Raised to be self-sufficient and hard working, they viewed teaching as a means to support themselves until they married and had children.

During the 1920s and 1930s, school trustees and superintendents continued to require certain moral standards of the women they hired. Leona Clark Williams remembers one time when she went dancing with her Uncle Vic while she was teaching at Lula. 'He picked me up and carried me up to Demarest to the dance. There was a lady over there, and she said, 'They'll fire her if they know she went to a dance'. So I went and told Uncle Vic to carry me home'.[26] All women remember the guidelines that trustees expected of teachers. 'When you taught under the trustees, you knew your trustees and they knew you', states Waters,

26 Ibid.

> They inquired. They knew your background. They knew your grandpa and your grandma. They knew if you went to church, but they wouldn't tell you you had to go. They knew what your life was like. Only one time before I got married in 1935 did I know a teacher who was immoral and got pregnant. That was a quite a shock to us in the 1930s.[27]

27 Waters, tape recorded interview by author, June 28, 1991.

Local trustees such as those at Chestnut Mountain and Lula expected certain moral standards of their teachers, notably church attendance and proper attire. Until World War II, Upcountry white women, in contrast to black women, had to quit teaching when they married. Teachers were to embody the values of the respectable members of the community such as temperance, hard work, and evangelical Protestantism. When trustees hired women who attended local Baptist or Methodist churches, they knew they were hiring women who avoided playing cards or drinking alcohol, who had been raised to work long hours, and who had little tolerance for behavior perceived as lazy or foolish in the classroom.

These women also shared professional status with the national construction of the educated New Woman. At the same time, they intentionally avoided some aspects of the image such as modern dancing, listening to jazz, immodest attire, and contemporary scholarship on psychology, evolution, and economics. As Waters stated, the trustees already knew that their teachers attended church so there was little need to require them to do so. For example, when Williams dated her future husband, Bill Williams, she claimed that,

> we probably could have bought the state theater in Gainesville because we went there every night. Well, there wasn't anything else to do in 1936, so we went to the show and went to the show and went to the show.[28]

28 Williams, tape-recorded interview by author, June 13, 1991.

Clearly, other young adults participated in different activities in the 1930s. Waters knew a single teacher who became pregnant, and Williams had met students at college who drank alcohol and smoked cigarettes. Yet women who became teachers regarded such pastimes as outside the boundaries of respectable behavior. Even if they had never taught school or been expected to uphold community morals by school trustees, these women would have undoubtedly followed similar values.

Like African-American teachers, white teachers claim to have known what was needed to be a good teacher before they ever took teacher training courses or taught in the public schools. Leona Clark Williams learned throughout her education the difference between good and bad teachers, at least from her perspective. She praises her teacher at the mountain school who worked with her on her reading, and her college English teacher who taught her about double negatives and put her on the debating team. On the other hand, Williams' experiences at the Franklin high school taught her about bad teaching. 'My English teacher in high school was as mean as the devil', Williams recalls,

> She told us that if you said a word incorrectly when you came in the class, it was five points off your report card. I'd get my paper back and it would look like it had been bled all over with all of this red pencil. I was afraid to ask her what a double negative was, so I just barely got by in English.[29]

29 Williams, tape-recorded interview by author, June 25, 1991.

What Williams discerned from her own school experiences was the importance of treating children equitably and the need for teachers to be accessible to students.

Moreover, most white teachers, similar to African-American female teachers, had experience in handling children. Some women, as one of the oldest children in the family, had to take responsibility for their younger siblings. Williams states,

> I had to get them to school. That was a big job. But that way I learned to work with children. Then when I took teacher training

at Tennessee Wesleyan, I didn't have any
trouble making an 'A' on my training
because I'd already been trained. You learn
the different types of children, and you learn
them good.[30]

30 Williams, tape-
recorded interview by
author, June 25, 1991.

Women emphasized pedagogical fundamentals such
as reading, history, spelling, geography, arithmetic,
and evangelical Protestantism. Beginning each day
with a prayer and a Bible reading, African-American
and white teachers demanded that their students do
their best. Education, in contrast to the beliefs of
some community members, was as important as a
meal or church attendance. They insisted that every
day of their students' lives counted and could be
used for improvement. Cotton culture's reliance on
hard work and self-sufficiency translated into
structured daily learning in academic fundamentals.
Weaving education with cotton culture's values,
teachers' craft evolved into a web of tradition and
modern changes. All teachers agreed with Leona
Clark Williams who believed that teaching entailed
caring for children as well as educating them.

Yet what black and white teachers appropriated from
their culture clearly undermined many of the values
they sought to sustain. By claiming the prestige to
instruct children, they undermined evangelical
Protestantism and family authority—the sources of
education in the past. They embraced modern
educational reforms such as consolidation that drew
students into the web of education and away from
their local communities. Just as the national
consumer culture allowed many of them to teach, it
decreased cotton culture's emphasis on interdependence and self-sufficiency. As their students
became part of consumer society, they gradually
privileged materialism and individualism. The torch
that teachers carried illuminated the paths of
consumption and acquisition.

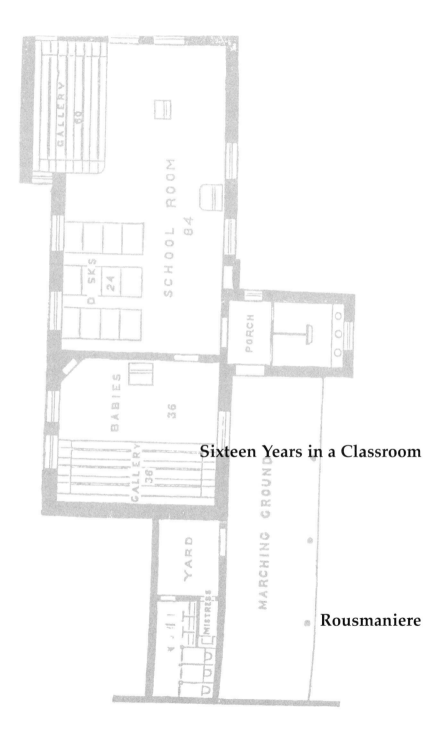

Sixteen Years in a Classroom

Rousmaniere

Sixteen Years in a Classroom

Kate Rousmaniere

I got a job teaching at the Hendricks School in the Town of Lake. That was the district of the Union Stockyards... Most of the children.. were those of English, Irish, and German parentage. They were, for the most part, alert, eager to learn; but the school itself was almost hopeless... I taught in the Hendricks School for twenty years.[1]

These sentences are almost the entirety of Margaret Haley's written account of her years as a classroom teacher in one school in late-nineteenth century Chicago. For most classroom teachers, these comments would be remarkable only in that they were recorded, published and survived long after the teachers left their classrooms. For Haley, however, the significance of these words is something altogether different, because after leaving the classroom, she became the leader of America's first and largest teacher union. Yet in all her later years as a teacher activist, she never chose to recount more than these few remarks about her own experience as a teacher.

Haley had more than enough opportunities to describe her experiences as a classroom teacher later in her life. A political organizer for Chicago teachers for almost forty years, Haley spoke about urban teaching and teachers on a daily basis. Furthermore, in what proved to be a futile attempt to publish her autobiography in her lifetime, Haley dictated her life story three different times.[2] At the height of her career as a labor leader, Haley gave hundreds of public speeches and interviews, wrote for her union newspaper, and was lauded for her life's work multiple times. But in none of those surviving manuscripts or transcripts did she offer any more insight into her years in her Chicago classroom,

1 R. Reid, ed., *Battleground* (Urbana: University of Illinois Press, 1982) p. 2

2 In the first three decades of the twentieth century, Margaret Haley led the Chicago Teachers' Federation to be the first teachers' labor union in American history. As leader of the predominantly female elementary teachers Federation, Haley fought for increased salaries, a stable pension plan and tenure laws, led investigations into teachers' working conditions and school funding, and negotiated an unprecedented affiliation between teachers and the industrial labor movement. Haley worked at the national level too, traversing the country to promote political activism among the nation's predominately female teaching force. For over thirty years, she was a dominant figure in American educational politics, challenging lawmakers, businessmen, and politicians to commit to improving the lives of teachers and students. The manuscripts for the three autobiographies are deposited at the Chicago Historical Society, with Haley's other professional papers. In 1982, Robert Reid published his edited version of her autobiography under her title, *Battleground*.

although she did reflect more on her earlier experiences teaching in rural schools, once confusing her experience in one of those schools with her work at Hendricks School. In addition, her minimal recollections are curiously contradictory: her assertion that she taught at Hendricks for twenty years cannot possibly be true as the school was built in 1884, when her official employment records with the school system began, and she left the school in 1900, having taken at least one leave of absence during those years.

For the biographer, Haley's avoidance of her teaching experience presents a greater problem than simply a sixteen year lacuna in her life story. The silence is especially frustrating because it is likely that Haley's political base as a union leader, her perception of urban teachers' needs, and her insights about how to organize Chicago's teachers developed in these years. At the very least, in those years at the Hendricks School, Haley learned both how to teach and how to be a teacher. But she left us with little understanding of the legacy of that experience. What might Margaret Haley have learned in those years about teachers and schools that later fueled her political work?

If Haley's own testimony is limited, the official records of the Chicago school board can be only somewhat more helpful. In Chicago, as in many American cities, school records are the official accounts of moneys spent in a school district and include reports on the construction and upkeep of school buildings and requisitions for supplies, repairs, and curriculum texts.[3] The records also document the staffing of public schools; salaries for teachers, administrators, and staff; teachers' names and home addresses; and broad statistical surveys of students in different districts. Other information can include the standard curriculum, official holidays, and the rules and regulations for school employees. By their very nature, these records epitomize the

3 The school records used for this paper include the *Biennial Report of the County Superintendent of Schools for Cook County* (1884-88); the *Annual Reports of the Chicago Board of Education* (1889 to 1896); *Proceedings of the Board of Education of the City of Chicago* (1890-1897); and *Rules and Regulations of the Board of Education,* Chicago (1896).

great gap between administrative record-keeping and people's actual lives. Chicago's school reports were intended to document a city school system over fiscal periods, and not the workings of each of the city's three hundred schools on a day to day basis. The sources are frozen in time and curiously unverifiable: they chronicle events that were intended to happen, but not how those events came about or how they were experienced by teachers or students. They offer no insight into work processes or social relations, no explanation of why certain supplies were needed, how certain facilities broke, how curriculum texts were used in classrooms, or who these teachers and students were and how they interacted.

Furthermore, these are written narratives only: while the board of education took formal photographs of some school buildings to illustrate their annual reports, the Hendricks School is not one of them, so that we have only spare architectural measurements to help us imagine what this school looked like to the thousand children and two dozen teachers who entered its doors for so many years. To make matters more challenging for the historian, while Haley taught in a single school building for sixteen years, the political districts around that building changed, making documentary sources for the school particularly difficult to track as it moved under the purview of different agencies.[4]

But if such static and one-dimensional sources can provide only an incomplete snapshot of a school and a teacher, can they still contribute elements for a panorama of images over sixteen years? Read as pieces of a sequence, these cool official narratives can offer surprising clues about the heart of a school as a living force. Supply and repair requisitions document the life span of a building, and suggest shapes, sounds, and images that provide dimension to a once flat narrative. Annual lists of names tell us something

4 The Town of Lake was a sprawling suburb south of Chicago. The Hendricks School was opened in that town in 1884. In 1889, Lake was annexed into the city of Chicago, adding thirty-three new school districts, over 30,000 pupils, and 700 teachers to the expanding city. The Hendricks School begins to be documented in the Chicago school records in 1890. H. B. Clark, *The Public Schools of Chicago: A Sociological Study* (Chicago: University of Chicago Press, 1897) p. 30.

about the changing character of the teachers' community. Moving outside the school to studies of the neighboring community, we can peer back inside the school windows and consider how life in the school was shaped by the noises, smells, and activity of the neighborhood around it. Haley's own fragementary recollections, pieces of her public biography, and other accounts of local and city school events can further flesh out the narrative.

Even our questions themselves can raise new dimensions and textures to our moving picture. What was not documented by the state and why not? What records were discarded as 'not important' and how did that lack of 'importance' affect teachers? Why did Haley herself leave some clues about her work and not others? Does her silence suggest a sense of failure or boredom as a teacher? Was the classroom experience finally not that important to Haley? Or was her silence a political tactic to chronicle her labor autobiography with the 'legitimate' political acts of a union leader, such as legal challenges, political negotiations, and economic deliberations? Or could her silence be simply explained by her own acknowledgment that she was not a terribly introspective person? With the sources once laid out as a kind of collage, with all their corruptions over time, can we still make some sense of what we see? Without 'torturing' those sources, can we make meaning from the way the surviving sources lie, and the partial story that they tell over time?

The Teacher and the Community

Margaret Haley began teaching in Chicago in September 1884. She was twenty-three years old, a relatively advanced age for a first year teacher, but the Hendricks School was not her first job. Since age sixteen, Haley had taught school in her home community in rural northern Illinois and in two small cities just outside of Chicago. As she recounted in her autobiography, by the time she came to Chicago she was already experienced with teaching in damp, under-heated schoolrooms, with student discipline problems, with scrambling to learn her lessons the night before she taught, and with working under an incompetent principal who had less than a high school education. Haley had also spent a few months studying at different teacher training institutions, most recently at the Cook County Normal School on the edge of Chicago, from which she convinced her parents and five younger siblings to move to the city with her.[5]

Haley's family was part of the upwardly mobile Irish-American working class, what became known as 'lace curtain Irish' to distinguish them from the destitute Irish famine immigrants who came to the United States some years after Haley's grandparents. Her father was a skilled craftsman and one-time owner of a stone quarry, and his children continued the upward class trajectory in Chicago civil service and commerce: the three Haley daughters became teachers, one son became a mailman, and the other two were skilled craftsmen. In the early 1880s, Michael Haley bought a house in Englewood in the Town of Lake, a suburb on the south side of Chicago which had been recently settled by middle class families escaping the increasingly congested city. The parents and six children lived in a roomy two-story wood frame house on a large lot, from which they watched the gradual settlement of the neighborhood, the construction of streetcar lines to the city, and in 1893 the famous Chicago World's Fair less than a mile from their home.[6]

From this comfortable setting, Margaret Haley went to work by taking a streetcar seventeen blocks north into an entirely different world: an urban neighborhood that one observer described as being so backward it seemed like a 'frontier'. The Hendricks School was a public grammar school housing grades 3 to 6, located on the edge of what

5 Haley in Reid (1982) pp. 3-29.

6 E. Skerrett, 'The Development of Catholic Identity among Irish Americans in Chicago, 1880-1920,' in T. J. Meagher, *From Paddy to Studs: Irish American Communities in the Turn of the Century Era, 1880-1920,* (New York: Greenwood Press, 1986), pp. 117-38 and E. Skerrett, 'The Irish in Chicago: The Catholic Dimension,' in E. Skerrett, E. R. Kantowicz, and S. M. Avella, ed., *Catholicism, Chicago Style* (Chicago: Loyola University Press, 1993), pp. 29-62; Reid (1992) pp. 22-29. A visual sense of Haley's neighborhood in Englewood is available by looking at city residential and commercial maps located in the Illinois Regional Archives Depository (IRAD).

7 J.R. Barrett, *Work and Community in the Jungle: Chicago's Packinghouse Workers, 1894-1922* (Urbana: University of Illinois Press, 1987) p. 19. The Hendricks school was located on the far east side of the Stockyard district, in a neighborhood that was often referred to as Canaryville. See G. E. Holt and D. Pacyga, *Chicago: A Historical Guide to the Neighborhoods* (Chicago: Chicago Historical Society, 1979) pp. 132-39.

8 H. E. Wilson, *Mary McDowell: Neighbor* (Chicago: University of Chicago Press, 1928) pp. 26-27.

9 D. L. Miller, *City of the Century: The Epic of Chicago and the Making of America* (New York: Simon and Schuster, 1996) pp. 218-24.

was known as Packingtown, the residential community of workers hired to slaughter cows and pigs and pack their meat in the infamous Chicago stockyards. This was the world of industrial poverty that Upton Sinclair wrote about in his 1906 muckraking novel *The Jungle*, a community in which in 1889 fifty-seven slaughtering houses and meat packing plants employed 20,000 workers, primarily first and second generation European immigrants.[7]

Contemporary observers described Packingtown as a dreary urban community of 'gray streets, gray houses, and smoke-laden air', marked by devastating squalor and the ubiquitous odors of the packing houses.[8] It was an expansive industrial neighborhood of factories, animal yards, slaughterhouses, grain elevators, iron mills, slag heaps and coal piles, bordered by huge clay holes that the city used for garbage dumps, vacant lots used to dry the hair and skin of slaughtered hogs and cattle and that attracted hoards of blue bottle flies, and the notorious Bubbly Creek, a noxious cesspool for the sewage of the packing houses. The entire area was criss-crossed by forty three train lines that rattled and roared through the neighborhood on street level, clogging inter-sections and terrorizing pedestrians. Through the turn of the century, only a few main streets in Packingtown were paved, and the sewage and city water system were so backward that stagnant water created 'a thick, green, leathery scum' that appeared so solid that sometimes small animals and children tried to walk on it and were sucked under and drowned.[9]

But according to contemporaries, the most distinctive aspect of Packingtown was not the sights but the smells of the neighborhood industry built on the slaughter and packing of animal flesh. The famous Chicago winds blew a variety of odors out of the stockyards— the choking smell of burned flesh, feathers and animal hair, the stench of sour garbage, and the reek of thousands of hogs and cows.[10] Haley herself described the Stockyards district as a 'sprawling, malodorous neighborhood'.[11]

The Hendricks School was located on a major commercial street that led directly into the Stockyards eight blocks west. It was close enough to the plants so that even the slightest western breeze would blow the infamous aromas into open school windows, and the unpaved 43rd Street was busy with commercial traffic, the almost continual construction of new buildings, tourists en route to view the infamous Stockyards, workers going to and from work or to the hundreds of saloons that surrounded the yards, and boys' urban street gangs. A few blocks away from the school was Chicago's largest and most popular gambling house, owned by the son of the notorious Mrs. O'Leary whose cow was blamed for starting the great Chicago Fire of 1871. Adding to the bustle from the street was the clatter of three major railway lines that passed within five blocks of the school, carrying passengers to and from Chicago or doomed animals to slaughter. Church bells clanged from the Methodist church two blocks west and from the 160-foot bell tower of St. Gabriel's Catholic church two blocks south. And in the distance, the noise of the Stockyards itself infiltrated the school windows: 'thousands of cattle bellowing... hogs squealing, and so many men roaring'.[12]

As the odors and noises from the street poured through the school windows, so, too, did the culture and politics of a working class community. Haley's first students at Hendricks were primarily German and Irish, the children of skilled butchers and factory workers with full time employment in the Stockyard. But even though she later remembered these children as 'alert and eager to learn', they were hardly privileged children.[13] Families in Packingtown were crowded into wood frame tenements, the men eking out lives of ten-hour work days in the packing

10 M. McDowell, 'Reminiscing on Stock Yards Area,' (Foreword to 'Beginnings Frontier Town— Back of Yards,' (Feb 10, 1914). McDowell Papers, Chicago Historical Society, Chicago.

11 Haley in Reid (1982) p. 24.

12 Holt and Pacyga, (1979) pp. 133-35. Quote from L. C. Wade, *Chicago's Pride: The Stockyards, Packingtown, and Environs in the Nineteenth Century.* (Urbana: University of Illinois Press, 1987) p. 183.

13 Haley in Reid (1982) p. 24.

houses, women taking on piecework and boarders in already cramped apartments, children leaving school early to find work. Tuberculosis, consumption, diphtheria, and other infectious diseases ravaged the people of Packingtown, and Upton Sinclair described how the notorious Chicago winters swept through the fragile frame houses with 'icy, death dealing fingers'.[14]

14 U. Sinclair quoted in Miller (1996) p. 219.

Children's lives only worsened during the 1880s as the stockyards expanded. By the turn of the century, the Packingtown population included an increasing number of unskilled Bohemians, Poles and Lithuanians, whose cultural and language differences led Haley to refer to them unsympathetically as the 'Huns and the Vandals'.[15] A medical inspector in the 1890s found almost twenty percent of students at one Packingtown school below grade. They were poorly dressed, thin, anemic, 'and apparently neglected'.[16] Through the 1890s, Packingtown workers were the object of vigorous labor-organizing campaigns, and the main Knights of Labor organizer held meetings for his local in the Buckley School, a few blocks from Hendricks. The community was enlivened by regular mass rallies, literature distribution campaigns, and street skirmishes between strikers, scabs, and militia hired by the industries.[17]

15 Autobiography of Margaret Haley, (Chicago version, 1935) Box 34, Folder 4, p. 693, Chicago Teachers Federation Archives, Chicago Historical Society [hereafter, CTF Archives].

16 M. McDowell,'A Quarter of a Century in the Stockyards District' (1919), p. 17. McDowell Papers, Chicago Historical Society.

17 Wade, (1987) pp. 233-58.

18 Haley in Reid (1982) p. 25.

19 M. Murphy, 'Progress of the Poverty of Philosophy: Two Generations of Labor Reform Politics: Michael and Margaret Haley'. Paper delivered at Knights of Labor Centennial Symposium, Chicago, May 17-19, 1979. pp. 17-18. See also J. L. Thomas, *Alternative America : Henry George, Edward Bellamy, Henry Demarest Lloyd, and the Adversary Tradition* (Cambridge, Mass. : Belknap Press, 1983); A. Feffer, *The Chicago Pragmatists and American Progressivism* (Ithaca: Cornell University Press, 1993), esp. pp. 179-93, 208-11.

In the comfort of her home in Englewood, Margaret Haley and her family discussed the working class political activism of the 1880s and 1890s, which she later recalled would 'stir the minds and hearts of men and women', including her own.[18] Haley's father had been a member of the Knights of Labor, and he taught his children an innate distrust of monopoly capitalism and a faith in the power of the democratic state to control the unbridled interests of profit.[19] Haley's own readings in political theory taught her that in the industrial wars of the late nineteenth century, it was the responsibility of state agencies such as the public school to create a systematic and paternalistic civic apparatus. Her own observations of her students' poverty and the economic hopelessness before them could only have supported these ideas. Although a series of compulsory education acts and child labor laws in the 1880s required Chicago children aged seven to fourteen to attend public school, through the turn of the century about half of Chicago's children who entered primary school left before the required age. Thus Margaret Haley's sixth grade classroom was the last schooling that many of the Hendricks children would see before they entered the factories or the streets.[20]

We can imagine that Haley's experiences with poor urban children in the city schooling structure could have only reinforced her political beliefs. Later in life, as a union leader, she consistently argued that her work for teachers was not only for labor interests but 'far more truly... for the children of the city'.[21] She placed school reform at the center of municipal reform, arguing that 'the cause of the teacher is the cause of the people and vice versa, and their common cause is that of the children'.[22] We might say that she believed that with appropriate funding and support by the state, a city school like Hendricks *could* be an agency for poor children's social improvement, and not just a way-station in their desperate and hopeless lives.

The Teacher and the School
Margaret Haley started teaching in a school that was so new that for its first two years it was referred to officially only as the 43rd Street School. Hendricks was built in 1884 as one of four new schools designed to accommodate the children of the growing population of Stockyard workers. Located on a corner lot, it was a three-story brick building that in its style resembled a nearby factory more than a rural country school house. It was probably the largest building on the block, located in an area of residential tenements, working class cottages, and small

20 Clark (1897) pp. 99-100; Barrett (1987) pp. 19-117.

21 Haley in Reid (1982) p. 40.

22 Margaret Haley, August 3, 1901, box 36, folder 1, CTF Archives.

commercial buildings. On the first floor of many Chicago school buildings of the period, a hall ran through the center of the building, connecting to four or five classrooms, the principal's office, and an area where teachers picked up their classroom keys in the morning. A stairway led upstairs to more classrooms and one large room with a piano that doubled as a recitation room and assembly hall. The fifteen classrooms were rectangular, with walls painted a light tinted color and blackboards around at least two sides, cabinets to hold books and supplies, and rows of connected desks bolted to the floor with seatings for forty-eight students. Each room had a separate closet with seats where students could take off their coats and boots. There was a girls' and boys' playroom and outside playground, reflecting a popular social belief that coeducation was acceptable as long as the genders were separated for play time.[23]

This was how the Hendricks School looked on its first day of school in September 1884, but over time the building expanded with the community and aged with daily use.[24] Hendricks was designed to seat 715 students, but within a few years its enrollment had increased to more than 1000, so three rooms in the attic were rebuilt into classrooms, and new desks, bookcases, ink wells, and blackboards were ordered. But even these rooms did not provide adequate space, so in many classrooms students may have doubled or tripled up at desks designed to fit only one. Over the sixteen years of Haley's tenure, physical facilities were damaged or wore out, so that throughout the school year, the building janitor and engineer were in the basement banging away at steam pipes and plumbing, on the roof repairing the shingles, in the hallways fixing floor boards, or on the grounds painting the picket fence, repaving the sidewalk, and spreading black earth on the playground. Walls needed replastering, drafty windows needed to be caulked, and window shades needed to be mended.

23 The descriptions of the interior of a typical Chicago school building in 1897 is in Clark, (1897) p. 90. Other data about the school building was drawn from the 37th Annual Report of Board of Education, 1890-91 and the maps at IRAD. For comments on coeducation in American public schooling see D. Tyack and E. Hansot, *Learning Together: A History of Coeducation in American Schools* (New Haven; Yale University Press, 1990), p. 70.

24 The following information about school facilities and repairs is drawn from the Proceedings of the Board of Education of the City of Chicago, 1891-97.

Minor disasters occurred, including a small fire in the building and a storm that damaged the flag pole. At one point, the principal began to worry about vandalization of the building after hours so he requested locks for the rear hall door and for the outside gates. A building filled with young people strained under their energetic romping that teachers could not completely control: stairwell banisters were bent from children learning on them, window sashes were broken from too much yanking on them, drains were clogged with children's dirt, classroom desks were broken from some childhood fracas. The flag pole rope had to be replaced after ten years, indicating the strain of children tugging on it day after day. Exhausted from their long days at work, busy teachers lost their classroom keys and needed replacements.

Over the years, modern facilities were added to the building, and probably the most significant one for teachers and students was the replacement of an old pan closet toilet with a siphon toilet in the teachers', students' and principals' lavatories, thereby vastly improving the environment in and around those rooms. A new ventilating apparatus helped teachers keep the air in their rooms moving, and presumably addressed the problem of the dust and odors that infiltrated from the street. But even this new mechanism needed mending, because some grates rattled when the heat turned on, or possibly when the ground shook from a train passing nearby.

The Teacher in the Classroom
This was the place that Margaret Haley headed to every morning, taking a streetcar from her suburban home in Englewood into the heart of Chicago's poorest industrial neighborhood. For sixteen years of school mornings, from September to May, with a Thanksgiving holiday in late November and Christmas holiday in late December, she arrived at the building at 8:45, fifteen minutes before some 800

to 1,000 students gathered on the playground and crammed their way into the building, 48 of them filing into each classroom. In her own crowded room, the sixth grade teacher whom students called Miss Haley began class at 9 a.m. with a half hour opening exercise that included some singing. Through the morning, she taught fractions and introduction to geometry, political and physical geography, the history of the United States through the War of Independence, lessons in city and county government, reading, composition, singing, and drawing, and a course in physiology and hygiene with special references to the effects of alcohol and narcotics. To help her teach, her classroom was supplied with arithmetic and writing charts, a historical atlas, some Webster's dictionaries, an eight-inch globe, and maps of the world, the United States, and Illinois.[25]

25 Clark (1897) describes the curriculum of a sixth grade class, p. 46 and pp. 113-14.

For ten minutes a day, Miss Haley supervised organized physical activities in the crowded classrooms, leading arm, leg, and breathing exercises while students stood at their seats. While supervising her classroom, Miss Haley kept an eye on the classroom thermometers to keep the room between 65 and 70 degrees whether the air outside the windows registered below freezing or steaming hot. She was prohibited from using corporal punishment with her forty-eight ten and eleven year old boys and girls, and was urged instead to maintain a stern, but still caring approach of 'moral suasion' to maintain order. She supervised a fifteen-minute mid-morning recess and monitored students as they left the building at noon for lunch. Because she and many of her colleagues lived far from school, they probably stayed in the building for lunch, eating at their desks or in a makeshift teachers' lounge. At 1:30, the children were back at class until 3:30, and by 4 p.m. Miss Haley had closed her classroom, placing her room key in the proper position on the key board in the principal's office.[26]

26 *Rules and Regulations of the Board of Education*, Chicago, 1896.

This, at least, is what was supposed to happen according to the official teacher guidelines of the Chicago board of education. Other evidence suggests more variation in how lessons might have been taught inside Miss Haley's classroom. Given the required curriculum, the crowded classroom, and the problems raised by students' poverty and linguistic diversity, it is hard to imagine how any Chicago teacher devised anything but the most mechanical rote lessons for her students, and at least one observer described exactly that. In his scathing 1892 survey of American city schools, muckraker Joseph Rice found Chicago classrooms full of students glued to their desks, monotonously reading, writing, ciphering, and reciting from textbooks all day long.[27]

27 J. M. Rice, The *Public School System of the United States* (New York: Arno Press, 1969 originally published 1893) pp. 166-183.

But progressive pedagogy might have been more prevalent in Chicago schools than Rice saw, as less than a year after his observations, the Chicago Board of Education erupted in controversy over a charge that the city curriculum was driven by too many progressive 'fads', including too many courses in art, music, and physical culture.[28] Margaret Haley herself believed that even at their worst, Chicago schools were less restrictive than those in many eastern cities because they were lacking 'the melancholy attitude of Puritanism'.[29] In this she reflected a wider belief among Americans that the great mid-western city of Chicago was a raw and inventive cauldron of creative energy, free of settled traditions, a place where, according to Mark Twain, the residents 'were always rubbing a lamp, and fetching up a genie, and contriving and achieving new impossibilities'.[30]

28 Clark (1897) pp. 31-32, 77-78.

29 Haley in Reid (1982) p. 23.

30 Twain quoted in Miller (1996) pp.188-89.

This kind of inventiveness was exactly what Haley had seen in the year before she began teaching at Hendricks, when she was a student at Cook County Normal School. Under the direction of Francis Wayland Parker in a building near Haley's home in Englewood, the Normal School became a famous center of progressive pedagogy, emphasizing students' self- discovery and active learning in the classroom. Haley described Parker as someone who broke old traditions of education, freeing women teachers to use their minds in the same way that modern fashions had freed women's bodies from the corset. She was particularly inspired by Parker's lectures on the notion of the school as a social community, the value of academic freedom, and principles of self-discovery in interdisciplinary and interactive classes.[31] For the young Haley, Parker's education 'shook educational practices loose from the old foundations'.[32]

As an older teacher, Haley continued her studies in progressive education by attending a few terms at Catholic summer schools for teachers. The most influential of these educational experiences was at a school run by Dominican Sisters in rural Wisconsin where she learned about the school as a social welfare agency for the child. A visiting lecturer at this school re-affirmed her earlier education at Cook County that the elementary school classroom should not be 'a quiet, sad place, where little children fear to move lest they should disturb a nervous teacher', but it should be an active and social place where children learned 'from each other more than they learn from the teacher and where they learn by doing rather than by hearing'.[33]

But was Haley able to make her own classroom at Hendricks such an active and social place? Because she never described her own teaching style, we can only guess that she developed her educational theories in part by some practice. Furthermore, creativity may have been more likely for Haley than for many other teachers because for the entirety of her career at Hendricks, she worked under a liberal-minded principal, John W. McCarthy' who kept his teachers abreast of school politics and promoted the work of the newly formed teachers federation.[34] That Haley worked with this principal, and the same

31 I. C. Heffron, *Francis Wayland Parker: An Interpretive Biography* (Los Angeles: Ivan Deach, 1934); Reid (1982) p. 23; Rice, (1969) pp. 209-16.

32 Autobiography of Margaret Haley, (California version, 1935) Box 33, Folder 1, p. 2, CTF Archives.

33 T. E. Shields, *Teachers Manual of Primary Methods* (Washington D.C.: The Catholic Education Press, 1912), p. 35; J. Ward, *Thomas Edward Shields: Biologist, Psychologist, Educator* (New York: Scribner's, 1947), pp. 125-214.

34 Autobiography of Margaret Haley (Seattle version, ca. 1910-11) Box 32, Folder 4, CTF Archives.

assistant principal, for all of her sixteen years at Hendricks implies that the relations between the progressively minded teacher and her administrators were not conflictual.

Still, we cannot forget Miss Haley's crowded classroom, the exhausted and hungry students, the absence of supplies and space to lead creative lessons, the lack of parks or a safe neighborhood in which to take field trips, and the way that these material realities must have limited her ability to teach innovative lessons. We need to remember that Haley herself described her school in a sweeping statement as 'almost hopeless'. We can also imagine how Margaret Haley, the future teacher union leader, may have been politicized by the contrast between her own progressive teacher training and the restrictive working conditions in her school. Central to her union platform in the Chicago Teachers' Federation was the teachers' right to shape the classroom into a caring and supportive environment for children. A vocal critic of what she called the 'factoryization' of education, Haley argued that schools should be flexible enough to allow teachers to be creative and caring in the classroom. If the school could not 'bring joy to the work of the world', she argued, then 'joy must go out of its own life, and work in the school as in the factory will become drudgery'.[35] Did she know this because she had seen such drudgery in her own or other's classrooms?

The Teacher and her Colleagues

In 1895, Haley was one of 4,000 elementary and grammar school teachers in Chicago, up to one third of them Irish Catholic and all but eighty of them women.[36] Late nineteenth century Chicago housed the fourth largest Irish population in the United States and their prominence in civil service occupations and local politics furthered Irish-American women's access to local public school teaching positions.[37] Haley recalled that her own job

35 Haley in Reid (1982) p. 286.

36 Clark (1897) p. 96.

37 J. A. Nolan, 'Irish-American Teachers and the Struggle Over American Urban Public Education, 1890-1920: A Preliminary Look,' unpublished paper, 1994; H. Diner, *Erin's Daughters in America: Irish Immigrant Women in the Nineteenth Century* (Baltimore: Johns Hopkins University Press, 1983); J. W. Sanders, *Education of an Urban Minority: Catholics in Chicago, 1833-1965* (New York: Oxford University Press, 1977) pp. 130-35.

was promised to her through her cousin who lived in the neighborhood, and she herself probably played a role in securing a job at Hendricks for her sister Jennie, and after Jennie transferred to another school, the third Haley sister, Eliza. For much of Haley's tenure at the school, two other pairs of sisters worked there as well, and like the Haley sisters, they lived together. Such hiring practices reflected the informal community-based practices and concerns of late nineteenth century schooling.[38]

But if Hendricks was originally a stable, community based staff, as time went on, it became increasingly less so. Two years after it opened, half of the staff of the Hendricks School had been transferred, mostly to other schools in the same overcrowded district. So transitory was the staff at Hendricks, that in 1889, Margaret Haley was the only original teacher left at a school that had been in existence only five years. By her eleventh year of teaching at Hendricks, more than half the staff had been at the school less than five years. The mobile staff at Hendricks may have had two effects on Haley. First, because teacher transfers were not voluntary, their increase in number suggests that the demands of an expanding city school system may have taken precedence over the priorities of teachers and the community, presenting Haley with an early lesson in school board politics. Secondly, transfers undercut any sense of community and collective history among the adults in the building.[39]

Over sixteen years, the staff changed in other ways too. When Haley first entered Chicago schools, aspiring teachers needed only a high school diploma, and as late as 1897, more than 3,000 of the city's 4,000 elementary and grammar school teachers had gone directly from high school to the teacher's desk.[40] Teachers like Margaret Haley learned their trade by apprenticeship under older teachers, and secured their jobs by personal connections. School reformers tended to disapprove of these informal and localized

38 Haley in Reid (1982) p. 22; List of teachers' names from Board of Education annual reports for inclusive years.

39 M. Murphy, *Blackboard Unions: The AFT and the NEA, 1900-1980* (Ithaca: Cornell University Press, 1990) p. 42.

40 Clark (1897) p. 97.

training and hiring practices, and in 1893, the City of Chicago instituted a one-year training requirement and expanded the teacher exam to include a section on pedagogical theory as well as general knowledge. By 1898, reformers promoted a four-year college degree requirement for elementary teachers. One effect of these changes was the gradual discouragement of working class women from entering teaching and an increased number of teachers from the middle class who could afford the extra schooling. In 1880, four years before Margaret Haley began teaching, almost half of all Chicago teachers came from working class backgrounds, whereas by 1900 barely one third did. The proportion of teachers from immigrant backgrounds also decreased during that time.[41]

41 Murphy (1990) pp. 34-43.

Haley herself fit somewhere between the two cohorts: the daughter of Irish-Catholic working class immigrants, she had also attended a few semesters of teacher education and thus was probably more educated than most of her elder colleagues. Yet the haphazard nature of her training distinguished her from her younger colleagues' more systematic teacher education which emphasized a set body of scientific theories in education to be administered by a centralized school bureaucracy. This experience differed radically from Haley's own education as a community teacher hired through community networks, and a student of progressive, child centered pedagogy. As younger teachers entered the Hendricks School through the 1890s, Haley may have observed both the class difference and a different attitude about the occupation of teaching.[42]

42 Ibid pp. 34-43.

In 1897, at age 36, Margaret Haley was the most senior, and possibly also the eldest teacher in her school. The only people who shared her memories of the original 43rd Street school were her principal and assistant principal. At least one of her original colleagues from her first years teaching at Hendricks had died, and this possibly added to her sense of loss in a rapidly changing and increasingly youthful system. Over the years, her classroom had become crowded with more poor children from more foreign backgrounds, and school politics seemed to be working against progressive education and the notion of a stable community-based school. Haley's position of seniority and difference may have shaped her decision in 1897 to join the newly formed Chicago Teachers' Federation which had taken on its first battle: pensions for retiring women teachers, many of whom were Haley's friends and past colleagues. At the very least, 1897 was a year in which Margaret Haley might have believed that her classroom at Hendricks was an increasingly lonely and isolated place.

Conclusion

A snapshot of a teacher tells only a part of her biography: her face, her dress, a corner of the classroom during one second of the whole school year, her students at one uncharacteristic moment of immobility. But the work of the teacher does not happen only in the classroom in one second; it changes over time and through communities; it is shaped by large trends such as changes in school board regulations and student population, and by immediate daily events such as a rainstorm or a sick child. Teachers' work is regular and regulated, but it is also spontaneous and unrehearsed. Teachers are among the most literate of all workers, yet the nature of their work leaves them too exhausted to chronicle their day, and classroom papers are usually discarded because they are not considered important.

Thus we should not be surprised that the biography of a teacher seems less like a narrative of day-to-day events than a collage of images, impressions, incidents, and feelings. So, too, does the biographer seem less like a traditional historian and more like a scavenger, sorting through both the most intimate personal sources and broad institutional histories. Like the act of teaching itself, we should not expect to find clear, hard data to document what actually happened inside a school, whether we are asking this of a teacher who arrives home from work this afternoon, or a teacher who left the classroom ninety years ago. Rather, we should look for the broad ambiance of the experience of teaching over time and the meaning that teachers' work held for her.

Part 3
Raising Questions/
Seeking Answers

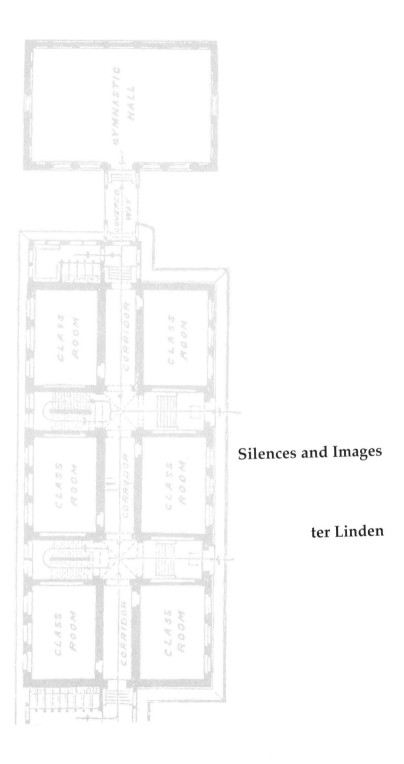

Silences and Images

ter Linden

Silences and Images: reading the past

Jaap ter Linden

This group of images serve as a test for the arguments within the book and come from a Dutch museum collection. One reading of them is offered here by the Curator of the Netherlands Schoolmuseum; alternative readings or new questions are to be encouraged.

Photograph 1 Traditional classroom. The light falls from the left, as it should be. The girls wear aprons, which was not usually the case in Dutch schools.

Photograph 2 Boys and girls. It seems to be the same school as in photograph 1 (e.g. tiles and desks). This is a first form - one can tell by the reading boards on the desks. With these reading boards came little tins containing cardboard letters.

Photograph 3 Detail. One wonders why they let the poorest child sit all the way at the front of the classroom. See the holes in his stockings, which one would not have been able to see if he had been allowed to stand.

Photographs 4 & 5 The same classroom in 1925 and 1926. School pictures are hung on top of each other. This is a unique situation, in conflict with the way the school pictures were supposed to be used.

Photographs 6 & 7 An open-air school. This is known from the literature. The photographs say it all - lessons outdoors, rain or shine.

Photograph 8 An open-air school as well? No – during the Second World War schools were requisitioned by the army and obviously sometimes lessons were taught outdoors.

Photograph 9 The Dutch East Indies, a boarding school.

Open classrooms, on the wall a school picture used as a basis for writing a composition.

Photograph 10 The school picture in detail. Education in the Dutch East Indies almost completely focused on the Netherlands.

Photograph 11 Indigenous school at Djocja. This is a school for Javanese children. The school pictures were made in the Dutch East Indies and were completely unknown to the museum.

Photograph 12 Who will find the answer to the question?

Reading the past

Reading the past

Reading the past

Reading the past

Reading the past

Reading the past

Reading the past

Reading the past

Reading the past

Eerste klas, Javaansche School te Djocja.

Reading the past

Reading the past

Contributors

Ann Short Chirhart, Ogelthorpe University, USA

Kristof Dams, University of Leuven, Belgium

Marc DePaepe, University of Leuven, Belgium

Philip Gardner, University of Cambridge, UK

Ian Grosvenor, University of Birmingham, UK

Lars-Göran Högman, University of Umeä, Sweden

Ulla Johanssen, University of Umeä, Sweden

Martin Lawn, Westhill College, UK

Jaap ter Linden, Nationaal Schoolmuseum, Netherlands

Valinda Littlefield, University of Illinois, USA

Jo Anne Preston, Brandeis University, USA

Kate Rousmaniere, Miami University, USA

Frank Simon , University of Ghent, Belgium

Harry Smaller, York University, Canada

David Vincent, University of Keele, UK

History of Schools and Schooling

THIS SERIES EXPLORES THE HISTORY OF SCHOOLS AND SCHOOLING in the United States and other countries. Books in this series examine the historical development of schools and educational processes, with special emphasis on issues of educational policy, curriculum and pedagogy, as well as issues relating to race, class, gender, and ethnicity. Special emphasis will be placed on the lessons to be learned from the past for contemporary educational reform and policy. Although the series will publish books related to education in the broadest societal and cultural context, it especially seeks books on the history of specific schools and on the lives of educational leaders and school founders.

For additional information about this series or for the submission of manuscripts, please contact the general editors:

Alan R. Sadovnik
118 Harvey Hall
School of Education
Adelphi University
Garden City, NY 11530

Susan F. Semel
Dept. of Curriculum and Teaching
243 Gallon Wing
Hofstra University
Hempstead, NY 11550